YAO

A LIFE IN TWO WORLDS

YAO

A LIFE IN TWO WORLDS

YAO MING
WITH
RIC BUCHER

miramax books

HYPERION

NEW YORK

CONTENTS

INTRODUCTION

When I was approached about helping Yao Ming write his autobiography, I was thrilled by the prospect of being part of such a historic project. I knew the story would go way beyond that of a great Chinese athlete and how he became an NBA superstar; sports, in fact, was merely the backdrop for something far more momentous. Yao Ming had single-handedly showed the world's oldest civilization that it could not only compete but also excel in domains beyond its own borders. In fact, he had influenced how *two* of the world's most powerful nations think of themselves and of each other. All this—plus his inspiration of unprecedented transglobal business and cultural alliances—Yao had accomplished with a personal effervescence that transcended every barrier.

It was captivating to watch Yao Ming defy all the skeptics and emerge from an inauspicious debut with the Houston Rockets in 2002 to become a force among the world's best basketball players halfway through his first season. That drama, given the conditions under which he learned the game and his struggle merely to make it to the NBA, was interesting in itself. But the truly tantalizing part of helping Yao tell his story was the opportunity to see and hear about events that resonated far beyond a bouncing ball and rattled our big blue orb. Part of Yao's charm is that he has steadfastly refused to think of himself as a historic figure, and yet, as you will learn here, he was aware that every one of his decisions would have a widespread cultural impact, the effects of which would be felt long after he retired, and he acted accordingly.

One other enticement for becoming Yao's Boswell: the chance to help this bright young man, who is uneasy speaking a second language in front of strangers, express himself fully, at last, to the legions of basketball fans and casual observers who have found themselves liking and admiring Yao without knowing all that much about him. I would be the conduit, the can opener, their cultural liaison. The only glitch in that plan, I realized as I prepared to fly to Shanghai in March 2002 to meet Yao for the first time, was that I didn't know much more about the People's Republic of China than the average NBA fan.

I knew there had to be valleys of subjects and events between the cultural peaks that had caught my eye as a casual observer—Jet Li, Free Tibet, *Crouching Tiger, Hidden Dragon*, Chairman Mao, Confucius, acupuncture, feng shui—but they were shrouded in fog. I scrambled to learn more before my trip. In a month-long cram course on Chinese language, culture, and history, I plowed through anything that seemed remotely helpful, a desperate hodgepodge that included Pang-Mei Natasha Chang's memoir, Sun Tzu's *The Art of War*, Ben-Fong Torres's autobiography, half a dozen travel books, and Dai Sijie's *Balzac and the Little Chinese Seamstress*. I listened to Pinyin tapes, and I read any magazine article I could find that seemed it might shed some light on China's twentieth-century evolution. Then I grilled friends and friends of friends if they had even the slightest China connection.

The end result: I now knew for a fact that there were valleys beneath all that fog.

If I had anything going for me, it was being a first-generation American whose first language was not English. I grew up in Ohio trying to reconcile my German heritage with being accepted by my completely American friends. My fluency in German returned during a term studying in Germany as a college sophomore, and I occasionally was mistaken for a native. I was going to China, then, with at least a little understanding of the difference between studying a culture and living it.

Yao embodies that distinction. Everything about him—from his square jaw, flattop, and immense size to his skills on the basketball court—defies the world's ideas about China and the Chinese. He's the equivalent of a blinking neon sign that reads: "ALL PRECONCEIVED NOTIONS ARE HEREBY NULL AND VOID!" In the end, that may prove to be his greatest accomplishment.

That first trip was on my own time and my own dime, a hastily arranged weekend visit to see the NBA-bound Yao play in his last Chinese Basketball Association regular-season home game. I'd been asked whether I thought Yao's story would make for a good book. I did and agreed to an exploratory visit, but there wasn't much more to it than that. Having covered the NBA for more than ten years, including trips to South Africa, Yugoslavia, and Turkey to write about other players who had used basketball to cross a cultural divide, I knew what awaited him here. This was my chance to see what, if anything, I could discover about what he was leaving behind.

Yao and I didn't exactly hit it off right away. We first met in the back corner of a hotel bar with NBA agent Bill Duffy, who approached me with the book idea, and Frank Sha, a Nike China representative who had grown up with Yao. We talked for maybe twenty minutes with Sha translating. Yao was drinking juice and wearing a gray Dallas Mavericks warm-up suit, a gift from Mavs president Donnie Nelson, a pioneer among NBA scouts in China. He seemed so wary that I didn't have the heart to pull out my notebook or turn on a tape recorder. I had a camera with me as well, and Duffy took a photo of us before I left. It shows Yao standing stiffly beside me, hands clasped in front of him. He did not smile.

I watched him play the next day in an unheated arena, the substitutes bundled in down jackets on the bench. Before the game, TV reporters stuck cameras and microphones in every non-Asian face and asked questions about the NBA and Yao Ming. The non-Asians present included Scott Layden, then the Knicks' GM, and Jerry Krause, then GM of the Bulls. No two NBA officials made more visits to scout Yao Ming, and when he was made aware of that, he agreed to meet with them privately during his predraft visit to Chicago. He did so for no other reason than to honor the special interest they'd taken in him.

Yao dominated the game despite looking out of shape. All the basic skills were there—passing, shooting, dribbling—and he was clearly the floor general, directing his teammates through each play, but two moments stood out. One was when he dived to the floor for a loose ball and instinctively flipped it behind his head to a teammate for an open jumper. The second was when the opposing center, a 6′8″ Eastern European, turned to face Yao Ming with the ball. Yao dropped into a defensive crouch and waved his hand as if to say, "Come on. Try me." They were glimpses of an effort and attitude he'd need a lot more of to stand a chance in the NBA.

The comparisons to Shawn Bradley, though, never applied. Bradley, a 7′6″ Mormon drafted after one year at Brigham Young University, entered the NBA after completing his religious mission in Australia and not playing competitively for a year. He had nei-ther Yao's thick torso, essential for holding position near the basket, nor his leadership qualities. Rik Smits, a 7'4" Dutchman with a sweet jumper who played twelve seasons for the Indiana Pacers, was a closer match, but he wasn't a leader, either, and didn't have Yao's fluid touch with his back to the basket. The greatest issue would be that the speed and strength of the NBA were many times greater than anything Yao had faced in China. I wondered if his ath-leticism—he's graceful and runs well for 7'6", but has average lat-eral mobility and a sub-par vertical leap—would allow him to adjust. I'd seen enough, though, to believe that, at worst, Yao would be a serviceable NBA center.

We met with Yao and his parents that night in the lobby of my hotel. The conversation lasted approximately fifteen minutes. There was an ease among Yao and his parents, as if they were three old friends, with Yao simply the youngest and therefore most deferen-tial among them. The family circle served as refuge from the rabid investment that all of China seemed to have in Yao Ming's not just reaching the NBA but also becoming a star. It struck me as pre-sumptuous, having seen the mediocre competition that had whet-ted his reputation. I flew home believing that, for all of Yao's ability, there were all sorts of ways he might be chewed up and spit out and the world would just keep turning.

Yao Ming's first NBA season, of course, was an unqualified success. He was selected by fans over Shaquille O'Neal as the Western Conference All-Star starting center and helped the Hous-ton Rockets challenge for their first playoff berth in four years down to the final week of the season before falling short. The lone disappointment was his finishing second to Amare Stoudamire in Rookie of the Year balloting.

But all that's through a purely basketball prism. Big picture? It might've been the most remarkable debut in league history. The NBA being a league of copycats, the league's Chinese talent pipeline would've been severely crimped, if not sealed, had Yao failed after the inconsequential showings of Wang Zhi Zhi and Mengke Bateer the year before. Instead, Yao had Allen Iverson referring to him as a "gift from God," coaches and other players anointing him Shaq's successor as the league's most dominant center, and Rockets owner Les Alexander predicting Yao would be bigger than both Michael Jordan and Tiger Woods combined. He endeared himself to the country in an Apple commercial, opposite 2′8″ "Mini-Me" actor Verne Troyer, merely by smiling. His "Yo, Yao" Visa commercial for Super Bowl XXXVII in 2003 spawned an instant pop-culture catchphrase.

All while legions of Asian-American basketball fans suddenly began packing NBA arenas, and NBA teams, in turn, began courting an entirely new fan base.

My first official interview with Yao for this book took place in an elegant but austere cherrywood-paneled home office just inside his front door, and nearly the entire conversation was conducted through his translator, Colin Pine. I expected to need a translator again when I met Yao in Hong Kong during a Chinese national-team tour four months later, but after we had had an hour-long conversation in English, I realized we could go without one. Yao might not have a dazzling English vocabulary or talk in long paragraphs filled with nuance, but he has an eye for detail and a natural affinity for storytelling. I'm told all that is far more evident when he speaks Chinese, but I found that his plainspoken English by no means inhibits his ability or desire to speak his mind and share his observations about life. What I've tried to do in this book is capture the way Yao thinks and speaks, without imposing either my own diction or an interpreter's. I tried to stay as true as

I could to his syntax and word choice, in the hope that readers could experience what I did chatting with Yao on the back of the Chinese national-team bus from Jian Jing to Beijing or, by the end, at a Japanese sushi bar in Seattle the night before the Rockets' last 2003–2004 regular-season road game.

Talking for hours and hours with Yao didn't completely burn off the fog obscuring my understanding of all things Chinese, but there was something special about having him as my guide. Even if it did mean he had to endure hearing me repeatedly say in clumsy Chinese, "Ching Jiang Ingwen," which means, "In English, please."

Walking in public at Yao's side also gave me a disturbing look at the power of fame. In China, it was akin to the onslaught of a locust attack. As he strode through an airport terminal, you could sense heads turning and then hear sharp intakes of breath from every direction, followed by stampeding feet. Fans would crowd around him, oblivious to me, snapping photos or thrusting paper and pen at him and begging for an autograph. The Chinese national team also routinely sprung last-minute public appearances on him until he refused to get off the team bus for one. When the team hurried back on the bus after being gone only five minutes, one of his teammates said, "It's a good thing you didn't go. It was complete chaos." During that five minutes, part of the crowd pounded on the sides of the bus and yelled for Yao to come out. He looked distressed, not wanting to disappoint his fans but sensing he had to draw a line on nonbasketball demands because no one else would.

There were parts of Yao's story that he couldn't have described in English or Chinese, either because he wasn't present for vital moments in the drama of winning his release to the U.S. or because he wasn't fully aware of all the circumstances. I brought in other voices, of those who are close to Yao or have worked with him, to provide the missing narrative. In the end, Yao is simply about courage and determination. Yao Ming has made, and continues to make, history. He is a flashpoint of profound cultural changes that will be felt throughout the world as China continues to open up and prosper. But what makes Yao special is that he has passed through a crucible of extraordinary events by steadfastly holding on to the solid, reassuring ordinariness of life. As revolutionary as every day of his life has been since the pursuit of his NBA dream began, he never has lost sight of the fact that his basketball career is only a phase and that his actions and attitude define who he is, not the events surrounding him. Maybe it's having been inordinately tall his entire life and thereby having always stood out, but I've never met anyone who takes such pleasure at just fitting in or being part of a crowd.

People inevitably ask what Yao is like when they hear that I've worked on this book. My stock answer: "Whatever you think of him as a basketball player, he's five times that as a human being." Those who've spent time with Yao invariably have a favorite anecdote about his kindheartedness or humility. Michael Goldberg, the Houston Rockets' attorney, can't forget how Yao called him just before boarding a flight back to China after his rookie season, to thank him once again for helping make his NBA dream come true. Or there's the one about Yao wanting to give each member of the Chinese national team one of his NBA trading cards. Rather than impose on the trading card company to send him the requisite cards, he had a friend go around to all the sports memorabilia shops in Houston and buy the cards he needed. As our relationship evolved from that first stilted meeting to one where we'd share a meal or watch a movie for the simple pleasure of hanging out together, my motivation to see this book written shifted from a desire to tell where Yao came from and how he got to the NBA to providing a glimpse of the thoughtful soul that survived the journey. As his second-year NBA coach, Jeff Van Gundy, says, "If you were going to have an ambassador for your country in a sport, you couldn't find a better one than Yao Ming."

Here, then, in Yao's words, is the story of how a tall, skinny kid from Shanghai, whose parents had higher hopes for him than playing basketball, became an NBA star and thereby a living symbol for a country of 1.3 billion people.

—Ric Bucher

CAST OF CHARACTERS

Yao Ming—The first foreign-born and -developed player to be selected number one in the NBA draft, and the best-known celebrity in China. An online chat with Yao in China crashed the host system when millions simultaneously tried to log on and participate. Expected to eventually surpass Tiger Woods as the world's most marketable individual athlete. Ranked twenty-fifth, just ahead of Woods and highest among all athletes, in the *Sporting News* 2003 list of the 100 most powerful people of 2003. Also ranked seventh among 101 most influential minorities by *Sports Illustrated* in 2003 and named one of the Top 100 most influential people in the world by *Time* magazine. Born on September 12, 1980, at Number Six People's Hospital in Shanghai. Weight and length at birth: 11 pounds, 3 ounces; 23 inches. Playing weight and height his rookie year in the NBA: 7'5", 292 pounds. Now listed as 7'6", 310 pounds. NBA.com's most popular international player and third most popular player overall, behind LeBron James and Allen Iverson, during the 2003–2004 season. Voted by the media to the NBA All-Interview second team after his rookie season even though he spoke almost exclusively through an interpreter. Second in Rookie of the Year voting behind Suns forward Amare Stoudemire but received more All-Pro votes. Passionate about cars, combat video games, and Shanghai-style Chinese food.

Yao Zhi Yuan—Yao's father. Played nine years as forward for the Shanghai basketball team wearing number 15, which Yao then wore for the Shanghai Sharks. Recruited out of a factory to play basketball; he was twenty years old and had never played but was 6'7". Worked for the Shanghai Port Authority inspecting boats after knee problems forced his retirement from basketball in 1979. Retired from the Port Authority when the family moved to Houston. Yao says his father has given him his sense of humor and serenity amid chaos.

Fang Feng Di—Yao's mother. Fang was a 6'3" center and captain of the Chinese women's national team that won the country's first Asian Championship in 1976. Worked for the country's Institute of Sports Research before moving to Houston to find a house and furnish it for her son's arrival. When the family was asked who the best player among them was, she replied, "I am." Considered the driving force of the family. Yao says he inherited his investigative and analytical side from his mother.

Team Yao—A group of five men who never had met—and probably never would have—but joined forces to facilitate and guide Yao Ming's NBA career. They are Erik Zhang, a thirty-something Chinese-born, American-educated businessman who served as chief negotiator and organizer; Bill Duffy, head of BDA Sports Management, who already was working on Yao Ming's behalf when he joined forces with Zhang; John Huizinga, a business school deputy dean of faculty and Yao's NBA agent of record; Bill Sanders, vice president of marketing for BDA Sports Marketing; and Lu Hao, Yao's Chinese agent, based in Beijing. All have other business interests and commitments, but they hold a three-hour conference call every Sunday morning to discuss Yao, his concerns, and their responsibilities to him that week.

Erik Zhang—Yao Ming's most trusted confidant and the mastermind behind his successful entry into the NBA as the number-one pick. As stereotypically Chinese as Yao is atypical: short, roly-poly, bespectacled, Zhang is a talented negotiator with a thorough understanding of Chinese culture, politics, and business, despite his family's move from Shanghai to Madison, Wisconsin, when he was a boy. Fluent in English, Mandarin, and Shanghaiese. Double-majored in economics and biochemistry at the University of Wisconsin, hoping to please his parents (his father is an engineer and his mother a medical doctor), but entered the University of Chicago business school upon graduation. A devoted fan of the Wisconsin Badgers basketball team, Zhang had only passing knowledge of the NBA when, in 1996, the twenty-two-year-old's girlfriend, Angie, introduced him to her enormous, basketball-playing distant cousin. Yao and his family soon enlisted Zhang to help him explore the possibility of playing in the U.S., at first for a college education but later in the NBA. Zhang formed an eclectic team of advisers to provide the expertise he didn't have. With John Huizinga's help, Zhang also enlisted a business class at the University of Chicago to create a marketing plan for Yao Ming. Their 500-page report included a three-month marketing survey in China and was distributed to, and referenced by, Team Yao as they developed their subsequent strategy. The report pinpointed six brand pillars that consumers could associate with Yao's image: hardworking, self-confident, respectful, talented, lighthearted, heroic.

Bill Duffy—Head of BDA Sports Management, one of the NBA's top two sports agencies in volume of total contracts negotiated. Met Yao Ming three years before he was drafted and introduced him to U.S. media outlets, exposure that helped promote

Yao Ming as a potential number-one pick well before he officially entered the draft. Stepped aside as Yao's potential agent of record for political reasons but remained a powerful orchestrator behind the scenes, then and now. BDA Sports Management handles all of Yao Ming's marketing and media access. Duffy was ranked twentieth in *Sports Illustrated*'s 101 most influential minorities of 2003, highest among agents in any sport, in part because of his comprehensive basketball connections in foreign countries. Played and roomed with former Boston Celtics star and Minnesota Timberwolves GM Kevin McHale at the University of Minnesota, then transferred to the University of Santa Clara, where he played with Kurt Rambis, who went on to a career with the Los Angeles Lakers. Duffy was drafted in the fifth round of the '82 NBA draft by the Denver Nuggets but waived at the end of training camp. A devoted father of five children (all under ten years of age when Yao entered the NBA), Duffy runs his company out of a custom-made, 7,000-square-foot house in the San Francisco Bay Area.

John Huizinga—Deputy dean for the faculty at the University of Chicago Graduate School of Business; economics professor; avid NBA fan; unreformed gym rat. Wrangled an invitation to a predraft workout for Yao Ming in Chicago from one of Zhang's business professors and wound up as his NBA agent of record. His economic tables for compensating the Sharks were essential in winning Yao's release at a reasonable price. Joined Team Yao while overseeing construction of a new $125 million campus. Negotiated Yao's NBA and Reebok shoe deals and is contemplating becoming a full-time NBA agent.

Bill Sanders—Nicknamed "the Colonel" by Yao Ming (as in Kentucky Fried Chicken's Colonel Sanders). As the head of BDA Sports marketing, he is the gatekeeper to Yao's calendar for media, marketing, and endorsements. (These obligations, plus games and practice, leave about thirty days free per year for Yao, Sanders estimates.) Cut his teeth as a guerrilla marketer for low-budget art-house movies, including *Eve's Bayou* and *Gods and Monsters*. Based in Los Angeles. Used his film-industry background to over-see Yao's commercial shoots, a challenging task because of Yao's aversion to playing the celebrity for celebrity's sake. Says Yao turned down $30 million in endorsements and chances to be on the cover of *Time* magazine and to be one of *GQ*'s Men of the Year during his first season. "He was turning down stuff other players dream of," Sanders says.

Lu Hao—Yao's China-based agent. Born and raised in Huai-yuan, a small township in Anhui Province. Played briefly in the 1980s with Liu Yu Dong, the most accomplished Chinese pro prior to Yao, Wang Zhi Zhi, and Mengke Bateer. Head coach of the Xia-men University men's team for five years. First met Yao while trav-eling with the Chinese national team during its training visit to Dallas in 2001. Previously a vice president of a Xiamen pro soccer club. Zhang chose Lu Hao as Yao's agent from a half dozen candi-dates after the Chinese Basketball Association—less than two months before the 2002 NBA draft—imposed a requirement that its players be represented by a Chinese-born and officially certified agent. Zhang says he picked Lu Hao because, when asked what he'd do if he was in America negotiating a deal for Yao and learned his son back in China was suddenly ill, the agent said he'd return to China to be with his son. Every other candidate said he'd remain in America to close the deal.

Colin Pine—Hired by Zhang as Yao Ming's translator from about sixty applicants. As a twenty-nine-year-old University of Maryland grad equally obsessed with basketball and China, he landed his dream job. Lived with Yao Ming and his parents the first season. Also served as their chauffeur, gofer, and general so-cial liaison.

Steve Francis—Former Houston Rockets high-scoring point guard and team leader. Nicknamed Stevie "Franchise," but in un-likely NBA-superstar fashion, gracefully handled the focus and at-tention swinging to Yao Ming upon his arrival. Suggested he might be the franchise but Yao was "The Dynasty." Observed that he and Yao were very much alike, except that Yao was 7'5" and Chinese. Was heavily criticized by everyone except Yao for not feeding the ball to Yao more his rookie year.

Michael Goldberg—Senior trial lawyer for Baker Botts, L.L.P., and general counsel for the Houston Rockets, he negoti-ated the franchise's right to draft Yao Ming with the Shanghai Sharks and Chinese Basketball Association. Hired by Rockets owner Les Alexander after winning Alexander's right to purchase a majority interest in the team from a powerful collective of local minority partners. Became acquainted with James Baker (the "Baker" in Baker Botts) when the former secretary of state joined the firm. Developed ties with the Bush family when the firm suc-cessfully represented them in the "hanging chad" controversy in Florida during the 2000 presidential election. These connections became useful during negotiations to win Yao's release to play in the NBA.

Bai Li—Head of Shanghai Media Group Sports Properties, which owns Yao's former team, the Shanghai Sharks. Entered the media business when a girlfriend's father, who ran a soccer team owned by SMG, put in a word for him. When the Sharks were promoted to the CBA's first division and acquired by SMG, he was assigned to set up their business operations. Has three uncles who have been prominent in the People's Republic of China sports world; one played for the national basketball team, one was a national triple-jump champion, and a third was sports editor of the *Tianjin Daily*. The first uncle, Bai Jingshen, was assistant coach of the women's national basketball team when Yao's mother played on it.

Chinese Basketball Association (CBA)—The governing basketball federation of the People's Republic of China and also the name of the country's fourteen-team—it was twelve teams when Yao last played in it—men's professional basketball league. Both the national organization and the league are run by the same officials out of the same office in Beijing, creating confusion in the U.S., where the national basketball program, with headquarters in Colorado Springs, Colorado, and the NBA, based in New York, are distinctly different entities.

Xin Lancheng—Former executive general of the Chinese Basketball Association. Presided over the excruciating process Yao was subjected to before receiving permission to enter the NBA. Subsequently reassigned after three years in office. Now in charge of event scheduling for the 2008 Olympics. Described as stiff, dour, and impersonal by those who had to deal with him in his previous capacity. Removed all the information files—including contract information on the pro league's players and coaches—from his CBA office when he left.

Li Yuanwei—Current secretary general of the Chinese Basketball Association. Gregarious and progressive, he employs a management style that is as open as his predecessor Xin Lancheng's was secretive. Spent twenty years as a professor, coach, and referee at the Beijing Sports University. Was deputy director of the CBA for five years before Xin Lancheng had him removed in 2000.

Liu Wei—Yao's best friend and teammate since they were twelve years old. Starting point guard for the Sharks and the Chinese national team. Plays the most Americanized game of any Chinese national team player besides Yao.

Wang Fei—Former Chinese national team and Bayi Rockets head coach; currently runs a basketball academy in Beijing. The most progressive coach in China after he spent a year in the U.S. attending games and practices of the Dallas Mavericks and the Oklahoma University, and Southern Methodist University men's teams. Fired after China lost the 2002 Asian Games title to South Korea. A quick and slender small forward with a nice shooting touch for the Bayi Rockets, he would've excelled in the kind of up-tempo offense he adopted from the Mavericks and unsuccessfully tried to employ with the Chinese national team. Developed such severe asthma after retiring as a player in 1993 that he is now forced to travel with a briefcase of medicine at all times.

Teyo Johnson—Oakland Raiders tight end who befriended Yao in the summer of '98 when they played on the same High-Five AAU team based in Johnson's hometown, San Diego. The two stayed in touch with occasional phone calls over the years. Yao called Johnson from China to offer congratulations when the Raiders drafted him. Johnson played both football and basketball at Stanford before leaving after his junior year for the NFL. Yao, who compared Johnson (6'6", 260 pounds) to Charles Barkley as a basketball player, invited Johnson to the 2004 All-Star Game in Los Angeles and afterward gave him his All-Star Game jersey.

Wang Zhi Zhi—The first Chinese player to be drafted and to play for an NBA team. (Sung Tao, drafted sixty-seventh in 1987 by the Atlanta Hawks, never left China.) Originally drafted thirty-sixth in 1999 by the Dallas Mavericks, he joined them on April 4, 2001, after the 2000–2001 CBA season and made his debut the next night against the Hawks, scoring 6 points. At the time he left China, he was named the country's most popular athlete in a nationwide poll and selected by the Asian edition of *Time* magazine as one of twenty-four Asian heroes. His career has been a disappointment ever since. He declined to return to China to train with the national team after the 2001–2002 season, arguing he'd be better served playing in a pro summer league and then joining the national team for the 2002 World Championships in Indianapolis. China left him off the team but later agreed to welcome him back to train for the 2003 Asian Championships. Wang refused. Spent the 2003–2004 season bouncing on and off the injured list with the Miami Heat, his third NBA team in three years.

Mengke Bateer—The second Chinese player to play in the NBA, Mengke signed with the Denver Nuggets as a free agent following the 2001–2002 CBA season. Made his debut on February 27, 2002, against the Golden State Warriors. First Chinese player to start an NBA game and first to win an NBA championship ring, playing forty-six minutes in twelve regular-season games for the 2002–2003 San Antonio Spurs. Was not part of the team's active playoff roster.

Carroll Dawson—Houston Rockets general manager and a native Texan, universally known as CD. Never wavered in his commitment to draft Yao Ming with the number-one pick, despite facing considerable skepticism from the Houston public, the media, and Rockets players. Compiled a tape of Yao Ming highlights and showed it to any player or reporter who strayed into his office, collecting converts one by one. "Even a blind man could see he could play," Dawson says, as he could attest, having been temporarily blinded after being struck by lightning while playing golf in 1990; his eyesight remains severely impaired. Hired as a Rockets assistant coach under Del Harris in 1980, he has spent his entire NBA career with the Rockets.

Rudy Tomjanovich—The Houston Rockets head coach during

Yao's first season. Has an international reputation, earned for his coaching accomplishments with the 1998 U.S. national team—which did not have any NBA players because of a labor dispute but won a bronze medal in the World Championships—and the 2000 U.S. national team, which won an Olympic gold medal in Australia. Diagnosed with bladder cancer late in Yao's rookie season, he recovered but chose not to return as coach and was replaced that summer by former Knicks head coach Jeff Van Gundy. Tomjanovich, who was with Dawson the day he was struck by lightning, remained with the Rockets as a college scout.

YAO

A LIFE IN TWO WORLDS

1

WELCOME TO
MY WORLD(S)

My name is Yao Ming. That's what everybody calls me, but in America the right way would be to say Ming Yao, because Yao is my family name. My dad is also a Yao—Yao Zhi Yuan—but not my mom. Usually in the United States, when two people get married, the woman takes her husband's last name. They did that in China many years ago, but now they don't because the government has said that women should be equal to men. My mom's name is Fang Feng Di.

This is only one of many things that are different in China today compared to long ago. In some ways China is becoming more like America, but I don't think they will ever be the same. That means I live in two places—one that is very new and different to me, and one that is very old and very different now, too.

It's hard for me to see all the changes in China, maybe because when I go back, I'm not trying to see them. I'm more interested in the things that I know will not have changed—the food and my friends. Or maybe I'm changing, too, and that's why I can't see what is different. It's hard for me to know. I feel the same on the inside, but maybe on the outside I'm different. As long as I change for the better, that's OK.

If you're reading this book, I would guess it's because you want to learn more about me. But I hope you can learn a lot more from it than that. Not many people have tried to do what I am doing, to be part of America and China at the same time. At least not many have tried to do it with so many people watching. One reason is that nobody was allowed to try before. Maybe that's the biggest change of all. Maybe that's an important lesson, too—that, with time, everything is possible.

I don't know if you'll learn everything about me and my life in this book, but I will give you as much as I can. I don't like to skip steps, so let me start at the very beginning, with my name as it is written in Chinese:

In English, a name can mean something else—for example, first names like "Summer" or "Jack" or last names like "Rice" or "Bell." It's the same in Chinese. My first name, Ming, means "light." To write it, you use two Chinese characters. The first character means "the sun," and the second one means "the moon." The two names together mean light all the time, day and night.

My last name, Yao, doesn't mean anything in itself. It's just a last name, like Jones. But the two characters that are used to write it, when looked at separately, do mean something. The first character means "woman." The second character means many, many, many—like a billion, only more. So that means more than Wilt Chamberlain, right?

If you know me, you know that's a joke. First, because I like to make jokes. Second, because I have been interested in only one girl since I was seventeen. When I tell people that, they don't believe me. Maybe I'm the only NBA player like that, but it's true.

There is another important difference between English and Chinese. With all Chinese words, the way you say them changes their meaning. If you say the word "shui"—it sounds like "shway"—it can mean "water," "sleep," or "who," depending on whether your voice rises, falls, or falls and then rises again.

Names are the same. If you say my full name the wrong way, it can mean "killer," or that I am a person who wants to take your life. That's the way a lot of Americans say it. To say it correctly, your voice must rise when you say "Yao" and again when you say "Ming." If you say it still another way, it means "incredible life." But translate "incredible life" into Chinese and you don't get Yao Ming; you get something different.

Maybe *that's* what this book is all about.

You should know that, at first, I said no to anyone who said I should write a book. There are many reasons. One is that I am a private person; that is my personality. Another is that I've always thought only heroes write books or have books written about them. It's important to understand the difference between heroes in the U.S. and in China. In the U.S., the heroes in movies and books almost always live. They face danger and they have the chance to die, but they don't. In China, the biggest heroes are those who have died for their country—not always (the first Chinese astronaut will be a hero no matter what happens), but usually. I'm not a hero. I don't think what I'm doing makes me a big hero. I'm just doing my job.

I also didn't think I'd lived long enough to have something important to say, and playing basketball in China, no matter how good you are, is not considered as important as I think it is in the United States. That's why I like to read books about history and biographies of important people in history. There are people who have faced more pressure than I will ever face. In Chinese history, the peasants revolted many, many times, but the dynasties changed only about ten times. If the leader of the peasants won, he would become the emperor, but there was little chance of winning, and he paid a big price for failing. His family would have a terrible reputation forever, and anyone directly related to him would be killed. That was the law.

Don't get me wrong; I don't see coming to the National Basketball Association as something revolutionary or see myself as a rebel. I am proud to be Chinese and proud that I learned to play basketball in China. I never want to lose my citizenship, and I will go back to live in China when my NBA career is over. I went through a lot to play in the NBA, but if I had to choose between playing in the NBA and playing for the Chinese national team, I would choose the national team.

Still, I like to read about people who have tried to make important changes because it makes what I face seem easier. I've never had to worry about what would happen to my family if I were to fail. And even though books of history and biography describe times that are very different from ours, reading about how someone under great pressure makes a decision can help me make my decisions. And sometimes reading about someone else just helps me not to think about the challenge I face for a little while. I know this, too: just because I'm in the NBA doesn't mean I can't still fail. People in China expect much more from me than just being able to say I played in the NBA. I expect more from myself than that, too.

At first, I didn't believe writing about my experience could help other people. Many Chinese are coming to the United States for the first time and trying to live in a new culture, but I had many advantages as a number-one draft pick that they will not. I wondered if my experience was too different for it to help anybody. But I have learned something from people who lived a long time ago, people whose lives were much different from mine, so I could be wrong about that.

I also wondered what people still living in China would think of me if I wrote a book. It is bad for someone Chinese to act more important than he really is. Chinese people have no respect for someone like that. They won't show it, but that's how they feel. A few Chinese athletes have written books, but they wrote them at the end of their careers, not at the beginning. Most Chinese people who have written books about themselves were great leaders in government who had retired. Or someone else may have written about them after they died. One exception would be a very important man, like the former general secretary of the Communist Party, Jiang Zemin. I don't think of myself as that kind of exception. I don't think of myself as a superstar yet, either, though maybe some day I will be. I am not planning to retire, either, although maybe I will have to after this book comes out. That's also a joke. I hope.

I finally decided to write this book because I saw the importance of my telling my story rather than having others tell it. You should know that not everybody helped me. Some people wanted to help only because of what they could get from doing so, and when they couldn't get anything, they tried to stop me. I don't know everything about those situations—some things I didn't want to know—so the people who helped me will tell you those parts of the story. I say "the" story, not "my" story. This is why, I think, it's OK for me to write a book. I don't think of it as being just about me. It's really about the people who helped me and how the world has changed to allow a player from China to be a number-one draft pick in the NBA. It's also a chance to tell the rest of the world something about my country and its people. Collective honor, the honor of the entire country, is very important in China. That's what I hope people will see in my work in the NBA. I also can send a message home about how a person can think of his country and still act as an individual out in the world.

I also wrote this book because other people were writing books about me. For a while a new one came out every six weeks in China. I had nothing to do with those books, and at first I thought, "OK, no problem, I can't stop them." But then I read one. It talked about me as though I've never made a mistake and made me sound like Mao Tse-tung. The truth? I have failed many, many times. You probably will learn more about those times in this book than the things I have done right. Everybody likes to talk about success, and the media has said many nice things about me, maybe more than are really true. But I think there's just as much to be learned from things that went wrong.

I wasn't worried about failing in my first year in the NBA. I just wanted to try. I didn't want to fail, and I tried my best not to fail, but the most important thing was that I tried. That has changed now, because I know I can play in the NBA. The summer after my first year I thought more about failing because the goal had changed. My rookie year was good, not great, but I did enough to push my goals higher. I became a starter, and I played in the All-Star Game, so doing less than that at any time in the future will feel like failure. I don't know how American fans think, but in China if you score 30, the fans want you to score 40. If you score 40, they want 50. After my first NBA season, the Chinese newspapers were talking about how many years it will be before I win a championship, how many years before I am the league MVP. This is what makes me think about failing. These are very big goals, but I will be looked on as a failure if I don't reach them. I could tell you that what other people think is not important to me, but that's not true. I have this chance to play in the NBA because of a lot of people. I don't want to disappoint them. It would be easier if I didn't care about them, but that's not how I am.

I think differently about failure than a lot of Chinese. In China, many people won't try to do something if there's not a high chance of success. Whether I win or lose, I think I can get a lot from the process of doing something. I can be afraid to fail or lose, but I can't let my fear stop me from trying. But it's very hard for Chinese people to risk defeat. There's a very well known saying from 2,000 years ago. The translation is "The successful are the kings and royalty; those who have failed are bandits and villains." Every Chinese person knows this expression, and too many live by it.

To me, this means that Chinese people can be too concerned about the result of what they do. There's another expression: "The winners always write the history books." Or you could just say that if you don't win, nobody will remember you. In the U.S., both Michael Jordan and Charles Barkley are famous, even though Barkley never won a championship. Charles still works, even if it's only on TV. I respect that he's still working. But he talks a lot and says many things I don't think he really believes; he just wants people to say, "Did you hear what Charles Barkley said?" Anyway, he is why I say that in America, if you work hard and don't make it, you can still be famous. But China has a long history, much longer than America's. In China, you're famous only if you win or die trying. Otherwise, people will forget you.

Another thing is that if you don't win, nobody remembers why. They just remember you didn't win—by forgetting you. It sounds strange, but it's true. If a coach or a team wins, they will say the coach or the players are great. But if there were injuries or a superstar player is missing and the team doesn't win, no one remembers that. It's the same for individuals, too. Take the players on the Chinese national team. They are all famous in China. They have all made it. But I remember when I went to the Shanghai Sharks junior team. We had sixteen players at the first camp. My best friend Liu Wei and I are the only ones who made it to the Sharks. We made it to the national team, too. We are known all over China, but no one remembers the rest of those players. Maybe some of the other fourteen were good enough but got injured or sick. Maybe a coach made a mistake in not playing them more. Maybe other problems stopped them from doing their best. There's a reserve player on the national team now who was a starter on the junior national team. The junior team was leaving the country to play in a tournament and someone forgot to get him a new passport, so he couldn't go. Maybe his career would have been different if that hadn't happened. No one thinks about any of that. It doesn't matter. Those that don't make it are gone. It's over for them.

Thinking about that makes me scared, really scared. That, I think, could still happen to me. If I'm lucky, I won't get hurt. If you get hurt, you're finished. If you don't win, you're forgotten. That's why I feel a lot of pressure. My first year I didn't care about Rookie of the Year or about being an All-Star or how many points or rebounds I had. I would have liked to win the Rookie of the Year award to show that the Rockets were right to pick me first, but the most important thing for me was to keep playing. I had some injuries, and there were times when I was very tired, especially after playing all summer for the Chinese national team, but I'm the only Rockets player who played in all eighty-two games that season. So now I feel that nothing new can hit me, because now I know what it feels like to play every game of a season. I know what it's like to play without a break, to struggle and then play well and then struggle again. I feel that I fought through everything and, in at least this respect, came out on top. In China, people say if you have a good start, you are halfway to victory. I think I made a good start.

But I don't think it's right just to look at a result. As I said, I believe the process is important. I did not win Rookie of the Year, but I did my best. Let me do it over again and I could play better, but I was not angry that I did not win. I did more than I thought I would or could do my first year. I would've predicted that I would average maybe 10 points and 6 rebounds, and I averaged 13.5 points and 8.2 rebounds. I did not think I would play in all eighty-two games; in fact, I thought I would not play at all when the season started because I arrived late to training camp. I certainly did not think I would start as many games (seventy-two) as I did.

I know that I represent China to a lot of people, even though I'm not 100 percent Chinese anymore, or, I should say, 100 percent like the average Chinese person. My parents and I live most of the year in the U.S. now, yet sometimes my father will say to me, in Chinese, of course, "The bicycle keys are over there. Oh, I mean the car keys." That is just an example of how China is different today. I don't think I would ever make this mistake. There are almost as many cars as bicycles in China now. But when Chinese people my father's age and older think about going somewhere, they think only of bicycles.

We were not poor, but my parents never had a car until we came to live in the United States for my rookie year. I grew up in Shanghai, which is like New York, and having a car there is very expensive. Taxis are cheaper. It's different in Houston. I have my own car, and my parents have one, too. Maybe I will also get one in China, but only if I'm there enough to use it and I can find one big enough for me. Big luxury cars in China are very expensive, both to buy and to keep. The most popular cars are Volkswagens because factories in China make them. No other car company does that. To buy a car from outside China, like a Mercedes Benz or a BMW from Germany, you must pay a high tax. With the long NBA season and traveling to play for the Chinese national team, I would only be able to drive my car in Shanghai for, maybe, a month. Right now it's not worth it.

This is one reason I feel that people in the U.S. can learn only 50 or 60 percent of what it is to be Chinese from talking to me or watching how I live. You have to go to China to really understand. Even in China my life is different from the normal Chinese person's; that's true for anyone living in Shanghai or Beijing now. Those cities are only a very small part of the country. Other Chinese cities are just as big, but the people live very differently there. And most people do not live in big cities but out in the country, like farmers. I don't think it always will be that way, though. The government is promoting the way the city people live in order to teach the people in the country that they must change, to show them the new world. Too many people are still living in the old style. But it's really changing now, and it already has changed a lot in Shanghai and Beijing and other places in southern China.

Many Chinese are afraid of change, but the ones who live in the cities must show them there's no reason to be afraid. It's just hard to trust something when you've lived a certain way your whole life, especially when big change in China hasn't always made things better. China is the oldest civilization in the world, but sometimes it has changed and moved backward, not forward. Sometimes when it has moved forward, it has erased its past, and that was a big loss. If you read about China's history, you will know what I mean. Today many changes are coming from the West, and most Chinese people have been taught that the West is bad. Those are some of the challenges in getting all Chinese to trust the changes that are happening today.

So if you want to see China as it has been for many, many years, you'd better hurry: it's changing every day. You can still see the Great Wall and the Forbidden City and other famous places, but you can't really know China just from looking at bricks or buildings. People tell you the most about what a place is like, and people in China are changing, too.

Maybe, in some ways, my thinking never has been like the average Chinese person's. I grew up in Shanghai, which is now the most modern city in China. You could live there even if you don't speak or read Chinese. And I've lived in the U.S. for a while now, so that has made me different. But I still think of myself as Chinese, and, of course, that's how people see me. Some people see me as all of China. That's a big responsibility, and at first I was afraid of making a mistake or doing something wrong. Now I've learned to relax a little bit. If you're careful about everything you do, that's not living a real life.

I think the result I am looking for will be there with hard work and a little luck. I've already found out, mostly on the Internet, that a lot of young Chinese have the same ideas. I think it's really good that there are so many young people in China who think like that.

One reason for this change of thinking is that my generation of

Chinese doesn't study Confucius the way our ancestors did. Confucius was a scholar and teacher who lived in what is now Shandong Province from 551 to 479 B.C. He taught the proper way to act, whom you should respect, and how you should approach everyday life. Learning is obviously good, and everyone and everything has something to teach. Confucius has been respected for a long time for good reason, but sometimes respect can be carried too far. Studying just one school of thought every day—whether it's Confucianism, Buddhism, Taoism, or Jeff Van Gundyism—can limit your imagination. If everybody thinks the same way, where do new ideas come from?

A lot of things Confucius talked about have to do with what is already known or what has been learned from other people, not going out and exploring and learning things that haven't been learned yet. One Confucian belief is that the lives of rulers and their advisers are the highest examples of virtuous conduct. It's a good idea, but you can see how that might not seem realistic to someone living in today's world. Another belief is that a son or daughter should not move too far away from the house he or she grew up in if his parents are still alive. That wouldn't work for most people today.

The traditional Chinese scholar's exam is based on an eight-part test that has nothing to do with creativity; instead it requires memorizing the Confucian tablets and repeating them word for word. To understand Confucianism is to understand exactly what he taught and to believe it. You don't ask if it's right for your life or not. You don't live by just some of it. In old China, it's not even all or nothing. It's just all.

However, there are teachings from long ago that I have found useful. Someone I've studied a lot is Zhuge Liang, a military adviser who lived from A.D. 181 to 234. His life is recorded in a book called *Mastering the Art of War* and in another, 120-chapter book, *Romance of the Three Kingdoms.* The title refers to the three kingdoms that existed during his time. Two were very poor, but with his help they worked together and always stopped invaders from the strongest kingdom. But after Zhuge Liang died, those kingdoms were easily beaten.

His teachings are different from those of Confucius because Zhuge Liang does not try to tell you exactly what you should do in every situation. Instead, he gives you beliefs you can apply to a problem. His theory is that you should use everything at your disposal—all your soldiers, all your captains, all your generals. Find a way to use them 100 percent. The challenge is finding the right way to accomplish this.

I don't know who first said it, but this proverb is something else I believe: A lion leading a lot of sheep can defeat a sheep leading many lions. The important part is that I must decide when I am a lion and when I must be a sheep. I don't believe you are always one or the other.

This sort of thinking was helpful to me when I got to the NBA. I had to use everything I had. Physically, I was at a disadvantage. Zhuge Liang, in real life, was like that, too. He wasn't very big or strong and his armies weren't, either, but he used his head to defeat people who were bigger and stronger.

I was tall, of course, but I wasn't very strong. It was easy to push me away from the basket, and it was hard for me to push other people away. I'm stronger now, but there are still a lot of NBA players who are stronger than I am.

Overcoming physical strength with mental strength is not a new concept in China. There is a Chinese saying that you must use the finest steel in the narrowest part of the sword for it to cut and not break. I had to find what my strength was in the NBA and use that as much as I could. I couldn't worry about how I looked or how other people played or what NBA centers before me had done. I had to block all that out. I would remind myself that even if my opponent was strong in many areas, we, as a team, had only one goal, and that was to get the ball in the basket. It didn't matter how we did it or what part I played in doing it. I must admit that this is not a common way of thinking in the NBA. A lot of players have grown up believing they must do everything for their team to win. In China, the first thought is how to work with everyone else to achieve your goal.

There is also a martial-arts novel that has helped me: *Xiao Ao Jiang Hu*, by Jin Yong. Translated it means, "The Smiling Proud Wanderer." Not everybody uses this book as guidance for how to live life, but I like the way the hero in the book lives. He is very principled in the way he does things. He knows what he should and shouldn't do in every situation. But he isn't an overly serious person. He jokes around a lot. He's relaxed, even when he's about to die. I know this is just a story, but it's a very famous one in China. If there's one thing I hope and strive for, it's that when I am in a very difficult situation, I can be as relaxed as he was.

The second thing I got from the book relates to the hero's martial skill. I'm not saying I want to practice that martial skill, just the philosophy behind it. As with all schools of fighting, there are different positions you can take to prepare for attack or defense. If I want to hit you in the face and I start with my fist held high in front of me, you know what I want to do. But if I don't do anything, then you don't know where I want to strike. You can't go in knowing what you must do, because you're not sure what I'm trying to do. I use that in basketball. If I'm attacking you, I don't want to make the first move. I want you to wonder a little bit about what I'm going to do. How a player reacts to that tells me something about him. He almost always will show me his strength. Then I can try to adjust to that. In any battle or game, you have to make it the kind you feel comfortable fighting, or the kind that is more comfortable for you than for your opponent.

It's easier today for Chinese people to decide what they want to study and how they want to live their life. I'm no expert on Confucius, because I haven't studied all of his teachings. Since I haven't done that, it's not for me to say what his influence on China and education has been. All I can tell you is that in the past, people in China studied Confucius very closely. I haven't and I am not alone in not having done so. If it had applied to me, I would have studied it more. If there were things I could use, I would use them.

What does this change of philosophy mean for China? Maybe in the future, the Shanghai market will not be known for selling copies of Rolex watches and Louis Vuitton bags but will offer original Chinese watches and luggage. But the old way has existed for several thousand years. It could be a thousand years before it's completely changed. One example of the way the process has begun: now some Chinese use watches, even though they are a Western invention.

Many Chinese people are afraid to change rules and ideas that have been passed down for thousands of years, or even decades. I think this is why: If a law or a thought comes from the ancestors and doesn't work, then it's their fault. But if you change it and it fails, it's your fault. This goes back to the fear of failure. It's as if some Chinese believe not being at fault is more important than finding a way that works. Nothing works all the time. No one gets it right the first time, every time. Sometimes you must fail. Sometimes you must make changes. This is life.

I've always believed that if I'm successful, I will be a big success, and if I'm a failure, I will be a big, big failure. It's interesting
to try to do something nobody has tried before. It is like going to
a place you've never been before. Everything is new and exciting,
and no matter what, you will learn a lot. But the process of getting somewhere is the same wherever you are or whatever you are
doing. If you want to get to the second floor, you must take one
step at a time. If you know where your target is and it's far away,
don't always look at it. Just look at your feet and walk your walk.
And then one day you will lift your head up and put your hand
out and see you are very close.

I'm also not afraid to say what I think I can do, which does not
fit with many Chinese people's idea of humility. I can be a humble or modest person. I just don't like the Chinese way of being
humble, which is not to say anything. When I was with the Sharks,
I would say, "We have to make the playoffs" or "We should get this
victory" or "We are going to win the championship." I would say
it only when I believed it, and I don't say it every time about
everything, but it doesn't matter; it's not very Chinese to say such
a thing, ever. In China, teams and players say nice things about
each other. They play very hard against each other and try to win,
but before they play, they almost give themselves a reason why
they might not win. Even when I was playing in China, I started
saying, "We will beat this team" or "We will win the championship." A lot of people weren't happy about this. But this is who
I am. If I succeed, I feel that saying what I wanted to do helped
me. And if I fail, I will feel that it brought me down. Either way, it
makes me try harder to succeed than if I said nothing.

I was that way in China, but I am more that way now. I can't
help it; I'm here, I'm getting used to a new life, and I have to
keep changing.

FANG FENG DI (Yao Ming's mother*; translated): *That is the difference between who Yao is and who I am. I never predicted how I was going to do. If I want to win a championship, I won't tell anyone. I'll just try to do it. When I was captain of the 1976 women's national team that won China's first Asian Championship, I was happy, of course, but the articles at the time singled me out as the reason. I felt embarrassed because anyone in my position would've done what I did. Morally, it wasn't something special that I did. Yao is more flamboyant and confident. I was surprised by his aggressiveness in the NBA. He'd never shown that before—his combativeness, getting technicals, and dunking in people's faces. But I've never worried about his turning bad. I look at him within the team, and he doesn't act special or expect special treatment. I'm just proud that he usually accomplishes what he says he plans to do.*

I never saw my mom play basketball, but my coach for the Shanghai Sharks played on the men's national team at the same time she played for the women's team, and he said my mom played very hard, like a tiger.

My father was a little bit softer as a player. That's why he never went to the national team. That's what my Sharks coach told me. But he said my father's shot was pretty good. Some people shoot the ball soft. He shot it like a rocket. *Ssssshhhsssh.* No arc, but it went in. I've seen it. The Sharks have been around for only eight years, but before that there was a professional team in Shanghai. There was no name; it was just Shanghai's team. That's the team my dad played for. There are a lot of players, like him, who are retired but still like to play. So every Wednesday the old players play

---

*See Cast of Characters for a list of the people whose comments appear throughout the book.

against the Sharks' junior team. I think that's good. That's where I got to play against my father a lot. I was bigger than him then. My dad always shot from the outside. He didn't want contact with me inside. But I still didn't dunk on him. I was too skinny. Besides, somehow it doesn't feel right to dunk on your dad.

The first time I played against him, it felt like the first time I played against Shaq. I was not with the Sharks' junior team yet. I was still a student, maybe ten years old and 5′11″. My dad is 6′7″. That's why I say it was like playing against Shaq. How could I push him out? I couldn't. How could I shoot over him? Forget it. I couldn't do anything against my dad the first time I played him.

I played against my mom once, too. I was older then, maybe fifteen. It was right before a Sharks' junior team game. I wanted to warm up, so we played one on one. She had a hook shot, but she's only 6′3″. She couldn't use it against me: I blocked it every time. It was just for fun, but I beat her. It wasn't close.

My parents were my best coaches, even though they never really practiced with me. We talk about basketball all the time—after every game I've played, even my first year in the NBA—but I can count on one hand how many times they have actually played with me.

I once said I just wanted to be a basketball player, I didn't want to be the face of a whole nation. But remember the movie *Spiderman*? Before the uncle dies, he says, "With great power comes great responsibility." I believe that. If I'm making a lot of money, I have a responsibility to play well and improve myself. If a lot of people watch me play, I have a responsibility to talk to the media. Beyond that, every player should also do what he can to help people away from the court. He can't help everybody—he must know that, too—but he should do what he can.

I have learned that I can't make everybody happy. My problem is that I want to try. I know the history of China and what it means to people there for me to be successful. It's almost hard to believe that we are the oldest civilization in the world and that we have the most people and yet very few Chinese have become famous in other countries. The way I look at it, it's a great honor to represent China to the outside world, and I appreciate the support of so many Chinese back home. When I came to the NBA, I put an advertisement in the Shanghai newspaper that said, "How does a single blade of grass thank the sun?" That was my way of telling the fans how much they had helped me.

That's why it's hard when, wherever I go, especially in China, so many people want me to sign an autograph or take a picture. I am honored that they want my picture and autograph, but I also want to have a life and achieve the goals they have for me. If I had signed every autograph and stopped for every photo that I have been asked for in China, I would not have had the time or the energy to play a single game. So I've had to learn how to say, "No," or "That's too much." Sometimes, when I think of how big my country is and what the people's hopes are for me, I feel as if I can't carry that burden. I have carried it so far, but there were times during my first year in the NBA when I wondered if there would be a day that I couldn't and would collapse. Now I feel like that only every once in a while. If I were an American and playing basketball, I believe I would be playing just for me and my family and maybe my friends. If I failed, I would have to worry only about hurting myself and them. But in my country, many people believe that if I fail, it says something about all of China. Maybe this is only in my head, but sometimes I feel as if I'm carrying those millions of Chinese with me, that my failure will be their failure. However, I am starting to not think that way. I've also learned that pressure is like a sword. You can either point it outward or direct it at yourself. You can see pressure as a weight on your shoulders, pushing you down, or a hand on your back, pushing you forward. You just have to make it work for you and not against you.

If I want to remember what my life was like before, I just have to go to the apartment I share with my parents in Shanghai. It's designed especially for tall people—big furniture, very high showerhead, high doorknobs, high counters, even a high toilet. People who are not very tall say they feel like kids again when they visit. When my friend Erik sits in one of our chairs, his feet don't come close to touching the ground. Anyway, we have a trophy case in the living room that holds a picture of me and my parents. We are at a restaurant in Shanghai at sunset. It's my sixteenth birthday. I am standing between their chairs, leaning forward, smiling. No one else is in the picture. I look so different in this picture. My smile is a real smile. I still smile today, of course, but my face is not the same. There are wrinkles from worry and from being tired. I can tell you one reason why: from 1997 to 2000 I never had a vacation. I've still never left Shanghai, ever, to do anything except play basketball. Some day I will, but I don't know when. It could be a long time.

The way I think of it is professional player, professional job. Sometimes when I'm tired, I'm happy that there are commercials and billboards that show me smiling. They do what I can't—smile twenty-four hours a day. One reporter asked me about seeing my picture everywhere, and I told him that the Yao Ming in the pictures is better-looking than I ever could be. That Yao Ming, I said, could make movies.

It is a gift to be able to smile through anything, and I think Magic Johnson has it. A friend of mine had his photo taken with Magic Johnson at the All-Star Game. It was the same as all the other pictures I've seen of Magic: the man with the perfect smile. You could take one photo of him, attach it to a photo of every person who wanted a picture with him and the result would be no different than if you actually took each one of them together. Kobe Bryant, I think, is a lot like that, too.

I don't have this gift. When I'm tired, I can't hide it, on or off the court. That's another reason I don't think I could make movies, even though I've had offers. I'm a bad actor and it would be impossible to find a stunt double.

After my first year in the NBA, I had twenty days at home in Shanghai. It was like heaven. I gained twenty pounds. (I wanted another twenty days, but not another twenty pounds.) A good time is always too short. Shanghai is my home, but our apartment there almost feels like a hotel room now. I'm never there long enough to get back that feeling of home.

Looking back now, my first year in the NBA felt like a highway, a long highway; I couldn't see the end or even how far I had to go before I could rest. When you can't see the end, the road seems longer. There were times when I felt that I needed to stop and get gas, but the signs said I still had 500 more miles to go. The good thing is, I only sometimes feel like that now.

LI YUANWEI (general secretary of the Chinese Basketball Association; translated): *The demands on Yao to be part of both the Houston Rockets and the Chinese national team every year is obviously a big problem and an important one for us to think through and try to resolve. I can't speak for the NBA and its eighty-two-game schedule and preseason games and playoffs; I can only speak for what the Chinese Basketball Association will do. As I see it, there are only two things Yao is obligated to do—play as a national team member in the most important international tourna-*

ments and also help promote basketball, the national team, and Chinese basketball. Aside from those two requisites, we should try to find a way for Yao to adjust and rest in order to prolong his career and protect his health. The current situation is a problem. It's too mentally and physically exhausting for him. But it's something we have to sit down and think through, so that while he fulfills his obligation to the NBA and the national team, he's still well protected and well rested.

To look after individual interests is a policy not only of the CBA but also of the central government of China. The party secretary basically said this at a recent party congress. It wasn't always that way, but the party secretary said this has to be a central point of development in the Chinese society of the future.

A lot of people think Yao eventually will have to make a choice between the NBA and the CBA. I think he can do both. Yao already has done a good job with that. The reason he doesn't have to make that choice is that he understands the benefit of having both. Yao couldn't have the influence and impact he has without the support of 1.3 billion people. The interest people have shown in him reflects his value in society. I think Yao understands that. That said, he has multiple obligations, and most players don't, at least not every year. I believe an accommodation can be made for Yao to find the rest he needs. His career will not be shortened because of both obligations.

The thing about Yao Ming, the reason he is so successful, is not just that he's tall and skillful. It's because he has made a lot of right choices. He has made choices that endeared him to 1.3 billion people in China. That's why he is so influential and successful. That won't change.

The Internet is one place I go to relax. I spend a lot of time on the computer, either playing games or reading bulletin boards and sending messages. I will chat about everything, life and basket-ball. On one Web site, I use my real name as my screen name, but I don't think too many people really believe it's me. That's good, because it means I can be just another person. I don't have the chance to do that very often. I also have another screen name that I use; all I'll say is that it's from one of my favorite computer games.

What I hope people, and especially my countrymen, get from this book is that process is important—any kind of process—and that in achieving a goal, finishing the process is very important. And there is something to be learned even if you don't reach your goal right away. No one thought I'd be in the NBA when I started playing. I didn't even think that. But here I am. The important thing is not that you're prepared to accept failure. It's that you are not afraid of it.

2

A BOY IN CHINA

The dream of playing professional basketball is not a big one with young boys or girls in China. I didn't always dream of being a basketball player. When I was a boy I just wanted to be famous, but it could have been as a politician or a scientist or an army general. I just wanted to do something important.

The chance of a kid in the U.S. growing up to play professionally is very small, but the chance for a kid in China to have a basketball career is even smaller because there are many more kids but only fourteen level-A pro teams. (You can't really call the lower levels professional.) The money in China also is much less than what an NBA player makes, so that's not part of the dream. The top players in China don't make much more than the NBA developmental league (NBDL) players make, an average salary of $30,000. But when a player in China retires, his body hurts the way any professional player's body hurts, and then he has to go out and find a new job. What kind of job can you get when your best skill is bouncing and shooting a ball?

That's why my parents never wanted me to become a professional player, even though my dad was one for nine years and my mom played for the women's national team. Their experiences playing are why they didn't want me to follow them. They wanted a better life for me.

They knew when I was young that I would grow to be very tall, but it didn't matter. To their way of thinking, being over 7 feet tall might make it that much harder to get a normal job, so an education would be even more important.

The reason they knew I would be tall is that it is a Chinese custom to X-ray a child's hand and measure the bones to determine how big they will become. I was only 5'5" and ten years old when they X-rayed me and said I would grow to be 7'3". I was very happy and excited at first. When I got a few years older, I thought about how I'd have a lot of problems being taller. I worried that I wouldn't find a girlfriend. I also worried about how tall my kids would be, since kids are usually taller than their parents.

I never felt uncomfortable with my size, though. I can't tell you why, but my parents helped. When I was in school and my mom would walk with me, if I didn't stand up straight, she'd slap me on the back and say, "Straighten your back." Of course, some kids made fun of me, but it didn't really bother me. Everybody has been made fun of for something.

Finding clothes my size wasn't a problem because I could just wear my dad's old stuff or buy men's clothing. Tailors are not expensive in China, either. By the time I was taller than my dad, I had a contract with Nike, and they gave me stuff to wear. I've never needed a lot of clothes; I wear mostly T-shirts and warm-up suits, anyway. I have about a dozen dress pants now, but I wear them only when it would be wrong to wear a warm-up suit or shorts.

The only real price I can think of for being so tall as a kid is the cost of riding the bus. In China, they make you pay once you reach a certain height. Kids shorter than 1.27 meters—that's a little under 4′2″—didn't have to buy a ticket when I was growing up; they could ride for free. I can't remember ever riding for free, it was so long ago. I had to pay, or my mom had to pay for me, even before I started going to school. I was five years old and already 1.47 meters tall, or 4′8″, the first time I went to school.

My mom took me to see a very famous coach when I was around twelve. It wasn't her idea; a friend told her she should. I didn't know why I was there. He told me to turn around and walk away from him, and then he had me walk back. That was it. Then he told my mom that I would never be a good basketball player. My butt was too big, he said, and I didn't have good balance. (He didn't tell me any of this; he just told my mom.)

He also told her there was another young player who did have what it takes to be great: Wang Zhi Zhi. His mom had played on the national team when my mom was on the national junior team. "Her son will be much better," the coach told my mom. "He has big hands and long legs. He can run and jump."

I never knew any of this when I was growing up. A few years later, though, I joined the Sharks' junior team. The coach didn't say anything about his prediction. A few years after that I went to the Sharks' first team. Still this coach said nothing. A year after that, I was invited to try out for the national team. Then I went to the NBA. That's when this coach began to tell everyone he had discovered me and that, when I was young, he gave money to my school every year. From what I've been told, he gave money to the school one year, the last year I was there. That made my mom unhappy. That's when she told me what he had said the first time she took me to see him.

My mom was not disappointed by what the old coach said at the time he said it. My parents wouldn't stop me from playing if that's what I wanted to do, but their hope was that I would want to be good at something else. More than anything, my mom just wanted me to go to college. In China, a player in any sport who wants to be professional stops thinking of school at a very early age. You start practicing hard when you are twelve or thirteen years old and go to school for only three or four hours three times a week. In America, you can do something one year and then do something else the next year, or you can go to college and still think about being a pro. In China, it's one or the other, and once you decide what you want to do, that's it; it's not easy to change. My mom thought if I went to college, then I could stay in the city, find a job, find a girlfriend, take her out, then find another one, maybe change girlfriends four times a year, have a good life.

But basketball wasn't something my parents played because they loved it. They played because that's what they were asked to do by the government.

My mom told me a story about playing basketball during the Cultural Revolution that is still hard for me to believe. During that time, the national slogan was: "Learn from the workers, farmers, and soldiers." Those people were the most respected. Sports were not considered important, but Mao Tse-tung liked basketball because it relied on working hard and working together. Basketball in China was still not very good, though, because no foreigners were allowed to coach or teach. Chairman Mao certainly would not have wanted American imperialists poisoning the people's minds about how to play the sport. So who were they going to learn from?

With the national slogan in mind, the athletes worked in the factories or carried bricks as part of their re-education. The factory workers and farmers and carpenters were in charge. Players would work in the morning and then practice in the afternoon—if they could find a place to play. The gyms were very poor, and players were always looking for a decent court. They didn't play many games during the Revolution; they just practiced a lot. The purpose was to learn how to be a better Communist Party member and a better citizen; learning how to beat another team was not the goal. No matter what job you had—basketball player, singer, reporter, soldier—whatever you did had one purpose, to serve the Revolution.

Here's the part hardest for me to believe: The basketball team manager also would have factory workers, farmers, and soldiers come to watch practices. Afterward, he would ask them what they thought the team should do to improve. More shooting? Better dribbling? More defense? Since the workers didn't know much about basketball, they'd usually tell the players they just had to work harder and never give up.

It sounds funny, but the people at that time didn't know any better. This is what they were told to do. Even though the workers didn't understand a lot about basketball and might have made some strange suggestions, they felt they had a great responsibility, that since they had been invited there, they had to do their best to help. It's not like they had a choice. It would have been very dangerous to refuse. But most Chinese people also feel a strong sense of duty to their country. I will always play for the national team for the same reason. That's why it's hard for me to understand why some NBA players don't want to play in the world championships. It seems that in the U.S. sometimes individual glory is more important than national honor. There should be a balance between doing something for yourself and doing something for your country. The Cultural Revolution just took this idea too far. In some ways, it feels like history has played a joke on us Chinese.

YAO ZHI YUAN (Yao Ming's father; translated): *I started playing basketball when I was twenty years old. I was a factory worker, hammering electrical parts together. That was actually a good job during the Cultural Revolution, because factory workers were considered the highest social level. Farmers were the second highest, then soldiers, then scientists. Businessmen were the lowest. I know some will say my son grew up to be a businessman of sorts, but I don't see him as one. Anyway, that was a different time from now. It's better the way it is now, and I'm proud of what he has become.*

When local government officials saw how tall I was, they suggested that playing basketball would serve the country better. So I went to play for the Shanghai basketball team.

After only two years of playing, I began to have problems with my left knee. That forced me to put more weight on my right leg, and after six more years, that one hurt, too. I retired from basketball when I was twenty-nine. After that I was given a job at the Shanghai harbor, inspecting ships that wanted to dock there. This time I didn't swing a hammer but a permit stamp. I worked at that job until we came to America for Yao Ming's rookie year. Having to live half the year in Houston and the other half in Shanghai, the thing I miss most is my job. I had power. A boat needed approval to dock, and if you wanted to, you could always find a reason they couldn't.

I was lucky, though, to get that job. Once athletes in China stop playing, they often have to start at the bottom. They usually don't have any skills, they're years behind people their age who started working regular jobs sooner, and you can't make enough money in any sport not to work when you're finished playing. We didn't want that for Yao Ming. That's why, at first, we didn't want him to go to a sports school.

I played with a real basketball for the first time when I was nine years old and went to the junior sports school in my district of Shanghai. My dad gave me a toy basketball when I was four or five years old, but I didn't think it was that exciting. I had other toys that I liked much better. They took me to see the Harlem Globetrotters when I was little, too. They were fun to watch, but it's not like I wanted to play basketball because of them.

In China, when you are nine years old, there are two kinds of school in each district—a regular school and a junior sports school. You are not picked for the junior sports school because you have shown you can play a sport. If your parents are tall or strong, or if when you are young, tests show you will grow up to be tall or strong, then you are invited to go to the junior sports school. Since both my parents were tall and played at a high level, I knew I would be invited. My parents agreed only because playing basketball in a junior sports school can improve your chance of getting into college; it counts as extra points on the college entrance exam. From what I hear, it's the same for high school players in America: playing a sport doesn't help if it hurts your grades, unless you're a really good player. Then it can do more for you than good grades. Some things are the same everywhere.

But that's why my parents let me go to the junior sports school—because they thought it could help me go to college.

The education in the district sports school, for kids ages nine to twelve, is not too different from the regular school. There also is a city-wide sports school that takes kids at that age from all over the city. This school is for the kids who government officials already know can grow up to be professional players. The city-wide school has better equipment, better coaching, better places to play and practice. I could have gone to that school, but my parents didn't want me to go.

LIU WEI (member of the Shanghai Sharks and the Chinese national team, and Yao Ming's best friend; translated): *Yao and I*

met for the first time on the basketball court in middle school, play-
ing against each other. Neither one of us went to the city-wide ad-
vanced sports school, because neither of our parents wanted us to
grow up to be basketball players. I was the better player then. He
already was tall, almost 2 meters, but he could not play very well.
His skills didn't really develop until he went to the Sharks' junior
team. It's funny, but because I grew up with Yao Ming, I've never
looked at him as being unusually tall. He never had a growth
spurt; he just started taller than most kids and kept steadily get-
ting bigger.

Once we became friends, we spent a lot of time playing com-
puter games together. I was best at the fighting or combat games,
while he'd always win the shooting games. We never had a lot of
money, so every week we'd collect what we had and go to a video
arcade. "Streetfighter" was our favorite back then.

I was thirteen and a half when I learned I had the chance to play
professionally. That's when the Shanghai Sharks invited me to try
out for their junior team. They were still not called the Sharks at
that time; they were just the second-division Shanghai basketball
team. Two years before I moved up from the junior team, they finally finished second in the second division. The first two teams
in a division move up and the bottom two teams move down, so
Shanghai was finally a first-division team. That's when they became the Sharks, because first-division teams must have a nickname. The second-division's first-place team that year is now in
the third division. They ran out of money, so all their good players left.

CBA teams can get their players from anywhere in the country,
but most players choose to stay close to home. For a long time the
army team—the CBA's Bayi Rockets—had an advantage because

they looked for players all over the country and invited them to join their junior team. All a player had to do was agree to join the army. It was a good deal because Bayi players never had to worry about money or actually going to war. They even sent my mom a letter when I was twelve asking if I knew where I wanted to play. I could've joined the army system, but she didn't want me to go. She still hoped I would stay home and go to the university in Shanghai.

The Bayi Rockets' advantage in getting players is a big reason why they won the CBA's first five championships. But it's different now, at least for the Sharks. In the mid '90s, when the first division became big, Shanghai's team had only local players, like every other team except the army team. But now players all over China know about the Sharks, and because Shanghai is a big, modern city, the team has become very attractive. If a player joins the junior team but isn't good enough to play professionally, the team will get him into a good high school or college. The Sharks have that kind of power. Not every team does. So a lot of families want their sons to go to the Sharks.

It was still not easy for my parents to let me join the junior team. The coach of the Sharks at that time was a friend of my parents, and he talked to them a lot about letting me play. He assured them I wouldn't be wasting my time, that he would help get me into a good university if I didn't want to play for the Sharks or if I wasn't good enough. Since I like to take things step by step, not skip over anything, there is a part of me now that is disappointed I never had a chance to go to college. I am actually an honorary student of a college in Beijing, even though I've never been to a class there. I still hope to go to college, maybe after I retire, and study international business relations or something like that.

But I wasn't thinking about any of that when I got invited to join the Sharks' junior team. It is a big honor just to make it to that level. It is also the only way to have a chance to play for the Chinese national team. I hadn't always dreamed of playing in the NBA, but I always hoped to play on the national team. One reason is that the first famous person I became aware of was China's Olympic gymnast Li Ning. He won three gold medals in the 1984 games. True fame, when I was a kid, meant doing something big for your country, like winning an Olympic medal or being a great army commander. China, despite being so big and having so many people, hasn't done very well competing in sports against the rest of the world. People in China know this and think about it, even if they don't talk about it. So when someone is successful outside China, it is a big accomplishment. But for a long time there was little chance to compete outside China, or at least outside Asia.

The first step on my road to changing that began once I joined the Sharks' junior team. There was little time for school after that. We practiced almost ten hours every day for the first six months, four practices a day—6:00–7:30, 8:30–11:30, 2:30–5:30, and 6:30–8:30. This was just training camp to make the junior team. After six months the coach said, "OK, from now on we will practice only four hours a day." That's still a lot, but after ten hours it seemed like nothing. We were very happy.

LIU WEI: *I try not to think of those early junior-team days. All I remember is that we were constantly running and training. I don't think my hair was ever dry, for six months straight. But it's not an accident that Yao Ming and I both came out of the same district and rose to the top. We always had each other to lean on or to push harder. I don't know that anybody else had that. Even after he went to the NBA, when I lost four games in a row playing for the*

Sharks, he called and calmed me down and gave me some advice. We won five in a row after that.

My parents helped me become a better player even if that wasn't what they wanted. When I played for the junior team, I was very soft. I did not go to the paint. I always wanted to shoot open shots from the outside, the same way my dad played. I'd shoot fade-aways and pump-fake a lot. But I'm a center. If I don't go to the inside, nobody else has a chance to get open.

I remember once when I was fifteen, I went to a Sharks game with my parents. I was still on the junior team, and the Sharks were still in the second division. They were playing the Beijing Ducks, who had a center named Shan Tao. (Mengke Bateer joined the Ducks a few years later, and the two of them were known as the Twin Towers. This was before San Antonio's Twin Towers, David Robinson and Tim Duncan, but after the Houston Rockets' Twin Towers, Hakeem Olajuwon and Ralph Sampson. We need some new nicknames for teams with two big men.) Shan Tao had a low-post move using his elbow. He'd turn holding the ball up and his elbow out, which forced the defender to back up or get hit in the chest or face with Tao's elbow. The extra space allowed Tao to shoot a jump hook without getting it blocked.

My mom took my hand and said, "Do you see that move?"

I said, "Yeah, I see it."

"You're soft. Try to use that," she said. When your mom calls you soft, you listen. I started going harder to the paint after that.

My father also told me a very important thing. It's why I don't like to hold the ball a long time and don't like players in the paint who do. Every time you have the ball and no chance to shoot, he said, move quickly right after you pass the ball because the defense will watch the ball, at least for a little bit. That means they're not concentrating on you. In that second or two, you can move into a better position. It's a small thing, but it's very important. I still use it today.

I've learned at least one thing from every coach I've had. My father had a teammate, Wang Chong Guang, who was only 6'4" but a great coach for big men. He told me a lot about playing center; he just told me too early. It wasn't until I was older that I understood what he had showed me. He was the first to tell me that when I'm on defense, I must read the other team's offense the same way I read their defense when I have the ball. He also told me how you can make fakes on defense the same as on offense. What is important, at both ends of the floor, is to get the other team worrying about what you're doing to them instead of thinking about what they want to do to you.

I was on the bench a lot my rookie year with the Sharks. No player likes to sit on the bench, but Wang Chong Guang made me look at it differently. Sometimes, he said, it can be an advantage to be on the bench at the start of a game because it gives you a chance to study the other team's offensive players. You can watch what they like to do or find out if they're feeling good or bad that night or see what they don't do well. Then, when you go into the game, they may not know anything about you, but you will know a lot about them.

FANG FENG DI: *After the Chinese national team qualified for the 2004 Olympics by winning the 2003 Asian Championships, reporters asked Yao Ming how he felt about the tournament. He said, "I helped accomplish the dream of many of my teammates who never have been to the Olympics." He also mentioned the previous national team coach, Wang Fei, who was disgraced when the team lost to South Korea in the Asian Games a year earlier. Yao Ming* said Wang Fei taught him many things that he did not understand as a young player but that were very useful once he came to the NBA. He was grateful that Wang Fei had opened up that world to him before he got there. I was touched by his answers. I'm proud that he's always thinking of others, that he has a team spirit and sensitivity. Yao Ming always has remembered his roots.

Some people believe the one-child rule in China created a lot of spoiled children, particularly boys. "Little emperors," we call them. As parents, we didn't want to create a little emperor; we just thought it was important to raise him morally, that he be an up-standing person. It was important that he be educated and be able to make a contribution to country and society. The reasons he turned out as he did are a combination of things—his personality and the way his father and I were raised and our experiences. Equality is a big theme in our family. We loved him as much as any parents would, but it's difficult to know how much influence we had because Yao Ming was always such a good kid. Personal-ity-wise, he never did anything growing up to earn a serious scolding.

Yao Ming, in fact, was too nice in some people's eyes. One ex-ample is from kindergarten. The teacher called me in on parents' night and told me that Yao Ming was too idealistic. She said, "You have to teach him survival skills." Because of his size, he's always had a big brother mentality. His class would take a bus for a group outing and he would give up his seat. Or if they had to clean windows at the school, he would volunteer. Maybe he be-lieves he has to do more because he's always been bigger than everybody else. He's always helped out as if it were an obligation because of his size.

His teacher was worried that Yao Ming's idealism and helpful-ness would make him susceptible to people's taking advantage of *him. I told her we didn't know how else to raise him because that's how we were taught to act.*

Yao Ming's junior team also had a parents' night, and the team officials asked if I had any thoughts. My only concern, I said, is that my son not develop bad habits. I knew that players on the pro team drank, smoked, gambled, and hung around with women. Yao Ming was thirteen when he left home, so he deserves a lot of the credit for not developing those habits.

I never really got a chance to pamper him. Pampering to me means overlooking serious character flaws. Yao Ming never presented a problem with any of that. He never hung out in bars, and he never used his size to get his way or bully anyone.

My mom talks about how good I was as a boy, so I don't know if she has forgotten this or just doesn't want to know about it. When I was ten years old, I went to a video arcade for the first time. I loved video games right away, but I had no money, so I'd steal my mom's money. For two years, she didn't know. At first I'd only take 1 RMB, which is about 12 U.S. cents. You could play some video games three times with that. Then I took 1½ RMB, then 2. Slowly I took more and more. The last time I took 100. That's when she found out. My parents started giving me an allowance every month after that. It wasn't much of a punishment, but I guess they didn't see anything wrong with my wanting to play video games. In general, my parents weren't as strict as most Chinese parents.

In China, many parents will order their kids to learn something outside of school—music, painting, dancing. The kid doesn't get to choose; the parents decide. My mom never ordered me to do anything like that. She just let me try whatever I liked. All she wanted was that I not learn to do something badly or the wrong way. Regular school was different. If I didn't do my homework, my dad would smack me. My mom also pushed me to read and study at home about things that weren't taught in school. It wasn't that hard to get me to do those things because I was interested in history and geography. I wanted to know about the world outside China, and I wanted to know what China was like long ago.

Even when I went to the sports school to play basketball, my parents never said, "You must win the championship" or "You must be the best." Some kids would tell their parents, "I got a good score. I got 95 out of 100 on my test." And the parents would ask, "Why didn't you get 100 points?" Or the parents would ask, "Who was first in your class?" If the kid said somebody got a better score, the parents would say, "You must beat them."

My parents never said anything like that. The only time they'd say something was when my score was below 60. Then I'd get smacked.

That's why it's not that hard to live with my parents even now. It's relaxing for me to be with them. I don't have to worry about their telling me I did this wrong or that wrong or I should have played this way or that way. When I come home and the door closes, I know I'm safe and there will be quiet.

Kids grow up differently in the U.S. than in China. In China, parents will say, "This is the way you do it." In the U.S., it seems as if parents give the kids many choices and let the kid decide, perhaps telling them why one way is better than another. My parents were like that before we ever came to America. They didn't mean to be like American parents; they just turned out that way. I would say, from my experience, that the way my parents chose is the best way to do it.

I also spent a lot of time living away from my parents when I was growing up. When I joined the Sharks' junior team at thirteen, I started living with the rest of the players at the Sharks' training facility during the week and going home on weekends. On Saturday night I'd go home, and on Sunday night I'd return to the team. I did that until I was seventeen. That's when I went to Beijing for the junior national training camp. Then I could go home only every three or four months.

I was born in 1980, so by then Mao Tse-tung's Cultural Revolution (1966–1976) was over, but you could still feel what life had been like during that time. Chairman Mao once said, "More people, more power." What he didn't think about is more people, more food.

There were rations on everything when I was little. The government gave you tickets to buy food. They weren't food stamps because you still had to pay. The tickets didn't mean you would get food, either. You had to have the tickets just for the chance to buy food, if there was any left. Once you used up your tickets, that was it, even if you had more money. There were tickets for everything—food, clothes, radios. Very few people had cars—we didn't, as I said earlier—but I remember that we always had a TV.

ERIK ZHANG (agent for Yao Ming): *I grew up in Shanghai during the hard times. In 1978, two years before Yao was born, my father won a company lottery to buy a TV. The government allotted a certain number of each product to each company. The company directors would hold a lottery to see which workers would be allowed to buy the product. Winning the lottery meant my father had to stand in line overnight outside the store because there was no guarantee that there was a TV for everybody who had a ticket. The TV turned out to be black-and-white with a 9-inch screen. My parents would set it up outside so as many people as possible could watch*

it. Sometimes there would be 200 people gathered to watch that
9-inch black-and-white TV.

There was no more ration system after 1985, but some people still collected those tickets, just to have them. They're worth a lot of money now. There's a place in China you can trade them. When I was a kid, I collected them for a while, but I gave up. I didn't have the patience. When you look at the pictures and writing on the tickets, though, you can imagine what China was like then, and the thought process of the people. There were pictures of Chairman Mao and talk of the greatness of Chairman Mao. He was like a god to a lot of people in China. They thought Chairman Mao would never die. Even now many still have him in their hearts.

My first home was a small apartment in Shanghai. I lived there with my parents and my grandfather on my mother's side. That grandfather died in 1999, a year before I went to my first Olympics. My father's parents didn't live too far away, and I'd go see them every Sunday if I had time, which was most of the year. I might talk a little with them or watch TV. Most of the time I'd watch them play mah-jongg with the neighbors.

I got sick when I was seven years old. There was something wrong with my kidneys, and I had to take medicine. But they gave me the wrong medicine, and I got even sicker. As a side effect of the medicine, I went deaf in my left ear. I didn't know I'd lost my hearing until one day the phone rang. My dad picked it up. It was my mom, and he gave me the phone to talk to her. I put the receiver to my left ear, then asked my dad why my mom wasn't talking.

I hadn't noticed anything wrong before that. I wouldn't say it's a problem today. The only problem is that when I sit with someone to talk, I ask them to sit on my right side. When a coach or player talks to me during a game, I will always turn my head so I can use my right ear to hear what they're saying. The first English word I really learned was "Eh?" It has the same meaning in every language.

YAO ZHI YUAN: *We took Yao Ming to the hospital to see if there was something that could be done to restore his hearing. The doctor gave us hope that there was. First, he said the ear tube was blocked but could be cleared when he got older; it wasn't a big problem. As he got older, we'd take him to the hospital regularly for therapy. They'd blow compressed air into his ear, trying to make the ear canal bigger, they said. But every time they tested his hearing, it was only 60 percent. It wasn't getting worse, so they hoped that meant it eventually would get better. By the time he got to middle school, it was too late for anything to change.*

I was twelve years old when I started learning English. America and China were on good terms by then, so learning English made sense. A lot of Americans already were visiting China, and a lot of Chinese were moving to America. My mom told me that, to help prepare for my future, I must learn English and how to use a computer. People learned English to go into business or to study in the U.S.; she thought I could use it in business. She wasn't thinking of basketball or of me going to America at that time.

The first word I learned—not counting "eh?"—was "cake." I drank a lot of water every day when I was little, so my mom also taught me how to say "I want some water" in English. I didn't know which word was water, or what each word meant. I just knew that saying those four words would get me water. It was when I started to play for the Sharks that I really began to learn English. We had a lot of American players, so I had a chance to use it. I also came to the U.S. for two months during the summer of 1998. I didn't learn to speak a lot of English at that time, but that's when I learned how to speak "basketball English"—pick and roll, pick and pop, the paint, bounce-pass, back-cut, things like that.

I can still remember that when I was a kid, America was not considered a good place to go. "Down with American imperialism!"—I heard that growing up. I was told America was a bad place and Americans were bad people, especially because of the Korean War. Maybe some people in the U.S. don't think of China as being part of the Korean War because they sent what was called a voluntary army rather than the regular one, but Korea is very close to China. The Chinese leaders said they did it for our country's protection. I don't know much more about the Korean War than that we were the good guys, and the Americans were the bad guys, and we helped the North Koreans. And that the Americans thought they were the good guys and the Chinese were the bad guys and the U.S. helped the South Koreans.

I watched a lot of movies when I was young, and the ones about the war made Americans look very bad. U.S. soldiers were always running away or acting like cowards. I don't know if they were really American actors or Chinese actors who just looked American; they all had on a lot of makeup that made them look very strange. As a child, you believe everything you see in the movies.

One movie was supposedly based on a true story. It's about a Chinese soldier on a base near the end of the Korean War. He's the last one left; everybody else has died. He radios the Chinese air force and says, "Open fire. I'm the target." And then he grabs a bomb and runs into the middle of the U.S. soldiers. The planes use him as a target and he dies. That's how the movie ends. That's what it takes to be a hero in China. (See why I don't think I'm a hero or want to be called one?)

There was a lot of bad stuff about Americans in our school text-books, too, but by the time I was a teenager, there was less and less. This had something to do with how my thinking changed.

That's also when they started broadcasting NBA games in China. You could see Americans in the stands, and they didn't look or act like we had been taught. We had been told they were all poor and didn't have enough food to eat or clothes to wear. They were happy and smiling. You could just feel they weren't as bad as we were told. So that was a start. That's when I began to see that people can be different, but that doesn't mean one way is right and the other is wrong.

3

COMING TO AMERICA

The first time anyone talked to me about going to the U.S. was in 1996, when I was sixteen, but that was for college, not the NBA. At the time, I was in a year-long training camp for the Sharks' junior team. I had officially made junior team when I was thirteen and a half, but we didn't play many games, so every year seemed like one long training camp. My goal was to make the Sharks' senior team as soon as possible so I could get a good pair of basketball shoes. As a junior player, I didn't have any in my size (18), and I didn't have a contract with a shoe company yet. That's how I met my "cousin," Erik Zhang. Erik's home in Shanghai was fifteen minutes from mine, but his family had moved to Wisconsin when I was two years old, and we had never met. He was Chinese but was going to school in the U.S., and someone we both know asked him if he could find some shoes that fit me in America and bring them back to China. Erik asked me once over the phone, "Do you want to go to the United States to play basketball, maybe in a university?" At that time I really didn't want to. I just wanted to play in the CBA and on the national team. That was my dream, and it included playing with Wang Zhi Zhi as a teammate. But a friend of my mom's thought going to school in the U.S. would be better for me because at that time Shanghai was a level B team, not level A. Shanghai basketball just wasn't very good.

"OK, just go and meet Erik," my mom said. "It's no problem. Just talk to him."

So we went to his house in Shanghai. His mom worked at the University of Wisconsin, and that's where Erik was going to school. I went on the Internet for the first time that day so he could show me the Wisconsin arena. It looked big.

"Before I saw you, I thought you had a thirty percent chance of playing basketball in the U.S.," Erik said. "Now I think you have a fifty percent chance." But I still didn't want to go. I wanted to play in the CBA. I don't think at that time anyone in China had dreams bigger than that.

ERIK ZHANG: *Yao Ming's mom was concerned about education more than anything else, so I told her about the NCAA and how it worked. I was mainly looking to help my alma mater's basketball team. So, of course, I showed them the University of Wisconsin Web site. I think it intrigued them a little bit. At the time, nobody, not even Yao, expected him to make it to the NBA.*

I became aware of Yao through my wife, Angie. I hadn't heard of him before that. We're not really cousins; Angie and Yao are. She's a distant cousin on his mother's side. But then again, you can say everyone is your cousin, in a way, can't you? The truth is, Yao and I claimed to be cousins for reasons I'll explain later. We met that day mainly because I had heard casually from one of Yao's first cousins several months earlier that Yao Ming needed shoes, and I offered to help find some in the States and take them back to China with me. They were very difficult to find. Maybe if it had been basketball season, it would have been easier, I don't know. I searched almost all the shoe stores in Madison, some in the Milwaukee area, and some in Chicago. Eventually a friend of mine who owns a shoe store in a very out-of-the-way Wisconsin town agreed to go to a Nike warehouse in St. Louis and find a pair for me. They were the previous year's model, but I was pretty sure that wouldn't matter to Yao.

He and his mom came to my parents' house in Shanghai to pick them up. This was in 1996. He rode a bicycle to my place. I knew he had to be over 7 feet tall already, because I had a childhood memory of a teammate of Yao's father and a friend of my parents. We have this old house built in the '30s. This teammate of Yao's father is about 6'9". When he walked in, the doorway was just above his head, but he didn't have to duck. Yao actually had to duck underneath. I asked him about his basketball aspirations, and it was obvious he hadn't thought much about the NBA. He seemed kind of shy. He was more worried about how he was going to survive on the Shanghai team. His mom was more concerned about his getting a good education, not being trapped as an unsuccessful athlete in China. The school system kind of forces you to miss out on life. So his mom was asking me all sorts of questions about universities. I guess I pushed that idea a little bit. Hey, I was recruiting for Wisconsin. If he had an NBA dream, I was trying to wean him off it. Look, I said, this is how many teams are in the NCAA, this is how many teams are in Europe. Each year you have players from all these teams eligible to be drafted and only sixty players get picked and fewer than half of those make it for longer than three years. So your chances are not very good. You should listen to your mom and really look at education as the number-one priority. If you make it, you make it; if you don't, you have something to fall back on.

If you were Chinese at that time, you just didn't think of going to the NBA. Our best professional player then was Hu Wei Dong, and he couldn't have played in the NBA. He had bad knees, and he was a power forward in the CBA. Maybe if his knees hadn't hurt and he could've played small forward or shooting guard, he would've been good enough for the NBA, but that's about it. He was not very big but really strong. Mengke Bateer couldn't move him. In China we say northern guys are much stronger than southern guys. I think maybe southern China is like the West Coast in the U.S. and northern China is like the East Coast. But Hu Wei Dong is from the very, very far south. He was an exception.

STEVE FRANCIS (Houston Rockets guard): *The guys that I knew that played in China never talked about Yao. They always talked about Hu Wei Dong. So the first thing I did when I had the chance was to ask Yao, "What's up with Hu Wei Dong? They tell me he's like Michael Jordan."*

"Ahh, he's so-so," Yao said. That's his favorite word.

I said, "What do you mean?" He thought I was talking about what kind of player Hu Wei Dong was right then, not back in the day.

"He was a rookie when my dad was still playing," Yao said. "Now that he's a little older, he's not that good, but years ago he was very good."

Like I said, he's big on details. Be careful when you ask a question; he'll get all literal on you.

TERRY RHOADS (Nike's former director of marketing for China): *Nike China relocated its headquarters from Guangzhou to Shanghai in the summer of '96, and that's how I got my first glimpse of Yao Ming. We had a sponsorship agreement with the CBA to outfit all of the A league teams with shoes and apparel, so we were excited when the Sharks were promoted from the B league to the twelve-team A league that fall. It meant we had a home team.*

I didn't just meet Yao Ming, I played against him. We had a hard-core group of Nike employees who played pickup every week at a local gym, so to officially kick off our new relationship with the Sharks, we asked them to meet us for a shootaround. When the Sharks showed up, they didn't look too impressive—mostly 6'4" guys with a couple of 6'8"ers. But the last one in was Yao Ming, who at that time already was 7'3" and 230 pounds. We joked that he had chopsticks for arms and legs, and while he stretched, we whispered to each other that he probably was just another tall stiff, all height and no skills.

Then he stepped onto the court and started knocking down jumpers. He kept moving back and kept knocking them down. There were no real basketball experts in our group, but we reacted like giddy kids. We decided right then and there that we were seeing the future of Chinese basketball. Remember, as of 1996, China had produced only one NCAA Division I player, Ma Jian, who played two seasons ('92 and '93) at the University of Utah.

Yao was wearing the pair of size 18 shoes he had gotten from the women's national team center, Zheng Hai-xia. I hadn't made it to my desk the next morning before the Nike China GM asked how long it would take to get those Adidas shoes off Yao's feet forever. The basketball guys in Beaverton express-mailed a few pairs of shoes made for Alonzo Mourning, even though I'm sure they didn't think we actually had a player who could fill them the way Zo did.

I left China for the first time in 1997 to go to the Nike camp in Paris. That's where I met my first NBA star, Tim Hardaway, who was one of the camp counselors. He looked like the rest of us—two hands, two legs, one head—but he was quicker than anybody I'd ever seen, especially the way he dribbled the ball. His footwork, his hands—all quick. He would challenge everyone to play one-on-one until he was too tired to move. I don't remember who the best player in camp was because I didn't know what good basketball was then. There were eighty-five players at the camp, and I wore number 85. I wasn't worried about how good Hardaway was because at that time I was just thinking I'd play in the CBA. I didn't think I'd see anyone like Hardaway again.

YAO ZHI YUAN: *The trip to Paris made a big impression on Yao Ming. He was there for only six days, but he learned a lot—not just about basketball, but maybe about himself and his place in the world of basketball. He found out there are a lot of great players outside of China and how good a player could be. He knew for the first time where he stood among the best young players in the world. He thought, "I'm not that good, but I'm not that bad." When he went to Paris, he learned what was possible. There was no way to really know that until he left China. Then when he went to the U.S., it was more about learning how to improve his game and reach the level he'd seen in Paris.*

The winter after I went to Paris, I broke my left foot. This was near the end of my last season with the Sharks' junior team. I jumped for a rebound and landed on somebody else's foot. I sprained my ankle on that play, too. I think if I hadn't gotten hurt, they would've brought me up to the Sharks before the season ended.

Instead, I finally joined the Sharks the next season, didn't get hurt, and averaged 10 points and 8.3 rebounds. I didn't win Rookie of the Year, just like in the NBA—but the CBA didn't have a Rookie of the Year award at that time. Now they do. They also have moved the CBA All-Star Game from after the season to the middle of the season, just like in the NBA. The two leagues are looking more and more alike.

The next year, I broke the same foot again, this time in a pre-season game in December. Someone stepped on my left foot just before I tried to move. I didn't play until the end of the season, the last twelve games. When Houston first saw X-rays of my feet, they saw that my left foot had been broken a couple of times and were worried I might have serious problems and not be able to play. They had their team doctor fly to Beijing and check me out.

The doctor said I was OK, but I can tell you I haven't jumped the same since the second break. Not that I could jump high before then. The first time I tried to dunk, I was thirteen years old and about 6′2″. I didn't miss by a little, I missed by a lot. Dunking wasn't that important in China, so I didn't worry about it. A couple of years later I tried again and still couldn't do it. Then one day when I was fifteen, about six months after I'd last tried, I was walking across the court to put a ball away after a junior Sharks practice and decided to try. I surprised myself. I did it. I was about 6′8″ then. The Chinese always say, "You don't want to think about it, you just do it. That's how you become strong." But when I tried again the next day, I missed.

It was after that season, playing for the junior national team, that I dunked in a game for the first time. I had fallen down near our basket, and the other team went on a fast break but missed the layup. Someone threw me the ball, and I was all alone. I remember I jumped really, really high. My head was at the rim.

The next time I dunked was playing for the Sharks in my second game as a rookie. We were down by 10 with a minute left and won! I scored 7 points, including a dunk while being fouled. A guard drove and passed the ball to me, and I made it even though someone bumped me.

I know I can't jump very well, but I feel lost at the start of a game when I don't jump for the tipoff. I'm almost always the tallest player on the court, so it feels strange to watch someone smaller jump center. I've had time to get used to it; even before I joined the Rockets, there were times I didn't jump center. When both Wang Zhi Zhi and I were on the national team, he would jump for tipoffs because he can jump much quicker and higher than I can. He even won the CBA dunk contest during his last year playing in China. In my rookie year with the Rockets, our power forward, Eddie Griffin, jumped center, except for the first time I played Shaquille O'Neal. Eddie started to line up to jump when Stevie pushed me in the middle and told me to do it. That meant a lot. It showed he had confidence in me. It was almost like a movie the way he did it, waiting until the last second and then pushing me in there. Very dramatic.

I first thought I might be good enough to play in the NBA when I was eighteen years old and came back to China after two months of playing in the U.S. I never expected to play as well as I did. As a junior player, I had played against players in China who were two and three years older, and when I joined the Sharks senior team at seventeen, the players were as much as five and six years older than me. I struggled because they were so much stronger and had been playing much longer. In the U.S., I finally played against players around my age, and it made a big difference.

The trip started in Indianapolis with a Nike camp. Then Liu Wei and I went to Dallas to join an AAU team called High Five. That team traveled all over the country playing in tournaments. That was when you could take players from anywhere and put them on one team. Now it's different, I guess: you have to live within 100 miles of your team's home city. Dallas is where I first

met Teyo Johnson, who is now a tight end for the Oakland
Raiders. Teyo and I have been friends ever since.

TEYO JOHNSON (tight end for the Oakland Raiders): *I flew
on a red-eye into Dallas. When I got to the hotel and gave my
name, the girl at the front desk said, "Oh, you're with the big Chinese dude." I thought, "What, I've joined a team of foreign-ex-
change students?" I went up to the room and knocked, but when
no one answered, I stuck my key in the slot. Just then Yao Ming
answered the door. In his underwear. Tighty-whities. And all I
could see was up to his chin in the doorway. He and Liu Wei were
sacked out. He let me in and went back to bed. They had a cot set
up for me. I called my mom right away and whispered, "There's
this 7'6" dude in my room, and he's Chinese!" She said, "Yeah, the
Mongolians and Huns can be really big." I didn't know what to
think until we went to practice the next day. That's where I found
out—this dude could play.*

I played everywhere in those two months. After Dallas we went to
Stetson University in Florida; AAU summer leagues or tournaments in Orlando, San Diego, Phoenix, and Augusta, Georgia; and
Michael Jordan's camp in Santa Barbara. We didn't know where we
were or where we were going most of the time. At Stetson I worked
out every day with Lee Scruggs, the center who played at George-
town. He's playing now in the NBDL, the NBA's minor league. The
coach working with us was Tates Locke. He had just become a
scout for the Blazers, after many years as a college coach.

I played with High Five for the last time in San Diego. We
stayed in dormitories at United States International University.
The High Five camp was in a big building right next to the campus. On the other side of the highway there was a military base

with fighter jets; we could see them landing and taking off every morning as we walked from the university to the High Five gym.

I played against Tyson Chandler for the first time in San Diego. He was only fifteen years old, and people were already saying he could play in the NBA. He dunked on me and he played very well, but I played good defense, and I had a good jumper already then. I was three years older, but after that I thought, "Some day I could be good enough to play in the NBA, too."

TEYO JOHNSON: *We lost that game by one point. I thought Yao destroyed Tyson. He threw one of his shots back to half-court near the end of that game. Yao was hitting his jumper, too. Even then he could shoot and I could tell how athletic he was. I knew he'd get tougher and that's all he really needed.*

TYSON CHANDLER (forward and center for the Chicago Bulls): *The first time I saw him, I thought, "That's an amazing man." I was always the biggest guy around, but he towered over me—a big dude with a soft touch who could pass the ball. I hadn't played with any foreigners at that time. Being on the court with this huge man, someone who didn't know English and came all the way from China, was just a crazy experience for me, so it had to be a crazy experience for him.*

The whole game he was just knocking down his jump shot, showing no emotion. Then I came down, dunked on him, and screamed at him. Awww, man, I didn't know what he was saying, but the next time down he clapped his hands, called for the ball, backed everybody down, and threw it down. Nobody could do anything about it.

The other thing I learned in those two months was that you had to shoot as much as you could. "Look for your own shot"—I learned that fast. I had no choice. Nobody passed the ball. It wasn't a very good team. We had good players, but we didn't play together. The one really nice guy on that team was Teyo. They say he's 6'6" and 260 pounds now, and I think he was close to that already then. Our rooms at the university were right next to the pool, so we spent a lot of time goofing around in the water. I really liked that because in China, once they knew I could be a good basketball player, they didn't want me to swim. They thought it was too dangerous. They would've been really worried if they had seen Teyo body-slamming me in the pool.

TEYO JOHNSON: *I played point forward on that team, and I'd get ten assists a game, eight of them throwing the ball to Yao. What he liked most, though, was just hanging out, because it was the one time in his life he was allowed to be just another teenager.*

We couldn't communicate, but we connected. We've been boys ever since. I didn't see him again for years, but I'd call him every six months or so and set up a three-way conference call with a transla-tor. He called me from China the day I was drafted by the Raiders to congratulate me, and when I saw him at his second All-Star Game, he gave me his jersey. The way I see it, we're friends for life.

After San Diego, I went to Jordan's camp and worked as a coun-selor, but we played every night. In the trophy case in my home in Shanghai, I have two pictures of me with Jordan. One is the picture he took with everybody who worked or played at the camp. The other is of me walking off the court and Jordan patting me on the back. I'm smiling, but I look very skinny. One reason is that I had only $200 for the whole two-month trip. Liu Wei took something like $150 with him. The first two weeks, we didn't need to pay for anything; Li Yaomin, the Sharks GM, took care of us. But after the

Nike Camp in Indianapolis, he went back to China and took all his money with him. We were two young Chinese kids without any money, playing in places like Augusta, Georgia, and Orlando.

So for two weeks, Liu Wei and I ate nothing but 99-cent double cheeseburgers and the free breakfast they had in our motel lobby every morning. We made sure to get there very early.

When another coach from China came over to check on us, he said, "You look skinny."

"Of course," I said.

LIU WEI: *Actually, Yao Ming ate two cheeseburgers every day while I had one. Since I was injured and couldn't play, we decided he needed more food than I did.*

I guess Li Yaomin didn't know that in America a player has to pay for his own food. Maybe he thought it was like in China, where there's always a free buffet for the players at every hotel or the team pays for everything. I'm hoping that's what he thought. The High Five coach, Rle Nichols, lent us each $100 after we used up our own money. Rle is 5'6" and I couldn't speak English then, so we called him "Little Coach" in Chinese. I don't know where he is now, but I still owe him $100.

After Jordan's camp in Santa Barbara, Nike took me to Portland to relax. They let Liu Wei come with me. We went to a batting cage and I tried to hit a baseball. Out of ten swings, I hit the ball maybe once. Maybe. They also took us to Jet Ski on the Willamette River. I liked it, but that was pretty scary—maybe the scariest thing I've ever done.

TEYO JOHNSON: *He had me flown up to Portland, too, to hang out with him. Nike was going after him hard then already.*

He showed no fear Jet Skiing that I could see. When I was riding on the back he'd gun it, take a sharp turn, and fling me off the back. He got a kick out of doing that.

LIU WEI: *When we went to the batting cage, he took more than ten swings and didn't come close to hitting the ball, not even once. The best part of the Jet Skiing was when Yao Ming fell off and couldn't climb back on. He finally had to grab the back of my machine, and I towed him back to the dock.*

TERRY RHOADS: *A year later, Nike signed Yao to a four-year contract for $35,000 a year with bonuses that could take it up to $50,000. They'd already signed Wang Zhi Zhi to a similar deal for $50,000 a year. That's not bad money in a country where the per capita income is $1,000 a year. And since Yao's salary with the Sharks was around $20,000 a year, the Nike China staff liked to joke that Yao was a full-time Nike employee and part-time basketball player, since we paid him double what the Sharks did.*

When we finally flew back to Shanghai, there was a lot of media waiting at the gate. I'd been away two months, and I hadn't had a haircut the whole time. My hair was so long, I thought I looked like Dr. J or Ben Wallace. And even though we ate better in San Diego and Portland, I was still really skinny. Big hair, skinny body. When I saw myself on TV, I thought, "That's me?"

Being dragged by a Jet Ski was one of the few times I was behind Liu Wei. When it came to basketball and moving up, I was usually one step ahead of him. I was picked to play for the Shanghai junior team a couple of months ahead of him. It was about the same going to the Sharks, except I was starting as soon as I got there and he was on the bench at first. (I was starting but not playing a lot of minutes.) The one team he made before I did was the junior national team. He went a year ahead of me, because the junior team already had Wang Zhi Zhi at center. I joined the junior team when Wang went to the senior team, but I played only a year with the juniors before I moved up to the senior team. Liu Wei didn't join me until three years later, because the senior team already had enough point guards.

It didn't matter what teams we were playing for or if we were playing together; we were always friends. When I watched *Band of Brothers,* it made me think of going up through the basketball ranks with Liu Wei. A lot of people go in together, but then one is gone, then another gone, then another. Then at the end, there are just a few survivors left. The fewer the survivors, the more special it is.

If I helped him join me at the next level, it was with motivation. I'd show him my jersey. He did the same thing to me when he made the junior national team. That hurt because it was the first uniform either of us wore with "China" on it.

"See this?" Liu Wei said, showing me his junior national team jersey. "Feels niiiiccce."

The fall after we spent our summer in the U.S., we both played for the junior national team. But in between I had been training with the national team. They cut me on the last day before they left to play in the 1998 Asian Games.

Liu Wei and I had been playing together for a long time by then, and we talked a lot about basketball. We became really good friends in 1997. So we had chemistry. Nobody said it, but both Liu Wei and I believed it. We'd had only one fight the whole time we played together, not long after we became friends. It was during the '97–'98 season and we lost a game to the Jiangsu Dragons. I told him what he should have done differently, and he told me what I did wrong. The fight didn't last long. We got over it, and in the end it made us better friends.

The junior national team coach at that time, Ma Lian Bao, was in the army and later coached the Bayi Rockets' youth team. He's a good guy, and he's not very old, but he did things his own way. One of those things was not to let me and Liu Wei play together in training camp.

Now, I wasn't one of China's dominant centers at that time. I was just a second-year player in the CBA. The talent of the players on the junior national team was similar enough that you couldn't know who the starting five should be. There were three or four point guards on the team, but I was the only true center on the roster, so you'd think I would have been in the starting lineup. I wasn't starting for the Sharks yet, but other than Liu Wei and myself, nobody else on the junior national team had played in the CBA yet.

Ma Lian Bao knew we were good friends and had chemistry, so I'm not sure why he wanted to keep us apart. As a player in China, you would never question the coach about something like that. My guess? He wanted to make sure he had control of the team. Maybe he didn't feel threatened, but he was an army officer, and in the army having command is more important than anything else. If two players are good friends, maybe he thought that would give them power over him. I don't think he did it to hurt the team; I think he really believed he was somehow making us better. Maybe he thought Liu Wei and I tried to get the ball to each other too much or trusted each other more than the other players, but no one ever said that, and I don't think that if you'd watched us, you would have seen proof of that.

Once competition started, we were both in the starting lineup, and we won the junior Asian Championship, so maybe it wasn't that important. As I said, I liked the coach; I just didn't like that idea of his, and I've never been able to forget it.

There's one thing Ma Lian Bao taught me that I'll always remember. "Your basketball IQ has to be better than your basketball ability," he said. "If you have a high basketball IQ, you can see the chance for a shot or pass. Even if you don't have the ability to make that pass or shot, you can work on getting it. But if you have the ability without the IQ, you can't ever make the right pass or take the right shot. Then your ability is worth nothing."

I always played hard because I felt an obligation to become as good as I could and one day bring honor to China playing for the national team, but I didn't really enjoy playing basketball until I learned how to pass the ball and make the most of my teammates.

The change didn't come because someone showed me or told me something I didn't know. It came because the Sharks started putting different players around me, and I had to learn how to use them.

When I first joined the Sharks' senior team, other teams rotated centers in and out of the game just so they'd always have someone fresh to defend me. The season before I played in the 2000 Olympics, the Sharks added two very good American players. One was a shooting guard, Michael Jones. He wasn't fast, but he was a good shooter from 17 feet. He never missed an open shot. The other player was Montreal Dobbins, a power forward. He was a good rebounder and very strong, but his touch sucked. He couldn't make free throws or a jump shot, but he could score from 3 feet and closer. He was only 6'7" or 6'8", but the CBA is not like the NBA. At that time there weren't many players who were very strong inside. Only Mengke Bateer and Wang Zhi Zhi were like that. When we played the Beijing Ducks, Dobbins would guard

Bateer and just push him out of the paint—he was that strong—and on offense he was a very good duck-in player.

That meant we were better when I was at the high post and Dobbins played on the low block. When he'd post up, I'd always throw him the ball because he was so strong, he could get real close to the basket. The game became very easy because I'd take the other center outside and then give the ball to Dobbins two feet from the basket. That made it harder for teams to wear me down.

It sounds simple, but it was all new for me. Before that time I was just trying to score on my own. The year after the 2000 Olympics we replaced Jones and Dobbins with two Americans who were even better—George Ackles, a 1991 second-round pick by the Miami Heat, and Damon Stringer, who had played at Ohio State and Cleveland State. Damon was only a year or two out of college and really, really fast. He plays like Earl Boykins—a point guard in size, but really a shooting guard. Damon is not as small as Boykins, but he's just as fast, and he could shoot. (The first time I played against Boykins, who is 5′5″, I thought a fan had run out of the stands to try to take the ball from me.) Not too many teams have a point guard 5 inches taller than their shooting guard, but we did that season, with Damon at shooting guard and Liu Wei the point guard.

Ackles was already about thirty-four years old, I think, when he joined the Sharks. He couldn't shoot, but he could rebound and block shots and score on hook shots. That year we also had a 53 percent 3-point shooter, Sha Wei Guo. Wei Guo, in Chinese, means "defends country." But he wasn't a defensive player, not even a little bit. Every time he was on defense, I had to be ready to help stop his man.

The CBA allows every team to have only two foreign players. They are usually two of your best players, but the difference between them and the Chinese players is not that great. We had players from a lot of different countries play for the Sharks during my career, including Americans. There's a reason Americans come to play in China, and it's usually because they're not good enough to play in the U.S. or in Europe. But the first ones I played with still acted like they were the best. They wanted to be stars, or thought they should be. If there was a disagreement about how to play, they'd say, "All of you are wrong, and I am right." Our first foreign player was from Lithuania, the second from Russia, the third from the U.S. I'm not going to say his name, but he was a guard who had played in a Hong Kong league before he came to us. He was a good shooter, but he didn't pass the ball. He was on the team at the same time as the Russian player. Coach Li would tell the U.S. player to drive and pass the ball out for another player to shoot, but he never would; he'd always try to score himself. That year a lot of people from the media were always coming up to me. He would come over and talk to them about me or for me. He didn't last with our team very long.

In my first couple of years in the CBA I wasn't very strong, so we would get at least one big foreign center to help me around the basket. They'd do the work on defense, and I would go to the low post on offense, wait to get the ball, and try to score. I still would have to play very hard, and I'd get very tired. But by the 1999–2000 season I was getting strong enough that we could bring in American drivers and shooters, because I could play in the paint at both ends and I was starting to draw double-teams. That meant more work for me on defense—but not much more, because there weren't too many good centers—and offense was much easier. I didn't have to stand on the low block and fight for position all game long. If I didn't score, I didn't have to worry; I knew my teammates could.

The 2000–2001 season is when I really started to enjoy the game. If opponents didn't double-team me quickly, I could score easily. If they double-teamed me, I knew my teammates could score if I passed them the ball. Until that season we were one of the better teams in the CBA, but we had no chance of winning a championship. That year we were better than every other team except the Bayi Rockets, and they were only a little bit better. I felt a lot more relaxed because I really had only one team to focus on to reach my goal.

WANG FEI (former coach of the Chinese national team; translated): *The first time I saw Yao play was his rookie year in the CBA. He was already over 7 feet tall but very skinny. What stood out was his passion for the game. He played hard. And although he was skinny and didn't have much skill or know much about the game, that attitude made him very different from a lot of young players in China. He was willing to show his emotions—not in a way that was out of control or meant to embarrass the other team, but if a teammate made a good play, he'd let them know. That probably doesn't sound too extraordinary to someone in the U.S., but it's very unusual in China. I always wanted players like that, but they are very hard to find among Chinese players. It's not in their nature. It's a cultural thing. They tend to be very reserved, almost passive. Yao is the type of player I hope other Chinese will emulate. His personality is spontaneous. It's not something he's trying to be, he just is that way.*

I selected him for the national team in 1998. Both Mengke Bateer and Wang Zhi Zhi were already on the team. Yao looked up to both of them, almost as idols and big brothers. From a technical and physical standpoint, he wasn't a match for either of them at that time. I coached him very briefly then. Yao's transformation into a great player was gradual. It wasn't like one day the switch flipped and the light went on in his head. When I met him, he had no post game or footwork. He was like a blank piece of paper. But every year he got better.

I still hope to go to college for an education, but I think it was better for me to get ready for the NBA by playing in the CBA than in the NCAA. The first time I met Carroll Dawson, the Houston Rockets GM, I asked, "If I had played in the NCAA, how much better would I be now?" He didn't think I would've been any better as a player, only that I would've been more comfortable off the court because I would have already spent time living in America.

If I had played in the NCAA, I would be more mechanical and predictable, because centers in college play only inside and around the basket. Maybe I would've lost my 15-foot jumper or not learned how to pass the ball facing the basket. Maybe. All I know is that the CBA taught me how to do everything, because at first I had to block shots, then I had to score, and then, when everybody started double-teaming me, I learned how to use my teammates. For the Sharks to win a championship, I had to develop all my skills.

I know the CBA level of play is lower than the NCAA's. I also know the early rounds of the playoffs in China aren't challenging, and when the CBA first started, even the championship round was only two games. If both teams won once, the champion was whoever scored the most points altogether. The second year it went to best of three games and the fourth year it went to best of five. It was best of five every year that I played in the finals.

But when you play to win a championship, it doesn't matter what league it is, the pressure is the same. If I had played in the U.S. in college, I would've played for Wisconsin, and I don't know if we would've played in the NCAA finals every year. In the CBA, I played in the championship round against the Bayi Rockets three years in a row. That experience is very valuable. My Houston teammate, Steve Francis, played on two different junior college teams and at Maryland for a year. He played in the national junior college tournament twice and led Maryland to the NCAA quarterfinals. But he's never played in a game that could decide a championship. He'd never played in a pro playoff series before, either. It's not Stevie's fault that he didn't have that experience in college; I probably wouldn't have, either. That's what I mean. There is a lot that Chinese basketball doesn't have and can't provide, but it gave me something I probably couldn't have found anywhere else.

4

THE WORKOUT

I felt I'd lost something when I chose not to be in the 2001 NBA draft. That was the year Wang Zhi Zhi became the first Chinese player to play in the NBA, after being drafted thirty-sixth by the Dallas Mavericks in 1999. That's really why I wanted to go, because he had finally joined the Mavericks for the last few games of the 2000–2001 season. Then I thought to myself, "It's not over. I still have a chance. I'll only be twenty-one years old. I can go next year."

That was the same summer the Chinese national team went to Dallas to train for the 2001 Asian Championships. An American reporter asked me, "Why weren't you in the draft this year? Maybe you would have been a first-round pick."

It wasn't the first time I'd thought about that question. I had asked myself the same thing all summer. By then I was confident everything would work out, so I made a joke. "So what?" I said. "That means next year I'm going to be a second-round pick?"

I believe I could've done in 2001 what Wang Zhi Zhi did in 1999 and entered the NBA draft without everyone's approval, but I didn't want to go to the NBA or leave China that way. I also thought it was important that I be picked high in the first round, and my goal was to be the number-one pick. At the time I had to make my decision in 2001, I didn't know who would have taken me or at what number, but number one didn't look very likely. Weeks or months before the draft, most players are told by a team, "If you're there when we pick, we'll take you." But with questions about who my agent was and if the CBA and Sharks were ready to let me go, nobody was saying that. I could have been a second-round pick, just like Wang Zhi Zhi.

I also believed that my chance to go wouldn't be lost by waiting a year. I remember that Erik had told me and my mom, "In the United States, they've heard about you now." He couldn't believe how many people knew about me, and he said that meant the Sharks would have to answer to a lot of fans if I wasn't in the next draft. So we decided to use the year to talk to the team and the CBA and to get everyone to agree that it was time.

WANG FEI: *The year Yao Ming went was the right year for him to go to the NBA. He was more mature physically, psychologically, and in his skills. I know he was upset that he didn't go in 2001, but he made another big stride from 2001 to 2002. If you look at his statistics in the 2001–2002 CBA season, you can see that he made a big improvement over the previous season. It's not like he leveled off and you could say it was a wasted year.*

I could've entered the draft in 1999, too, just like Wang Zhi Zhi. An important official with the Sharks—I don't want to use his name; let's call him Mr. X—really pushed me to enter the 1999 NBA draft. I'm now almost certain, though, that that was only what Mr. X wanted, not the Shanghai Media Group, which owned the Sharks.

I really didn't want to go in '99, either. My dream then was to play on the national team, play with Wang Zhi Zhi, win the Asian Championship, play in the CBA, and, if possible, win a championship there, too.

But Mr. X said Evergreen Sports, a U.S. agency from Ohio, had spent a lot of money on a plane ticket and hotel and food to send someone to Shanghai to sign me to a contract. So we had a meeting at Shanghai's OTV building (OTV is a TV network in the Shanghai Media Group). We talked for a long time, just the team official and my parents and me. He talked about a lot of money. He showed me a contract. I now know that a normal NBA contract between a player and an agent is two or three pages, and NBA rules say an agent can't get more than 4 percent of a player's salary. The Evergreen contract they gave me was only one and a half pages. It said that Evergreen would get 33 percent of everything I made—a third of my NBA contract, endorsements, everything. That didn't include anything the Sharks would get as well. I had no way of knowing at that time that this was not a normal contract.

We were there for four hours. After we got back home, Mr. X called me there and asked how I felt about the contract. I said I didn't want to sign it. He said, "It's a good chance for you. You could go in the first round of the draft!"

For three days, he called me almost every hour. I turned off my cell phone and he called me at home. You have to understand: I was nineteen years old, and this was an important team official telling me I should do this. I didn't know what would happen. I didn't want to sign with Evergreen or go to the NBA at that time, but I also didn't want to hurt my career in China. It was almost unheard of for a Chinese player to go against his team, and I didn't know what Mr. X might do. My feeling was that the Shanghai Sharks could control me, like I was something of theirs that could be sold. Because it was Mr. X speaking, I thought the Sharks must want this. I didn't find out until much later that it was only what he wanted.

Evergreen and Mr. X kept asking me to come to the hotel where the Evergreen agent, Mike Coyne, was staying. "Let's just talk," they said. I went, along with my parents. They kept us there until three o'clock in the morning. I just sat there and listened. I felt that I had no choice—either sign or they wouldn't let me leave; sign or no one knew what might happen to my career. So I signed. As we left the hotel, my mom said, "I feel like we just sold ourselves." As soon as I found out from the NBA I could end that contract, I did.

BILL DUFFY (agent for Yao Ming): *The day in '99 after Yao Ming was forced to sign that contract, a Nike official called me. He and other people at Nike were down, distraught, upset. "Well, let me see a copy of the contract," I said. I looked at it and told them to get the NBA Players Association involved because Yao Ming had rights. Billy Hunter, the president of the players' union, saw the contract and said it was ridiculous: you don't have to pay this much money, there are rules and regulations, and so on. Then they asked me to get a legal opinion, so I had two attorneys look at the contract, and they both felt it was invalid not only from the perspective of the Players Association but just on its own merits as a legal document. It was a personal services contract that could be terminated by Yao Ming, which he did.*

The whole thing was ridiculous on two levels. First, how do you represent Yao Ming against the Sharks and then represent the Sharks in terms of their compensation, which is what Evergreen was trying to do? It never made sense, but Evergreen tried to package the whole thing together. Second, I've always known that the

way agents work is that if you recruit a player, you build a rela-
tionship, and the player on his own volition wants you to represent
him. This is not a product; it's a human being.

I first heard about Yao Ming after he played Tyson Chandler in
San Diego. I finally met him in Shanghai during the winter of 1999.
I went to see him practice and even shot around with him a little bit.
I was intrigued.

We were really ready to have him go in the 2001 draft, but then
the Evergreen thing came up again. Even though Yao Ming had re-
voked the agreement, they were claiming they still had a contract
with him. That scared everybody off, and when the Sharks rejected
him coming over, that was the lowest point. It was all set, there was
momentum, he was fired up to come over, and then the resurfacing
of the Evergreen contract fiasco prevented it from happening.

I still remember what that Evergreen contract said: they would
bring Yao Ming to America and promised to give him food, a car,
English lessons, a driver's license, an apartment, and a laptop
computer. All that for 33 percent. I found out later Evergreen
didn't even have a license at that time to be an NBA agent.

ERIK ZHANG: *Yao's family had asked me to evaluate agents*
for him in the winter of 2000–2001. Michael Jordan's agent, David
Falk, seemed to me the strongest agent out there at the time. I didn't
know Duffy then, so he wasn't among the agents I evaluated. I rec-
ommended to the family that they start with Falk, and I set up a con-
ference call between Yao's parents and Falk. I translated every word
of the conversation. It went OK. They just thought Falk was a little
too businesslike. I personally thought Falk's pitch was pretty good,
but Falk speaks fast. If you don't understand English and there's
something you like about him, he sounds confident. If you get a bad
feeling about him, he sounds very abrasive. He's not like Duffy, who

always speaks very softly. I've joked that Duffy always makes me feel like someone in my family died and he's trying to console me. He's very soothing, very gentle, and very sincere.

Falk was pushing me for a decision, and so I was pushing Yao's parents. That's when they said, "Well, we don't think he's better than Duffy." I said, "Who the hell is Duffy?" Yao's parents said they didn't tell me about Duffy because they didn't want to influence my research. I wasn't sure what to think, but once Duffy and I met, we hit it off almost right away, and everything was OK.

Sports agents were a new thing at that time in China. Some soccer players may have had them, but no one in basketball did. There wasn't enough money, there was no CBA draft, and the teams had all the power. When it became certain that I was going to the NBA, the government made new rules: every player must have a Chinese agent, even if he leaves the country, and every agent must take a test to get a license.

I had met Duffy three or four months before I first met the agent from Evergreen. I'd heard about Duffy from other people even earlier than that, so I felt I knew something about him before he started helping me. With Evergreen, Mr. X said he would find me an agent, and a week later I met the Evergreen guy.

When I talked to Evergreen, it was only about money: if I go to the draft, how much money I could get, they could get, and the Shanghai Sharks could get. When I talked to Duffy, he always talked about what the NBA was like and what I needed, like weight training and rebounding better. That's why I believed him. We talked a lot on many nights over the years, and I just had a good feeling about him. I know now that an agent's job is to worry about your money, too, because that's how the agent gets paid, but I wouldn't want an agent who worried only about money. No matter what happens, Duffy helped me reach my dream, and so I will always call him a friend.

BILL DUFFY: *My father was stationed in Taiwan in 1965 and '66, and I spent kindergarten and the first grade there. My adopted younger sister is half-black and half-Taiwanese. The formative years of my life were spent in Asia. I loved the culture, the food, everything. Having been exposed to Eastern thought and philosophy that early, I was a really big fan of the TV show* Kung Fu *when we got back to the U.S. I loved how Kwai Chang Caine always had a solution for every situation. He was cool and calm, and I adopted that demeanor for myself. His influence, to be honest, is why people think of me being that way. I also have an appreciation for the Eastern concept that the solution is balance. So anything involving China is a comfort zone for me. But my involvement with Yao was never guaranteed. Because of the time difference, I was on the phone from midnight to 4 A.M., and one problem after another would come up. I'd hear about more roadblocks and new setbacks, and begin wondering if it was all worth it. Then I'd talk to Yao Ming, and he'd say, "Hey, Bill, how's the family?" And I'd think, "I can't quit on this guy. I have to see this through."*

ERIK ZHANG: *When we started hitting different roadblocks late—meaning April—in the 2002 push to get Yao Ming to the NBA, I decided to do two things: put the idea out there that I was Yao's cousin and arrange for him to have an NBA workout in the United States. The reason for saying we were related was to prepare for the potential resistance from the Sharks to me as Yao Ming's negotiator. Most Chinese people are moved by the family concept. The club could argue it had Yao's interests more in mind than some business student from the U.S., but how could they say that about a family member?*

*I think Fang Feng Di suggested I be called a cousin. We were reading
Web site chat rooms and message boards to gauge public sentiment,
and there was a very favorable response to the idea of Yao's relative
representing him. In another time and place, maybe this little white
lie wouldn't have been necessary, but with the way the Evergreen situation had gone, we couldn't be sure. The Sharks clearly had an advantage since they were able to dictate their view to the public
through several mediums, so we felt we had to use whatever we
could to offset that.*

No matter what happened, I couldn't see a reason to play another
season in the CBA. There were no challenges left. If I had to stay
in China for another season, I would've played with the national
team but not in the CBA. I had done everything I could do there.
I averaged 30 points during the regular season and made 21 of
21 shots in one of the championship games against the army
team. I was the leading rebounder, scorer, and shot-blocker in the
league. I won the MVP award for both the regular season and the
playoffs two years in a row.

I won those awards even though individual records or awards
were not the most important thing to me. The most points I ever
scored in a single game was 48. Sun Jun, a player from northern
China, set the CBA scoring record with 70. His nickname, translated, means "The King of Tigers." He's really slow and can't
jump, but he's very smart. His shot looks terrible. He shoots the
ball like a volleyball player, using both thumbs from over his
head. But it always goes in. He was on the national team for the
2000 Olympics and he still plays in the CBA, but he has retired
from international competition.

Anyway, the day he scored 70 points, I scored 42. I thought after that game, "Maybe today I'm the scoring leader." When I heard

what Sun Jun had scored, I said, "What!? Seventy?" But at least I had led in rebounds that day, with 32. I didn't say I don't care about individual performance; I just said it wasn't the *most* important thing.

Looking back, I think I could've broken Sun Jun's scoring record. In the game when I scored 48, I had 36 in the first half. Their center couldn't stop me, so they'd just let me score and then tried to fast break every time to try to even the score. We led by only 6 points at halftime, 54–48, so their plan was working. But I started passing the ball more, and we got back quicker on defense and won the game. I already knew I was the best player in the league. I didn't need the most points and rebounds to prove it. Maybe that sounds like I think too much of myself, but you have to understand the level of basketball in the CBA. It is not very high, so it's not saying I'm special to say I was its best player. I'm not making anybody mad by saying it, either. And I never would have said that while Wang Zhi Zhi was still in the CBA; I might have thought it, but it would have been too questionable to say.

The 2000–2001 season is when everything changed for me. I learned how to lead a team. I started telling my teammates where they needed to be and how they needed to get me the ball. The first game of the season, we played the army team, the Bayi Rockets. It was like playing the national team: seven of their players, including Wang Zhi Zhi, were on the national team. We lost, but something had changed. The score was closer than ever before, and for the first time we knew we could play with them. And I discovered that what really interested me about the game was finding a way to use my teammates, to balance my skills with theirs.

I became much more aware of statistics and personal numbers when I came to the NBA because it was a way for me to judge how I was doing. I wasn't at the top in the NBA but somewhere in the middle, maybe closer to the top than the bottom. The numbers helped tell me how much closer. They're also everywhere—on the scoreboard, on the locker-room chalkboard, in the pregame scouting reports. And now there is Coach Jeff Van Gundy. He can tell me how many minutes and seconds it has been since my last offensive rebound—without looking at a piece of paper. He knows statistics nobody else knows.

That's very different from the coaches in the CBA. When the league first started, they didn't even keep individual statistics. They thought it was bad for teamwork. Maybe that's true. Even now, a lot of arenas don't show individual statistics on the scoreboard. All they show is the score, the game time, and the real time. And sometimes the real-time clock takes up most of the scoreboard.

I told everyone at the end of the 2000–2001 CBA season that we would win the next year's championship. That sounds like a big thing to say, but I wasn't the only person who thought that. A lot of fans felt it was time. The only difference is that I said it.

I was a big reason the Sharks' fans felt it was time. They had seen me improve every year, and after coming close to winning the 2001 Championships—we lost, three games to one, to the Bayi Rockets—it was time. Basketball in China is not like in the U.S., where there's a lot of competition and a lot of teams closely matched. Put me on one of the worst teams in the CBA and it would instantly become one of the top four. For a long time the difference between the Bayi Rockets and every other team was 20 points. Then the Sharks slowly got better, and the difference between the Bayi Rockets and the Sharks and any other team in the league was 20 points. The Shandong Tigers won the 2004 CBA Championship, so maybe there are three teams now at the top, but back then there were only two.

I also knew that Wang Zhi Zhi would be in Dallas instead of with the Bayi Rockets, but that wasn't the reason I thought we'd win. In a perfect world, I would have liked to have won the championship playing against Wang Zhi Zhi.

Erik told me I would be able to go to the NBA whether we won the CBA championship or not. But if we hadn't won, it would have been a big blow to me. All my championships in China, or for China, feel the way the Lakers' championships must feel: they're expected. So winning is like if you buy a car and someone takes it and you get it back. It's not a surprise. You're not excited; you're relieved.

I decided to take a big risk with the championship series tied 1–1. After the second game, I said, "The Bayi Rockets are old; they can't play with us." I said this on TV. I just wanted to give our players some confidence. I knew that a lot of people thought the army team had better players than we did. They were old, but not too old to win. I thought maybe they would hate me and attack me for what I said, foul me every time. Our coach was scared. "You shouldn't have said that," he said.

We won the next two games to win the championship, so I guess it worked. But after we won, I said, "The Bayi Rockets are not really too old. They taught the Shanghai Sharks a lot. I'm sorry I said that. I just wanted our players to believe we could beat them." I made sure to say that on TV, too.

BAI LI (director of the Shanghai Media Group; translated): *I wouldn't say winning a championship was a condition for Yao Ming to leave; what everyone wanted was for Yao Ming to try to win the 2002 CBA Championship. You have to understand that Shanghai had never won a basketball championship. The Sharks had come very close, reaching the finals two years in a row, and with the ex-*

perience gained from that, it seemed that the team was finally ready to take the last step. They'd also lost in the finals both times to the Bayi Rockets with Wang Zhi Zhi, who was now going to be in the NBA. We felt Yao owed it to the Sharks, the city of Shanghai, and the fans to take advantage of this opportunity. It would've been very disappointing for everyone if he hadn't at least tried. It's difficult to say what would've happened if the Sharks hadn't won the championship, but my feeling is that if Yao Ming hadn't done it in 2002, that would've meant there were other things wrong with the team that were holding it back. If he tried three times and failed, at that point his need to develop as a player should have become the first consideration. In that scenario, I think the Sharks would've started looking for another superstar and another way to build the team, because obviously the team as it existed hadn't been able to get the job done.

ERIK ZHANG: *For whatever reason, the Sharks immediately announced at the championship award ceremony that they would let Yao go to the NBA, and that apparently upset the CBA because the Sharks had said nothing to them about making this announcement. The league is still very young, so the chain of command or protocol between teams and the league office hasn't been clearly established. I'm guessing it's a little like the Raiders and Al Davis in the NFL or the Yankees and George Steinbrenner in baseball.*

The reason I wanted to have Yao Ming work out for NBA people in the U.S. was more to give him leverage in China than to show U.S. basketball people what he could do. I knew private workouts were something that's done by every player who's serious about being in the draft, and that's the message we wanted to send—that Yao was serious about being drafted. I also thought showing that he could leave China specifically for an NBA-related event also would carry some weight with anybody skeptical about his really being available. But the main reason I thought a workout was important was that it would raise tremendous interest and awareness of Yao. People would be excited about the prospect of seeing him in the NBA, which meant there would be pressure on anyone in China who tried to prevent that from happening.

Some people advised us not to have a workout because Yao's deficiencies might be exposed and that could damage his draft position. But I already sensed there would be obstacles in negotiating his release with the Sharks, and I was sure the CBA would try to reassert itself, because the Sharks had undermined their authority with the announcement. There was still a chance the CBA might not have let him go at all because the Sharks hadn't gone through the right process. We needed all the firepower we could get.

As it was, the first thing the CBA did after the Sharks' announcement was to pass a rule that a player must use a Chinese agent to negotiate his way to another league. I think it's too much of a coincidence that they instituted this rule right before Yao was about to go to the States. The Sharks won the championship in mid-April, and the CBA gave notice that all prospective agents could take an exam in Beijing in early May. The twelve who did so are now the only official basketball sports agents in China.

LU HAO (Yao Ming's Chinese agent; translated): *The Chinese agent's exam was held in a classroom at a local university in Beijing. I'd say there were about sixteen people who showed up to take it, and everyone passed. They told us when we signed up for the exam what it would cover. It took about two hours and consisted mostly of basketball questions—what is a 2–3 zone, what is a pick and roll, where's the free-throw line. I had played professionally for a while and coached and taught basketball at Xiamen University, so* *it was particularly easy for me. The mock test I made for myself to practice turned out to be almost identical to the actual one they gave us. But only twelve of the sixteen who passed the test became registered agents because you also had to put up a security deposit of 100,000 yuan, which is about $12,500. That way, if you treated a client badly or screwed up in some other way, they could penalize you by keeping the deposit.*

BILL DUFFY: *Working out players before the draft is pretty standard for NBA teams. They usually bring a couple of guys in and put them through tests and drills to check their skills, give them a thorough physical, see how they interact on a personal level, and find out how competitive they are. We had originally planned to arrange a couple of private workouts for select teams, but the logistics were proving difficult, and Yao had a very small window between celebrating the Sharks' championship and reporting to national-team duty. We had planned to have one workout in the West for the Warriors and one in the East for the Knicks. Then the media got wind of everything, and it quickly became bigger than we had anticipated. We weren't sure we had the resources to deal with security, insurance, facilities, all that. When we turned to the NBA, they agreed to help if we would open Yao's workout to everybody. I had a contact at Loyola University in Chicago, which was centrally located from the NBA's view, so that's where we held it, about a week before the NBA draft lottery, which is when the order of the first thirteen picks is decided.*

I couldn't be publicly involved with the workout because we were afraid it would upset the Sharks and the CBA, so I worked with Erik behind the scenes. It was a big step, just being able to facilitate Yao's coming over to work out. Erik accomplished that. Finally, we just conceded and got the NBA involved.

The teams on our preferred list before the workout were Seattle, Portland, Chicago, New York, and Golden State. Seattle had gone over and scouted him extensively, and the city has a large Asian population. Portland fell out because the makeup of the team and their level of interest discouraged us. Golden State was intrigued, but they didn't really know much about Yao Ming. If they'd had the first pick, they wouldn't have drafted him. I don't think they would've taken him if they had the second pick, to be honest with you, because they never took a close look at him. It's funny now, because no team does more than the Warriors to market and promote when Yao is coming to town.

I couldn't go to the workout, and I never saw a tape, but you could tell by the reports the next day that people weren't overly impressed. That's because most people in the NBA and most people in the media like to point out what you can't do instead of what you can do. Since he was more perimeter-oriented and played kind of elusively, they thought, "Well, he has no post game" or "He's a 7'5" guy who can shoot. So what, we've got 6'9" guys who can shoot." All the teams I called leading up to the draft would say, "Yao Ming likes the perimeter too much." You just get tired of it. There's only one perfect player, and that's Michael Jordan. Everybody else has some deficiencies, but they still can be pretty good.

It was over for me when I saw Yao play in the Olympics in Australia. I like to think of myself as being on the cutting edge in terms of knowing NBA-caliber foreign talent, so I know the quality of big guys in Italy and Spain. When I saw him get 27 points and 15 rebounds against the Italian national team, I knew this guy could play. Bill Walton and I watched that game together. I was pumping up Bill before the game. "You just watch," I said. Yao was throwing outlet passes, bounce passes to cutters, scoring inside, turnaround jumpers. Bill went crazy. Whatever Yao did after that didn't matter, because now I'd seen him play against top competition. I knew what he could do.

Above all, the Chicago workout brought a huge amount of awareness. We didn't know yet what was going to happen with the draft lottery, and we didn't have formal permission for him to come out of China yet, but it created this huge buzz because he was finally here. It was in the newspapers, it was on SportsCenter. Even if they weren't impressed, they knew now he was real.

ERIK ZHANG: *I felt if we could demonstrate that Yao really was ready to play in the NBA, then no matter how many roadblocks were created, the fans in China would see his going to the NBA not as a single individual but as the entire nation making it.*

The tough part for Yao is that he didn't get a chance to prepare for the workout at all. Once the Sharks won the championship, there was a lot of obligatory stuff he had to do—government banquets, celebrations, parades, a whole bunch of ceremonial stuff. This also was the first basketball championship in the history of Shanghai. The owner of the Shanghai Sharks is a media conglomerate, so obviously they were going to work it to maximum effect, with TV interviews and all that. Yao was pretty exhausted and emotionally drained—first by the challenge of winning a championship and then by dealing with all that came after it. But there was no way to say to anyone, "He can't do this, he has to prepare for the workout."

After we won the championship, I didn't touch a ball for ten days. There was no time. After you win a championship, everybody wants to meet you, take photographs, have dinner, give parties. The whole team had to go to different places to do this. So many people wanted to see us that my flight to the U.S. for my workout was pushed back two days. That meant that instead of coming over for a couple of days and adjusting to the thirteen-hour time difference, I left Shanghai on Monday and arrived in Chicago late Monday night. My first flight from L.A. to Chicago was canceled, so I got into O'Hare very late, around nine o'clock.

Although I worked out for everybody on Wednesday, I had agreed to work out and have dinner with the New York Knicks and the Chicago Bulls alone. Team Yao and the Sharks wanted me to do something for those two teams because they had showed a lot of interest in me, more than any other team. They had come over to China to watch me play many times, beginning long before I thought about going to the NBA. I wasn't the one making decisions at that point; I was just following the plan Erik had for me, but I was happy to honor the Knicks and Bulls as they had honored me.

With the time change and excitement over finally seeing my dream of playing in the NBA getting close, I couldn't sleep at all Monday night. I spent the night talking on my cell phone to my girlfriend and other friends in China, because it was daytime there. I finally started to feel like sleeping just when it was time to get ready for the workout. Right before I worked out for the Knicks, I drank four Pepsis—I couldn't find any frappuccinos with cream— and asked for an hour to shoot before they started the workout.

I met Bill Walton for the first time as I left the hotel for the workout. Walton was wearing a very funny T-shirt—all green and red and yellow—and he had on a tie but his shirt had no collar. He gave me one of those T-shirts. I thought, "What is he doing?" We just talked for a minute or two. He's always been nice to me and helped me, but from that day I've thought of him as a crazy, crazy guy. That was my first impression, and it hasn't changed.

I have to say, that first private workout was very good. All I did was shoot, but I made 80 percent of my shots, and from 15 to 17 feet I didn't miss a shot. We were in a big gym with many courts.

I found out later it was Moody Bible Institute, which is where they have the regular NBA predraft camp for players who want coaches and GMs to see them. There weren't any other players there, so I didn't play against or with anyone, I just shot and ran up and down the floor.

At that time I could speak only a little English, but I remembered all the basketball words from my summer in the U.S.—pick and roll, pick and pop, wing, elbow, low post, duck-in. It's funny now how things work out. The Knicks assistant coaches at that time were Andy Greer and Steve Clifford. They had been hired to work with Jeff Van Gundy and stayed to work with Don Chaney when Van Gundy quit coaching for a while. Then when Van Gundy took the Rockets job, they left New York to join him—and me. I went to dinner with all of them after the workout. I needed a translator for that because they talked a lot about business. That's why, afterward, Knicks coach Don Chaney said he thought I couldn't speak English.

If you've ever played basketball, you know the first practice after a long rest is always OK. It's in the second practice that you feel the missed time. I don't know why that is, but it happened to me. That's why my big workout in front of everybody else was just so-so. In that workout, I did maybe 60 or 70 percent of what I can do.

I've never told anybody this, but another reason I played the way I did in the big workout is that I knew Chris Christofferson, the center they brought in to play against me. I had played with him before, in 2000, when I was with the Chinese national team and we trained for a few days in Portland. Chris was with the University of Oregon at that time and played against me in a practice game.

Erik told me Christofferson would be in the 2002 draft with

me. I thought, "If I play well against him, maybe nobody will pick him." I didn't want to do that to him. So there were times when I could have dunked and I just shot it instead.

I know a lot of the GMs there thought I didn't work hard enough, that I should've beat him up, but I thought, "That's OK. It's just a workout." I knew it was important for me, but I thought the most important thing was not to get hurt. One of the Clippers players who was there in the stands, Quentin Richardson, said that he expected to see a regular NBA predraft workout, where the players try to kill each other. I didn't know anything about what a regular NBA predraft workout was or how I was supposed to act. I also think this was different. In those workouts, nobody is there but the coach and the GM from one team. For this workout, the whole gym was full. All the reporters and media were looking down from a second-floor indoor track, and all the coaches and GMs were in the stands by the court. There was a group of Chinese officials who clapped every time I ran by them. I never thought the workout was meant to show my best. You could see that by watching me play with the Sharks or the Chinese national team. It's like when you go to buy a car. If you see it in a magazine or in a commercial, you wonder, "Does the car really look like that? Is it really that nice, really that fast?" You can't know until you go to the car dealership and see it. Then you can tell if you want to buy it. Maybe then you drive it. You don't drive as fast as the car can go, but you can still tell how it feels. I was the car. The workout was a test drive.

KIM BOHUNY (NBA vice president of international basketball operations): *I was with Yao Ming at his hotel before the workout. There was an issue about what he was going to wear—Team China gear, Nike gear, or what. We decided to have some generic NBA jerseys and shorts made just for the workout and express-delivered that morning. I had to find out if he was a triple-X or quadruple-X. We had both sizes made, and I called his room to have him come try them on. (He liked the triple-X better.) He asked me where the workout was going to be held, and I could tell he wanted to ask me something else, but then a bunch of people joined us. I could sense he was a little nervous. Then we had a brunch so P. J. Carlesimo, who was the coach working him out, and everyone involved would know what Yao was going to be asked to do. Finally, we were in the car on the way to the workout, and Yao was asking a lot of questions through Erik about the league and the players' union and how it worked. We held the workout at Loyola University and were getting close when he asked how many NBA people would be there. I told him there would be fifty or sixty, and there will be faces you may know—Jerry West, Pat Riley, Wes Unseld—but try not to be nervous. Then he asked me if there would be any media there, and I said yeah, there'd probably be over a hundred or so, including a camera from ESPN showing the workout live on air. I saw in his face that he was trying to prepare himself. That's when we arrived at the campus. The students had found out about the workout, and they were everywhere. It looked like there were thousands of them. I felt so bad for him. Here he was, having almost just stepped off a plane from China, and he was in every newspaper in the country, and the entire NBA basketball world was waiting for him inside that gym. It took real guts to handle it as well as he did. After that, I just felt in my heart that he was going to make it.*

P. J. CARLESIMO (former NBA Head Coach, current San Antonio Spurs assistant coach, coach of Yao's Chicago workout): *I'd only seen him on tape before the workout. There wasn't any one thing he did that made you go, "Wow"; it was just the sum total. He could put the ball on the floor, run, shoot, pass, and, oh yeah, he's 7'6" and 300 pounds. After the workout I heard people say, well, I don't know, he can't do this or that, and I thought, "What are you looking at?" I was laughing. These were guys I know around the league. If you watched for ten minutes, you knew he was going to be a force in the NBA. In the car after the workout, I was interviewed over the phone for a radio show. They asked me what I thought, and I said, "He's going to be an All-Star." The radio host said, "Really?" I'm not talking about being voted in by the fans or making it his first year. I just thought he'd get there.*

The hype that went into the workout and how he handled it is what really amazed me. Kids who are college All-Americans come in and work out in an empty gym for an NBA team and they're on pins and needles. Yao didn't look bothered by any of it. He was just delightful.

I was very nervous when I first went on the court, but the basketball helped me feel relaxed. Once I touched the ball, shot it, dribbled it, I forgot that there was anybody else there. It was nice to learn I could do that in such a strange, big-pressure situation. I'd played in big games before, of course, but never anything where everyone was watching just me. There wasn't a press conference after the workout, but Erik helped me write this statement:

It's been a dream of mine to play in the NBA ever since the first time I saw a game on TV many years ago. To almost touch that dream today fills me with a sense of joy that words simply cannot describe.

I am humbled and grateful for the unforgettable experience of the past few days. I would like first to thank the NBA for hosting this event in the great city of Chicago. The superb organization demonstrates a level of professionalism that I truly admire.

I would also like to express my sincere gratitude to all NBA teams for showing interest in me. I am honored by your presence. And I hope I have not disappointed you with my performance today.

Proper credit is also due to the members of media. The game of Cat'n'Mouse is stressful, but your resourcefulness and work ethic are something I think we players should emulate. Journalism is a profession I respect a great deal. Just give me some time to warm up. I look forward to taking each and every one of you to dinner sometime in the future, but the check is on you if your reporting makes me look bad.

Last but certainly not least, I owe the greatest debt of gratitude to the fans of basketball everywhere. You gave me the greatest job on earth. And I promise to repay your trust by respecting the game, and by challenging myself to be the best that I can be.

Let the good times roll!

Then I had dinner with Jerry Krause, former Bulls general manager, in my hotel. He was staying in the same hotel in a suite on the top floor. He has a house in Chicago, so I'm not sure why he was staying in the hotel. People say Krause likes to be very secretive and not let anybody else know what he is doing, so maybe that's why.

Krause had Chinese takeout food in the little white boxes delivered to the room. Before I knew Houston got the first pick in the draft lottery, Chicago was where I wanted to go. That was mainly because Erik lives there, and I thought that would make life easier for me. But after I talked to Krause, the Bulls GM, that's when I got scared. He wanted to do a good thing for me. He said that if I was tired after the NBA season to tell him. If that meant not playing for the national team, he would arrange for that. He would talk to the Chinese Basketball Association and tell them to let me rest.

That's what scared me. I wanted to play for the national team, and I didn't want the CBA to have problems because of me. That's why I didn't want to go to Chicago after that. Then I went back to my room and watched the Spurs play the Sonics in the first round of the playoffs. We made plans as if I were going to be in the draft. Bill—I called him "Beer" the first time we met—had a tailor measure me for a suit for draft night. The tailor told me the longest pants he'd ever made until then were for Dikembe Mutombo, who had 50½"-long pants. Mine were 54".

The next morning, I went to the Berto Center, where the Bulls practice. They measured my spine and tested my strength and how quickly I could move. I was really tired, so they stopped testing me before we were finished. I was told they would have drafted me if they got the number-one pick, so I must've done enough to make them happy.

JOHN HUIZINGA (Deputy Dean for Faculty and Professor of Economics at the University of Chicago Graduate School of Business): *I met Yao and Erik for the first time at that Chicago tryout. Erik called one of my colleagues, Mike Parzen, an associate professor of econometrics and statistics, and asked if he could reschedule his midterm. "Well, what's your excuse?" Mike asked.*

"I'm running this tryout for twenty-nine NBA GMs," Erik said.

"I guess that's a good-enough excuse." Then Erik asked if Mike would like to attend the tryout.

"Of course. Could I bring somebody with me?"

"Sure," Erik said.

*That's how I got invited. I'm a pro basketball junkie. I grew up
a Celtics fan in San Diego and chose MIT to do my grad work in
part so I could watch the Celtics.*

*I ran into an accounting professor from school, Roman Weil, at
the workout. "What are you doing here?" I asked. I figured Mike
had gotten him invited, too. It turned out Erik had invited him directly. Roman had written a best-selling accounting textbook that
apparently Yao's mom had used. She told Yao that he should try to
meet him. Roman was there to sign a couple of these textbooks and
send them back with Yao.*

*The next day I got a call from Parzen. "Would you like to go out
to dinner with Yao?" he asks. Hard question, right? We had dinner
in a private dining room in Yao's hotel after his workout for the
Bulls. They snuck him in through the kitchen. He spoke a little bit of
English. I don't think I'd ever had dinner with anyone so famous
they had to sneak them in through the kitchen.*

*Erik wanted to talk to several of us—Mike, Roman, myself—
about what was going on in China with Yao. He wanted us to help
him think through his strategy. He gave us a little bit of the history
of Yao's struggles to get out. If we were trying to get Yao out, he
asked, what would we do? It was a hard question because we knew
nothing about Chinese politics.*

*At one point during the discussion I asked Erik, "Have you
thought about how you're going to manage the draft?"*

"What do you mean?" Erik asked.

*"Well, Kobe didn't end up in L.A. by accident. There's a reason
why Steve Francis went to Houston and not Vancouver. There are
things you can do to influence where Yao winds up."*

*"All NBA teams are not equal," I added. "If it were me, I'd prob-
ably rather stay in China than play for the Clippers." Clippers
guard Quentin Richardson, who is from Chicago, had come to the*

tryout. Although I didn't know it at the time of our dinner, he said some not-so-flattering things about Yao to reporters afterward. He said he wasn't that impressed and that if Yao were on his team, they'd probably just take turns dunking on his head for the first few practices. Erik read that to Yao the next morning. Yao's reaction was "That's how teammates treat you in the NBA?"

"If you're on the Clippers," I said. All that proved to be lucky, because it gave me instant credibility with Erik.

Roman also is good friends with Gene Orza, one of the top guys in the Major League Baseball union. Erik had dinner with him and asked, "What would you be doing if you were me?" Orza said he'd get an agent to manage the draft. That obviously earned me more points.

Orza then gave him this big, long story about how a professional agent, and only a professional agent, can help with the draft, but Erik called me later and asked, "Would you help me manage the draft?"

"You know what Orza said," I told him. "Are you sure this is a sensible thing to do?"

"Given the situation in China," Erik said, "there's just no way we can go with a professional agent after what happened with Evergreen. Neither Yao nor the Sharks would feel comfortable. So anything you can do will be more than we could have done without you."

"All right," I said, "I'll do it." Then I spent the next ten days writing down every possible question I could ask Yao. What kind of coach do you want to play for? What kind of offense do you like to play? Does it matter to you if you live in a big city or a small city? How comfortable are you around the press? How important is it to you that your teammates are your friends? How important is it that you start right away? Do you care if you ever win an NBA championship? I'm trying to make a match for somebody I've met once when he was completely exhausted. I took his answers, or at

least what I could get out of him, and put that with what I knew about all the teams. I ranked all the teams pretty coarsely, just pluses, zeros, and minuses. Normally, though I was an NBA junkie, I didn't pay much attention to the lottery. But this time I paid a whole boatload of attention.

And then the lottery turned out how it did: Houston, Chicago, and Golden State got the top three spots.

BILL DUFFY: *What made the situation tricky is that I was in line to represent three of the top four picks, including Yao Ming and Duke's Jay Williams, and there was no clear-cut consensus on who the number-one pick should be. It depended on who got the number-one pick in the draft lottery, which was to be held about one week after Yao's workout in Chicago. If Chicago had gotten the first pick, I would've been going nuts, because Chicago was leaning toward Yao Ming, and that's where Jay really wanted to play. Part of an agent's role is to get his client picked both as high as possible and by a team that his client likes and looks to be a good fit. People were raising the question, if somebody who has the first pick could use both Yao and Jay, how does Duffy represent both? "Why don't we wait until the lottery selection and find out where things lie?" I said. "Maybe there's a valid argument not to have me represent both of them, but let's not do anything prematurely."*

After Yao's Chicago workout, I sat down with Erik and offered to step back publicly until we knew where everything stood. I knew that would help him deal with the people over in China, and it would relieve any concerns that I might be pushing Jay harder than Yao.

No one expected Houston to get the number-one pick, but once they did, there was no conflict. I knew they clearly needed a big man more than a scoring point guard because they already had

Steve Francis. Jay didn't want to go to Houston, anyway. Chicago was his first choice, and they ended up with the number-two pick, so it worked out perfectly.

When John Huizinga asked me all those questions, my first thought was "Getting drafted is not simple work." I'd never thought about what kind of teammates or coach I wanted. In China, a player doesn't have a choice in any of that. All I knew is that I didn't want Golden State to get the number-one pick because I knew they wanted a point guard.

It would be historic if I was the first number-one pick who was born and taught basketball outside America. No matter what happened, at least I would have that. That's why I wanted it. Song Tao had been the first Chinese player drafted by the NBA; he was selected in the third round by the Atlanta Hawks in 1987, but he hurt his knee and never came over to try out. Ma Jian was the first player to try out for an NBA team, going to training camp with the Los Angeles Clippers. Wang Zhi Zhi was the first Chinese player drafted and signed by an NBA team. When Mengke Bateer started for the Denver Nuggets in the 2001–2002 season, he was the first Chinese player to do that. In China, you don't want to be second in anything. When it came to the NBA, being the first pick felt like my last chance to be first.

5

THE NEGOTIATIONS

The day after meeting with Erik and the professors, I flew back to China knowing, or believing, that I would be going to the NBA. It was one thing for the Sharks and the CBA to decide I shouldn't go in 2001; no one from the NBA was really talking about me that much then, and even I wasn't 100 percent certain the time was right. But now almost every team had seen me in the U.S. and even if not everybody was impressed, nobody was saying I didn't belong in the NBA. After watching me work out at less than 100 percent, they were still talking about my possibly being the number-one pick. Since the Sharks already had said they would let me go, it was up to the CBA. Could they still say no when everybody else was saying yes? I didn't think so.

You would think that the CBA would be happy to see Chinese players going to the NBA, because it would make the CBA look good. But that had never been the thinking of the CBA or its teams. Teams didn't want their players to be stars. If a player became too famous and too many people knew who he was, the old CBA thought he'd become too hard to control. Even when I went back to China after the workout in Chicago, the Shanghai Media

Group wanted to do a TV show about the trip. I thought it was a good idea, but the CBA didn't want me to do it. I think the CBA was worried that if everybody saw how I had played and how much interest the NBA had in me, it would make it harder to get what they wanted from me in exchange for letting me go.

However, keeping me away from the media when I got back from Chicago backfired on them. When I landed in Shanghai, a lot of reporters wanted to talk to me. I had changed my phone number, but a couple of guys got the new one and called me. The CBA already had told me that if any reporters wanted to ask me questions, I should let the CBA know. So I told the reporters who found me, "I can't talk. The CBA says you must talk to them." I didn't really want to answer a lot of questions from a lot of different people about the trip, anyway, but the CBA made it their fault that I wasn't talking, not mine.

I can't see anything like that happening under the new CBA director, Li Yuanwei. If he had been in charge, I'm sure he would have wanted me to do the show with Shanghai Media Group and hold a press conference for the other reporters. Unfortunately for me, he took over after I came to the NBA. He's a very good guy and will make the CBA better, but he's going to need time to make changes.

ERIK ZHANG: *I had started negotiating with the Sharks to make sure Yao got to the NBA right after the disappointment of the 2001 draft. But when I returned to China in late May, about a week after the 2002 draft lottery, Mr. X suddenly began pushing really hard to get me out as a negotiator. I'm not sure exactly what inspired the change, but something happened while we were in Chicago. He was part of the group that went over, and we were supposed to have a meeting after the workout, but he completely ditched me. The next I heard, he was in California, supposedly meeting with other parties who wanted to represent Yao. One reason may have been that he had found other agents who were promising to give a bigger piece of Yao's earnings than I was willing to give. The problem was that those agents never had talked to Yao. Maybe he thought that if he pushed me out, Yao would have no choice but to select an agent who would be more accommodating. Mr. X started blasting me publicly. His mission, at that point, was to be able to select whoever was going to represent Yao. The thinking must have been, "How can we trust Erik to protect our interests?" My obvious answer would have been, "I'm not responsible for protecting your interests," but that's not the way they think. If you understand how sports developed in China, it's not really surprising they think that way.*

The Chinese sports system originated from a Russian model in the '50s and '60s, at a time when the interests of the collective were much, much more important than the interests of the individual. That sort of system allows a country with limited resources to channel what it has toward developing a few elite athletes. The transformation China has undergone since adopting an open-door policy in the late '70s is basically a change from a planned economy to a market-driven economy. That is naturally going to create more freedom for the individual. Individuals have choices now. What Yao's situation demonstrated is that such freedom was a little slower to come to the sports world than to other places. If Yao had been working in a Shanghai TV factory, for example, and a U.S. company had offered him a job, he could've left the next day.

There had been clashes of individually recognized Chinese athletes and this old Russian model before Yao. In the '90s China had a badminton player who was ranked number one in the world. The Chinese badminton federation wanted to control his endorsements, and he refused, electing to retire instead. He was twenty-three years old, and he never played again. There are other cases. The clashes just never have been so prominent, so public, as with Yao.

Mr. X began feeding stories to the media that I wasn't qualified to represent Yao. I was very careful not to counterattack, because I thought it would only make things worse. It was really a business transaction, so there was no point in making it personal. When a reporter asked me about the blasting, I stayed positive. "I think it will work out," I said.

After a while, the reporter who attacked me the most became suspicious. At first, he never tried talking to me, and I had no interest in talking to him. I figured he was in Mr. X's camp, dead set against everything. He had been writing an article every day, every one of them quoting the Sharks' official blasting me in a different way. Then one day the guy found me. "This doesn't sound right," he said. "Mr. X paints you as a vicious person and a money-hungry middleman. Why don't you rebut any of this?" So I told him why it's important that a player select his agent, rather than have one appointed for him, and what the role of an agent is. Remember, the concept of sports agents in China was still pretty new, and it's understandable that the club would feel threatened by this new entity. But after we talked, the reporter started asking questions. With editorial control being as it is, there was no way he was going to say anything on my behalf, but at least he started toning down his articles.

Mr. X then countered by bringing up the Evergreen contract, suggesting Yao Ming had committed to something already, so I was out of my mind trying to interfere. But that turned out to be a mistake, because I had a copy of the Evergreen contract.

The contract stipulated that Evergreen should get one-third of all Yao's income. The big problem was that the signatories to the agreement were only Evergreen and Yao Ming, nobody else. Now I knew Mr. X's plan was for the Sharks to get one-third and Yao to get the remaining one-third, but all this was done orally. None of the details were being made public; all Mr. X did was play it up really big that Evergreen and Yao had a contract.

So I went to Bai Li, head of the Shanghai Media Group Sports Properties, and pressured him. "There's no way you're letting Yao Ming go for nothing," I said. "But your signature is not on this contract, and you don't have a contract with Yao Ming. So how are you going to get your cut? Is it an agreement so disgusting you don't want to show it to the public? If not, there's only one conclusion people can reach: you just gave away the most precious asset in the club for free." I've always thought Bai Li was a good guy. I was sure he wasn't fully aware of how the negotiations had been going or what the Evergreen contract looked like. His first concern was running the TV station.

"There has to be a signature," he said. "Mr. X told me there was a signature."

"I have a copy," I said. "Why don't you take a look."

His face lost its color. There was silence for maybe five minutes. He stared at that contract for a long, long time. Then finally he muttered: "I'll take Mr. X out of the negotiation process." That's all he said. It wasn't smooth sailing from there, but whatever happened, winning that battle established that I was going to represent Yao Ming in negotiations.

BAI LI: *I was not aware of the details of the Evergreen negotiations until Erik showed me that contract. In Chinese business, a representative getting paid one-third of all earnings is not that extraordinary, but obviously it was a flawed contract. I also felt that the people negotiating for us were being too shortsighted, too wor-*

ried about the immediate short-term gains, and that there were larger benefits for the Sharks and the Chinese Basketball Association to consider. I met with Erik in New York in March to have preliminary discussions about what it would require for Yao Ming to go to the NBA. The CBA playoffs had not yet started. I had already used my business contacts to talk to several lawyers in both New York and L.A. about orchestrating the deal, but it became clear that they didn't know anything about the NBA or what Yao Ming meant to China. They were approaching it strictly from a business standpoint. I thought that could prove to be disastrous. I was beginning to believe that whoever it was had to have Yao's trust and understand his needs. But that person also had to understand something about the NBA, as well as the needs of the Sharks and the CBA. The more I talked to Erik, the more I realized who that person should be—Erik.

After Yao Ming's workout in Chicago, I met with a representative for the mayor of Shanghai. She made it clear that the mayor, and therefore the government, felt it was time for Yao Ming to go to the NBA, that the stage of basketball in China was no longer big enough for him. Chen Liang Yu was the mayor then and is the party secretary of Shanghai now. For Shanghai truly to be an international city, he felt it couldn't just have people coming in but had to have some of its citizens going out in the world and being recognized.

JOHN HUIZINGA: After the workout Erik knew that he would have to return to China to work on Yao's release before the NBA draft. He also knew he wanted someone here in the U.S. working on Yao's behalf while he was gone. Surprisingly, before the NBA draft lottery he asked if I would help him prepare for the NBA draft and follow through by dealing with the NBA teams in his absence. I agreed and Erik notified all the NBA teams. We did *our homework, the lottery came and went, and Houston had the number-one pick. That's when things got a bit crazy. There was a mountain of misinformation. The Rockets were hearing things that just weren't true.*

Carroll Dawson, the Rockets GM, called and started out by saying, "I know Yao doesn't want to play in Houston, but I just want you to know we're really interested, and we'd like you and Erik to come down to Houston."

There had been reports in numerous media outlets that Yao wanted to play for New York, Chicago, or Golden State. Based on my conversations with Yao, I knew his preferences had evolved to the point where these reports were no longer accurate. I told Dawson—everybody calls him CD—we'd be happy to come.

We took a 6 A.M. flight out of Chicago, so we were up at 4 and by 10 A.M. we were sitting in a small conference room at the Westside Tennis Club where the Rockets practice, meeting with CD, team president George Postolos, and owner Les Alexander.

That's when Erik and I find out that in a Chicago newspaper that day—and I am sure the timing was not coincidence—there is a story claiming that the Shanghai Sharks are very upset with the Rockets because they are talking to people who falsely claim to be representing Yao Ming, and if that's the way the Rockets were going to treat Yao Ming, Yao would probably be much better off in Chicago. Alexander asks, "How do you explain this, and should I even be talking to you?"

It was a little nuts, I have to admit. Here's this professor and this roly-poly little Chinese guy who claim to represent Yao, and the truth is, the Rockets have no idea if we represent Yao or not. I hadn't even registered as an NBA agent. Erik had told me if I did so, it would be tough for Yao back in China, but at the same time the NBA was telling me I couldn't meet with teams unless I regis-

tered. Erik finally told me not to worry, that the Chinese would still view me as a professor, and I eventually registered but not until after that first meeting with the Rockets. To their credit, they decided to believe us and talk anyway. They told us they'd had a scout watching Yao for several years now and were sure they wanted him.

"We'd be the perfect team for Yao Ming," Rockets coach Rudy Tomjanovich said.

I wasn't so sure. There were things about the Rockets we liked, but also things we didn't like. I asked Rudy if it was possible to change some of the things we didn't like. At the same time, I was thinking, "Who am I to say this to an NBA coach who directed the Rockets to two NBA championships?"

Rudy didn't answer my questions at first. He would give me an answer, but it had nothing to do with the question. I asked again, and he still didn't give me a straight answer. After I asked a third time, I guess he got the idea I wasn't going to give up.

At the end of the day the Rockets held a press conference. Then CD drove us back to the airport. "Guys," he said, "I just have to tell you, I've never had a meeting with an agent anything like this."

We weren't sure exactly how to take that, so we just assumed it was good.

MICHAEL GOLDBERG (Houston Rockets general counsel): *I was getting bombarded with calls from people supposedly on the inside telling me that if Erik and John were Yao's agents, I would never get a release from the Sharks. The calls were coming from various agents in the U.S., along with some Chinese people in Houston who I knew had ties with the Sharks. I just decided that if Yao wanted Erik and John, that's who I was going to listen to.*

CARROLL DAWSON (Houston Rockets general manager): *I had always thought that Bill Duffy was going to be the guy, so we weren't sure what to think when John and Erik came down. There was a lot of confusion at that time. There was a group out of the East, Evergreen, that kept calling me and saying, "You're never going to get Yao if you listen to those guys. There's no way you're going to get him out of China without us." They were telling me they had a contract with him and they were going to sue Team Yao—or what turned into Team Yao. Normally all that kind of stuff is settled way before a team even starts thinking about drafting a player, but there was clearly a fight going on for this guy. Once Erik and John came down to Houston, though, I was convinced they were credible. Erik was able to get Yao on the phone while we were talking, which was pretty convincing. Not long after that, I got a letter from Yao saying Erik would be his representative. I guessed it was Yao's signature; I mean, I'd never seen it before so I didn't really know. You had to trust your gut on a lot of things, maybe more than usual, when it came to making it all work.*

About two weeks later, we flew over to Shanghai to meet with the Sharks. They took us out for two or three days and showed us around town. It was meet and greet, that's all it was. They said it was time for Yao to go to the NBA, and they felt that Houston was the right place, but if we did get him, they wanted us to help them scout and find other players who might not make an NBA roster and would be willing to play in China. We actually sent them a tape of Yao's first replacement, a big kid out of Arizona named Dan Mc-Clintock. I sent them tapes of a few other players—I guess I sent about ten tapes—but I don't know what they did with those. I used to get faxes from them all the time about them coming over and requesting tapes. They stopped coming after Yao's rookie year.

I found Bai Li, the head of Shanghai Media Group Sports Prop-

Yao at two years old.

Five-year-old Yao
at the Great Wall.

Yao at the children's sports school. Age ten.

At the Sydney Olympics, 2000.

Yao with his parents.

With the
Shanghai Sharks,
2001.

At the CBA
championships.

Yao is chosen first at the 2002 NBA draft.

Signing basketballs,
February 14, 2004.

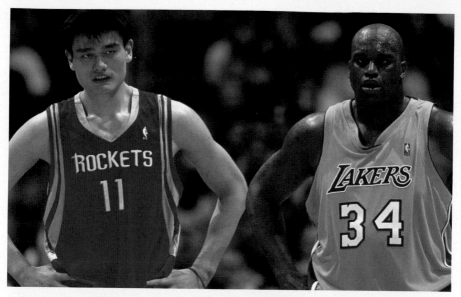

With Shaquille O'Neal at the 2004 NBA playoffs.

Battling Jermaine O'Neal at the 2004 NBA All-Star Game.

Team Yao from left to right: John Huizinga, Bill Duffy, Erik Zhang, Lu Hao, and Bill Sanders.

Yao with his translator, Colin Pine.

With assistant coach
Patrick Ewing during
the 2004 NBA
playoffs.

With Ronald
McDonald and
David Stern
announcing part-
nership with
McDonalds,
2004.

Talking to reporters
during the 2004
NBA playoffs.

Yao is the last runner in the Olympic torch relay in Beijing, June 2004.

erties, to be a very nice man, but he was the first one to let me know I was being suckered. We were using translators, so for all I knew the Sharks people didn't speak any more English than we spoke Chinese. But at one point the translator said they were talking about this guy who talks all the time, and I said, "Yeah, in Texas we'd say he was vaccinated with a phonograph needle." Before it could be translated, Bai Li was laughing his ass off.

MICHAEL GOLDBERG: *For Americans doing a business deal, it's "Let's do the deal and go." In China, you don't start doing a deal until you've established a relationship. I had time to sit with Mr. X in the hotel lobby after we arrived and just talk. There was no time for that with the CBA commissioner, and there was a noticeable difference. The commmissioner walked in and sat down at this long conference table, and there was just stone silence. He was waiting for me to start. It was pretty awkward. I knew Yao was practicing nearby with the national team, and when I asked if we could watch, the commissioner said, "Let's see how this meeting goes first."*

Hierarchy in China also is very important. I couldn't just be there as the Rockets' lawyer. So before we went, we made sure that everything being said publicly indicated that I was the chief executive going over there. I had a letter from Mayor Brown of Houston, introducing me, because he had just been there, and mayors in China have a very exalted position. I also got a letter from former President Bush, a former ambassador to China, who added a handwritten note at the bottom, "This comes to you, sir, from an old friend of the Chinese people." The part I may never live down is that Rudy and CD, as part of the hierarchy deal, had to walk behind me, carry our gift bags, and speak in the meetings only if I asked. When we got on the plane to come back, Rudy said, "I'm going to get you back for those bags."

We did get to see the national team practice after our meeting, and I got to take a picture of me shaking hands with Yao that proved extremely valuable not long after that. One thing about Yao— throughout the entire practice, he never looked over at us. He was practicing and wouldn't allow us to be a distraction. Some of the other players were looking over, but not Yao.

CARROLL DAWSON: *The smartest thing I've ever done is never waver about taking Yao Ming with the number-one pick. When we won the lottery and received the number-one pick and people started calling, asking if we'd trade it or take so-and-so, I said, "No, we're going to draft Yao Ming."*

When we got over there, we found out they watched ev-er-y-thing we did. They knew everything we'd done or said, and CBA commissioner Xin made a point of saying that they knew we wanted Yao Ming from the start. If we'd been wishy-washy, I do believe he would've sat in China another year. Cleveland probably would've had the choice of taking either Yao or LeBron James in the 2003 lottery.

Another big factor was having Rudy so well known in China. It was unbelievable how we'd walk down the street and people recognized him because our games had been shown over there and he'd coached against China in the 2000 Olympics. That helped, having a familiar face. There was a built-in trust established.

Even though I was confident I was finally going to the NBA, I couldn't really concentrate on getting ready to go. I still had a lot of things to do in China. I was split between thinking about the NBA and getting ready for the World Championships. I knew that the World Championships would be in the U.S. after the draft and that would be a big showcase for me. I just wanted to concentrate on the game, not the personal show, but I knew that, no matter what happened with the draft, everybody would be watching how I played very closely. I would tell myself every night before I'd go to bed—OK, not every night, but a lot of nights—not to get too excited about my personal goals and to think about the team. I can't say I was ready or even getting ready to play in the NBA. I was still thinking more about what I had to do for the national team.

In one way it was like my first year practicing with the Shanghai Sharks' junior team: I didn't know what I was practicing for; all I knew was that it was all for a game I would one day play in the U.S.—maybe in the NBA, maybe just in the World Championships. I didn't know if it would be both or just one, and in China, just like in America, we have the saying "Ignorance is bliss." My first year with the Sharks' junior team was my first time living away from my family. I was happy to be free. It was paradise, because I'd always lived at home before that. I could practice for a year because I knew there would be a game at the end, and that's why I was practicing. This was the same. I was getting ready for an adventure and the chance to do something I'd never done before, but I didn't know exactly what it would be. I also had to believe that if I was supposed to go, they would let me go. We also say, "A chance is given to someone when they are ready."

I was very lucky for another reason. At that time I had two goals. One was going to the NBA; the other was getting to know my girlfriend, Ye Li, who had agreed only a few months earlier to go out with me. I can't say that was the second goal, either. They were two equal goals that I had at the same time. I talked to Erik every day about what was going on with the CBA, but I didn't worry about it because any delay just meant I'd have more time with my girlfriend before I had to leave. And if, for some reason, I didn't go for another year, then that would mean another year getting to know her. That made a big difference. If I had had only the one goal, the NBA, maybe I would've been more worried when I'd find out something new about my chances of going or not going.

ERIK ZHANG: *After John and I met with the Rockets, two more roadblocks appeared. One was Wang Zhi Zhi, the first Chinese player ever to be allowed to play in the NBA. He had just finished his rookie year with the Dallas Mavericks and was talking about staying in the United States to prepare for the World Championships rather than return to China to train with the Chinese national team. At that time, Wang was the most popular player in the country, so for him to defy the CBA's wishes was a big problem. The CBA needed him to compete, but they couldn't have an individual player dictating terms to them or disregarding their orders, especially after they had let him leave with the understanding he'd come back when they asked. Wang and Yao are different people, but you can see why they'd be very uneasy about letting another top player leave for the NBA.*

The second roadblock was a statute written for players in non-team sports. In order to play in another country, the player has to hand over 50 percent of his earnings to the sports federation and other national sports organizations and then split the rest with his coaches and his club. The CBA pulled this statute out as a basis to ask Yao for compensation to leave. They weren't saying they expected Yao to give up that much, but it was a powerful bargaining tool.

This was not the first time I'd negotiated a deal in China. When I was in college, I had helped my father form a joint-venture company in China. It wasn't a major operation for my father, and he involved me just so I could get some experience. That company went bankrupt, just so you know how I did. But I learned a big lesson. I am, by nature, not a tough person, but sometimes you have to overcome your personality to get the best result. A negotiation is a chess game. People react for a reason, and you constantly have to be thinking as if you're in their shoes. If you do that, you can tell if they're bluffing.

I also wasn't someone who left China at ten years old and came back in my twenties to try to get a Chinese athlete out. My parents emigrated to the United States in the early eighties. My mom is a doctor and medical researcher, and my father is an engineer. He has his own company, which manufactures generators. From the very first day my mom came over, she worked for the University of Wisconsin. I pride myself on the fact that I know more about China than most people in my situation. I can communicate in Chinese— speak fluently, write legibly. I travel to China pretty much every summer. I have friends who are Chinese and came to the States when they were young and totally lost their language skills. They are foreigners now. Some have even experienced an identity crisis: are they American or Chinese?

So I understand Chinese society, past and present. I know how the game is played. That's why I never had any doubts Yao would get out; it was just a matter of when. Once the Shanghai club announced to its fans that Yao would be able to go, they would've angered a lot of people if they had taken it back. Sharks fans were looking forward to seeing him show the world what he could do. That's one aspect of Chinese culture that hasn't changed: you never want to lose face by announcing you'll do something and then not do it.

What I feared most was the effect of Wang Zhi Zhi's decision not to return. A country can't make policy because of one individual's actions, so I thought, at worst, it would delay Yao's entry into the NBA for another year. Missing another year would be very significant, but I believed that was as far as it could go. I also felt I knew the Chinese government's position. Indications already had been made that Yao would be allowed to leave, so going back on that would be difficult. If the CBA was defensive about Wang Zhi Zhi, it was because it can't make unilateral decisions. It has to answer to the Chinese general sports administration. The bureau of general sports administration is above them, and above the bureau is the head of the Chinese government. Every government organization has to follow certain guidelines for protecting or implementing Chinese policy. It was very difficult for me to fathom that China would be liberalizing everywhere else but that in this case, because of one guy, they were going to shut the door. I also don't think the public would've accepted as an excuse that because of Wang Zhi Zhi, the CBA would not let Yao out.

Yao already was promising to come back and play for the national team, which is something he wanted to do anyway. He agreed that he can be called back to China for four tournaments— the Asian Championships, the Asian Games, the World Championships, and the Olympic Games. That's in writing. The gray area is the amount of training he has to do. They had him for twenty weeks before the 2003 Asian Championships, and everyone agrees that that's too much. What is paramount with Chinese sports officials is maintaining discipline and control. With the liberalization of China overall, it's inevitable that individual players are going to seek more power. The question is, how are officials going to respond to that? Would they punish Yao for not reporting to training camp on time? It's possible. A lot of things are done to let everyone know who is in charge.

If the CBA didn't believe my promise that I would come back to play for the national team, it wasn't just because of Wang. Even before him, there were players on Chinese national teams in other sports who went to America or Europe and left their teams. There was no phone call, no mail, no message. They just didn't come back. At most, I'd say, five athletes have done that. None were basketball players. One was a female tennis player; I don't remember her name. Tennis is not very hot in China, so not a lot of people knew who she was. And after anyone leaves like that, the government blacks out their name. You can't find them in the record books or anywhere. It's as if they never existed. You wouldn't get in trouble for talking about the players who left, but no one would do that. There was no reason. They were gone, and someone had taken their place.

I don't know if the CBA believed my promise to come back, but I had the feeling they didn't, and that didn't really surprise me. I was used to it by then. It had been like that for a long time. After I joined the Sharks' junior team, we played a game in Taiwan. We had to change planes in Hong Kong, and after we went through customs, they took all our passports. Then when we landed in Taiwan, they gave us back our passports so we could write down the number on the entry card, then took the passports back again. When we were in America or Europe or anywhere, it was the same thing. Once we were there, we'd have one day to go sightseeing or shopping, and the whole team would go together. Every time I traveled outside China with a team, it was like that.

Before I went to the NBA, I had always had a business passport, not a personal passport. The business passport is good only for certain trips and at certain times. You can't go just anywhere with it, as you can with a personal passport. It's hard for me to say what the difference is, but it does feel different having a personal passport. I can't say it's good or bad. I know I can do things with this passport I couldn't do before, but I don't think about it. I know my power, but I don't want to use it. There's no point right now.

This, maybe, is the biggest difference: before I left China with my new passport in 2002, they ordered me to do things. Now they ask me to do things. Of course, I usually want to do what they ask, so it's not like I had to do things I didn't want to do or didn't think I should do. But when they ask instead of order, it feels a lot better.

JOHN HUIZINGA: *As part of preparing for all the potential draft scenarios, I spoke with people from the top four teams picking in the draft—Houston, Chicago, Golden State, and Memphis. When Erik and I got back to Chicago from Houston, we met with Jerry Krause and Bulls owner Jerry Reinsdorf. They told us they were hoping to find a way to keep Tyson Chandler and Eddy Curry, their two big men drafted straight out of high school and coming off their rookie years, and add Yao. I never really believed this story. When I spoke with Warriors GM Garry St. Jean, he seemed resigned to the idea that with the third pick he wasn't going to have a shot at Yao. I also knew the Warriors hadn't done much work scouting Yao, and everything I was hearing is that they wanted a point guard, which meant Jay Williams.*

I have to admit that coming back to my office and having my assistant tell me, "Jerry West called," was an unbelievable experience. West certainly was different from CD, who is this easygoing, down-to-earth guy. With West it's like the meter's running: he's got things to do, places to go. West said the Grizzlies were interested in Yao, and with his record of being able to build a team, Memphis was an interesting possibility for sure. What scared me was the possibility of Houston trading the pick to the Clippers or the Knicks, but I couldn't see the Clippers being that bold, and the Knicks didn't have anybody I could see CD wanting.

Our leverage was that nobody in the NBA, not even the Rock-

ets, knew what it would take to get Yao out of China. So we figured if a team that he wasn't interested in made a move to get him, they would face a lot of uncertainty. We would never lie, but given the informational advantage we had, there was significant room to encourage or discourage as we saw fit.

In late May 2002 Erik asked if I'd go to China with him. Becoming a negotiator in China wasn't what I'd signed up for when I offered Erik my help, but then I thought, "How often do you get a chance to be involved in something like this?" So I agreed. I ended up staying in China until after the NBA draft. It was a wild experience of elation, frustration, and, in the end, provided a real sense of achievement. On the frustrating side, on the night before our first meeting with the Shanghai Sharks, they call Erik and say if I, a non-Chinese, attend the meeting, they will refuse to negotiate. Our negotiating team ended up being Erik, Yao's mom, Wang Xiao Peng, (a lawyer), and Lu Hao, whom we'd hired as a Chinese agent, one of the CBA's prerequisites. Erik would excuse himself from the negotiations now and then and call me at the hotel on his cell phone. The first week I was in China, the Sharks refused to acknowledge my existence.

That week was anything but boring, though, because the Rockets had sent a contingent over a few days earlier to meet with Chinese officials and express their interest in Yao in person. I'm in China for the first time ever, walk into my hotel room after a crazy flight, and the phone rings. It's Goldberg.

"We've got problems," he says. "Come down right away."

I go to his room, which is just down the hall, and he tells me the Rockets orthopedic guy has looked at the X-rays of Yao's feet. "They're all messed up," Goldberg says. "He'll never play in the NBA. We certainly can't draft him."

The Bulls' doctor had checked out Yao before his workout at the

Berto Center. That report was then given to the NBA to make available to anyone who wanted it. I had been told the report showed evidence of where his foot had been broken, but that it also showed it had healed and there was nothing else wrong. "The report filed with the NBA says he's OK," I said.

"We saw that report," Goldberg said. "Our orthopedic doctor looked at the X-rays and read them very differently. The only way we draft him now is if you send him to Hong Kong to get his feet checked out."

The Chinese were not going to let Yao go to Hong Kong, and Erik and I weren't even sure we wanted Yao to be examined again. After some discussion, we agreed to arrange an examination in Beijing. Then, while we were arranging to find a hospital, sneak Yao in for tests, and get the Rockets to go to Beijing, we also tracked down the Bulls' doctor and told him what the Houston doctor said.

"I've seen a lot of NBA feet," he said. "You could look at the feet of virtually any NBA center and say, 'This guy is going to have problems' or 'I just don't know.' I've seen guys who have had worse feet than Yao and they've had long NBA careers."

MICHAEL GOLDBERG: *The NBA physical really wasn't complete. They had taken one X-ray that had a trouble spot on it and hadn't followed up. Our doctors saw that and said, "Hey, you're taking a big gamble here." So we flew over one of the leading orthopedic surgeons in the country. I had flown to South Korea, meanwhile, on some other business and now had to go back to China. But there was a problem: I'd used a single-entry visa to get into China, I'm in South Korea, it's Saturday, which means no U.S. consulate office is open, and I have to be in Beijing Sunday morning. I just went for it and bought a ticket. When I showed them my passport, they saw my visa was no good. I finally talked them into*

*letting me go, but I had to sign a release for the airline that if I
landed in China and immigration sent me right back, I had to pay
for the full ticket.*

*So I land in Beijing, go to customs; they look at my passport and
say, "You have to go back."*

*I said, "I'm from the Houston Rockets to bring Yao Ming to the
NBA." Then I showed them the picture I had taken when we went to
see Yao practice with the national team. It was actually just a pho-
tocopy of the picture. Suddenly a crowd of officials gathered to look
at the photo. There was lots of talking that I couldn't understand. Finally, they said, "OK, we'll make you a new visa." So I go into this
office and they take my picture and they let me in. I had to give them
a hundred dollars, too, but my point is, things are the same all over
the world: sometimes it's not what you know, it's who you know.*

*We pick up Yao in Beijing with this little car to go to the hos-
pital, and he has to squeeze in, but there's not one word of com-
plaint. The exam takes a couple of hours. Everything turned out
to be fine, but while we're waiting for the results, I call home to
talk to my wife and kids. I turned to Yao and said, "Would you
mind saying hello to my boys?" I don't like to push, and I knew
he was very self-conscious about his English, but he said, "Yeah,
sure." He spent ten to fifteen minutes talking to my boys. That's
when I knew we had something really special. Forget the basketball or the press or the international significance; we just had a
good kid.*

What many people probably didn't know is that my last contract
with the Sharks ended on December 31, 2002. Under NBA rules,
if no one had drafted me, I would've become a free agent and
could do anything or play for anyone I chose. But I didn't think
that would be fair to the Sharks. I wanted to acknowledge that

they had helped make me a good player, and I wanted them to get something for it.

The contract with the Sharks also wasn't the only one that could keep me in China. In the U.S., you let three months pass, your contract is finished, and you can leave and sign with anyone. In China, it's not like that. A team has control of a player until the people running the team decide they don't want him anymore. Then he's free to sign with another team if he can find one.

I also signed one contract with the Sharks and another contract with the Shanghai Sports Administration to play for Shanghai in the Chinese national championships. The championships take place every four years, and after you play in one, they sign you to a contract. I signed my first contract with the Shanghai Sports Committee in 1997 and then signed another one in the summer of 2001 to play in the 2005 national championships. That contract is only to play in the national championships, not to play in the years in between. That was another way I could be kept from leaving China to play somewhere else. If they said I could leave, then I could go play somewhere else and have to come back to play only in the fourth year. But if they said there's a problem and I can't leave, then I'd have to stay in China the whole four years, even though there wouldn't be any games to play during the first three years. The Sharks and the Shanghai Sports Committee work together, so if the Sharks didn't want me to leave, it wouldn't matter if I had a contract with them or not. The Shanghai Sports Committee would have used their contract to keep me in China to help the Sharks.

The short answer: it didn't matter if my contract with the Sharks was up or not. One way or another, I still needed them to say they didn't want me anymore in order to go to another team.

ERIK ZHANG: *If I had been negotiating for the Sharks, I would've wanted to keep the negotiations out of the public eye. So on our way to the first negotiating session, I made a bet with our lawyer. I said the first thing the Sharks lawyer will tell us is they want to keep the negotiations secret, that the negotiating process has to be confidential. I won the bet.*

"We'll act in a responsible way," I told the Sharks. "But we can not agree to keep the negotiations confidential." What I didn't say is "The public is our basis of support. Shut us off from it and you're chopping off our right arm in a fistfight." All I told them was we'd act in a responsible manner.

"No," their lawyer said. "You have to do this."

We'd already given in on John not being at the negotiating table. I couldn't give them this one. They finally relented. It was a small victory, but as things turned out, an important one in the end.

And even though John wasn't present, he played a very important role. The negotiations with the Sharks came down to compensation—how much was Yao going to have to pay them to be released. The final agreement proved to be very complex. We factored in the potential impact of injuries, future interest rates, and inflation, among other things. John and I treated it as a business-school finance evaluation project. At the start, I offered different proposals concerning what we were and weren't willing to accept. John had constructed a spreadsheet; if we changed a number anywhere in the equation, it would show how the entire value of the deal changed. If you change a number in year one, this is the new number twelve years down the road, or throw in a different discount rate and here's your new bottom line. There also was built-in protection should Yao be injured early in his career. Every day I'd take my laptop computer into the negotiations. But other than that it was like a regular negotiation. I think Yao got a fairly decent

*deal. Both sides signed a nondisclosure agreement, so I can't give
specifics.*

*We were down to one final point on the final proposal, but the
Sharks were dragging their feet. We knew the CBA wasn't going to
deal with us until we had an agreement with the team, and the
Rockets had given us a deadline of three days before the draft to deliver a release or they were going to trade the pick.*

*"That's it. We've come to an impasse, and we're running out of
time," I said. "Maybe it's your intention to drag things out forever,
but we're going to have a press conference in Shanghai this Saturday. We can either announce that an agreement has been reached
or we can tell the public why it hasn't been reached. In the second
case, we'll outline what we've offered and what you're demanding.
It's your choice."*

*I felt that the Sharks were using our time concerns against us
as leverage to make us concede the final point. This is where not
promising to keep everything confidential became vital; if we
had, we couldn't have threatened a press conference without their
countering that we had lied or negotiated in bad faith. But it still
wasn't an easy ultimatum to make. Not everybody thought the
press conference was a good idea, so we met at Yao's apartment to
talk it over. Yao was in Beijing, training with the national team.
Yao's mom, Fang Feng Di, didn't want to upset the team in any
way. Neither did our lawyer. It got pretty heated. But they understood that I had a lot to lose if all this failed. I plan to live in
Shanghai again one day. I have a lot of business interests there.
If this blew up or I went too far, everyone in Shanghai would
know. Yao's mom and the lawyer finally agreed to tell the club
about the press conference.*

*As expected, the club was very upset about that idea. We weren't
looking to embarrass the Sharks; we just wanted to regain some*

leverage. Things got heated again, but then Bai Li requested a twenty-minute break. The break lasted three hours. This was Thursday. The press conference was Saturday. The Shanghai Sports Bureau informed us that individuals couldn't hold press conferences, so I told them we'd just rent a hotel room and call it something else. On Saturday, we held our press conference, and we announced we had a deal.

I was aware of most of what was going on. I talked to Erik every day on the phone. Some days it was as if we were back at the starting point. There would be bad news, like "They've stopped talking to us" or "Somebody has to take care of their kids and can't come in today" or something else. But Erik told me, "Don't worry about anything. If you hear news and you think that 'Maybe I can't go to the NBA this year,' don't. I told you, it's a lock that you can go this year. Nothing can stop you from playing in the NBA." So I believed that.

I took any message from Erik that sounded bad for my chances to go to the NBA as something bad for China, too. If reporters found out about whatever went wrong and reported it—"They want a lot of money" or "Yao must go back and play a lot of games or they will cut him from the national team"—that would make Chinese basketball look really bad. In my mind, reports like that would be very contradictory with everything else that was going on in China.

I feel that what happened around me brought out a lot of what has been wrong in Chinese basketball. Whenever something strange came up, the Chinese officials would say, "China is special." If NBA contracts or European contracts are a certain way and Chinese contracts are completely different, they would say, "China is special. We must do it our way." They now say you must have an agent in China.

What other country says you must have an agent from their country to play a professional sport? I don't know of one. I don't mind using an agent from China; that's not a big problem. But that's what I mean when I say they have a lot of special rules.

JOHN HUIZINGA: *I was excited about what had been accomplished until we got to the press conference.*

"Where are the Sharks?" I asked.

"They're not part of it," Erik said. "They aren't going to comment either way."

"Do we at least have their agreement in writing?"

"No. But you are invited to tomorrow's meeting."

"Cool."

After the press conference we met with the Sharks to tie up a few minor details and have the Sharks send a fax to the CBA notifying them that Yao had been released from his contract. They offered us something to eat and were showing me pictures of the team winning the CBA championship. I look over at our lawyer, Wang Xiao Peng, and he really doesn't look well. He excuses himself, and when he comes back, Erik says, "We have to take him to the hospital."

I'm thinking, "The bastards! They've poisoned him!" It really was some kind of stomach illness for which the Sharks had no responsibility. However, the fact is that another day passed and we still didn't have the release agreement in writing, and I'm getting every excuse about the fax: the machine isn't working, so-and-so needs to sign it and he's at a meeting, etc.

I had planned to come over for a week, but things are really dragging out. At home I'm in charge of building a $125 million campus for the University of Chicago Graduate School of Business and that can't wait. So I'm having conference calls about it in the middle of the night. One of the guys from Turner Construction sees *in the newspaper that a John Huizinga is negotiating for Yao and says to himself, "That's odd. I know a John Huizinga, too." On the next call he asks me, "By the way, where are you?"*

"China," I said.

"You're that John Huizinga?"

Eventually I was confident the Sharks had sent the fax to the CBA and that the Sharks were behind us. I wasn't nearly as worried about the CBA as about the Sharks. Little did I know what we had ahead of us.

ERIK ZHANG: *There were different stages in the negotiating process with the CBA, but the critical one concerned whether or not Yao Ming would be drafted number one. The CBA wanted to accomplish two things: (1) make sure he was drafted number one or, if he wasn't, that it couldn't be attributed to anything the CBA did; and (2) not commit to anything that would tie its hands in negotiating final terms with the Rockets or Team Yao.*

CARROLL DAWSON: *When we arrived to meet with the Sharks, their offices were in a building shaped like a rocket. I took that as a good sign. We spent a couple days in Shanghai just saying hello to people and then went up to Beijing, where we met with Xin Lancheng, the CBA secretary general. That was much more businesslike. Yao was working out with the national team, and we asked if we could watch and then talk to him. The biggest surprise of the whole trip was when Yao walked over to us and said in perfect English, "Do you think I'm way behind because I didn't go to college for four years like most NBA players?" We really didn't do a whole lot of negotiating. We were just there to let them know we wanted to draft Yao. Nobody committed to anything, but everybody we talked to felt it was time for him to come over.*

ERIK ZHANG: *I think there was one other element at work: the CBA felt it should be at their discretion when and how Yao Ming entered the NBA. The NBA's position of power in the world of basketball raised concerns for the CBA that the NBA would dictate terms. I personally think that concern was justified. The $350,000 limit the NBA has for one of its teams to buy out a foreign player's contract is arbitrary and unrealistic. If nothing else, it forces a foreign team to shift the cost of entering the NBA to the player. In professional soccer, for example, a team can acquire a player under contract to another team by paying a transfer fee to the original team. Transfer fees among European pro teams often run into the tens of millions of pounds or dollars and aren't the player's responsibility. This is the model Chinese sports officials were familiar with and why they considered the $350,000 limit unfair.*

The trip over by Goldberg and CD really didn't accomplish anything, other than allow them to understand how difficult it was going to be to get Yao out. The CBA would promise Goldberg a meeting and then cancel it. Or they'd keep him waiting and waiting and then suddenly say, "OK, come into our office." He was touring the Imperial Palace and they said, "Be here in two hours." It was all about showing the NBA who was running the show. Goldberg kept telling me, "To a sane person, their behavior doesn't make logical sense." He's right, if you look at the dealings between the CBA and the NBA in isolation. But the CBA wasn't just trying to negotiate a deal to send a player to the NBA. And they weren't acting on their own. The only way to understand what they were doing was to look at where the CBA is within the society, what kind of external pressure they're under, what kind of internal pressure is exerted upon them, and how this whole thing of Yao going to the NBA fit into that. Then you'll realize that their response was very logical, because they had to answer to many different constituencies. This wasn't just about allowing a player to go to the NBA. This was about proving the CBA could handle a case of this magnitude.

I always believe the good guy comes out on top. I'm not saying the Sharks or the CBA were bad guys, but Yao, from a historical perspective, was clearly in the hero's role, a role he couldn't have assumed without the progress China has made. I felt he had reached the last step of a long journey to the NBA, that he'd already won all the major battles, gathered all the support imaginable, made all the right choices, so for someone to say at the last minute, "Hold it," well, I'd be disappointed if that was the world we lived in. Besides, for anyone to stop him at this point would've run counter to everything that China was trying to project to the world about becoming more open, integrating into the global village, and respecting individualism. What kind of message would it send if your best player wasn't allowed to realize his potential?

I always tried to reassure Yao by telling him, "You're not ahead of your time. We're beyond the debate of whether or not you should play in the NBA; it's only a matter of working out the details of how that will be achieved." There have been periods in China's history, such as the reform movement in the 1800s, where there were people within the Imperial Court who tried to reform the court in a way that would bring China into the modern age. But their ideas were way ahead of their time. If they were lucky, they got exiled, but more than likely they had their heads chopped off. "Yao, you're rolling along with history," I said. I had no doubt history was on his side, that he had been born at the right time—and that he would get to keep his head.

JOHN HUIZINGA: *It was like starting from ground zero once we began negotiating with the CBA. They didn't want to talk to me or Erik, only Lu Hao. There was a full week in which they said they couldn't talk to us at all because they were involved with the Wang Zhi Zhi situation. Needless to say this was frustrating and nerve-wracking because until the CBA issued a release to FIBA—the governing body of international basketball—Yao would not be free to sign an NBA contract. And Houston was understandably leery of using the first pick in the draft on someone they couldn't sign. That's why they had told Erik and me that if the CBA's release to FIBA was not a done deal three days before the draft, they would start looking for a way to trade the number-one pick. We knew that would make other NBA teams reluctant to draft Yao because it would have signaled that something was wrong. God only knows where Yao would have gone in the draft in this circumstance. The CBA eventually turned their attention to us, but I was getting nervous because it was one of those "We'll try to meet with you the day after tomorrow" kind of deals. Finally someone at the CBA told Lu Hao and Yao's mom that the CBA was ready to notify the Federation of International Basketball Association (FIBA) that Yao was released. That was four days before the draft and a day before the Rockets' deadline, so we thought we were golden. Elation, job completed. It was short-lived, however. Later that same day we learned that the CBA was not prepared to issue the release. We went from an incredible high to a state of "What's going on here?"*

The CBA's explanation was that when they finally looked at FIBA's release form, it contained some troubling language. The form said that Yao Ming had no obligation to play pro ball in China. But the CBA claimed it said he had no obligations of any kind in China when in fact he does—to play for the national team and pay both the Sharks and the CBA. But they insisted they couldn't sign it because it would mean Yao never would have to come back.

The next day we were as scared as we could possibly be. We

were out of time, the CBA wouldn't issue the release, and the rea-
son they gave for not issuing the release made no sense.

I'd already gone through a lot of frustration at this point. I wasn't about to let a little more beat me. I think the negotiations went back and forth at the very end because, while a lot of people in the CBA wanted to help, not everybody did. There were a few people who weren't thinking about what was good for me or for Chinese basketball. They just wanted to show they had power and to make decisions that were good for them. But in the end, I believe that this was a mistake, and how they are remembered will prove that.

We were ready to say to the CBA then, "OK, that's it, we just won't go." But the people misusing their power knew they couldn't allow that to happen, either. If that had happened, no matter what they might have given as the reason, the public wouldn't have accepted it.

In the end, the CBA got only a small percentage of my income, but I don't believe they deserved anything. That also makes me believe even more that the delays at the end were about power. The Sharks got a lot more money, but that's OK. I wanted to give the Sharks money. I spent eight years with them. So in the end, the Sharks got most of the money, and the CBA got all the bad press, because the reporters blamed them for everything taking so long.

A lot of players go into the sports school, then to a junior team, then to a team like the Shanghai Sharks, and on to the national team. OK, maybe not a lot of players, but a lot more than just me. I took the same road as everyone else, but I always felt something was different. Something always came into my life that changed me, allowed me to go to the next level more quickly. I always had Liu Wei at my side along the way and Wang Zhi Zhi in front of me, giving me someone to chase. Early on, I got a chance to go to Paris and see what basketball outside China was like. Then I got to go to the U.S., which showed me I was OK and that I had to get better. When I finally got almost as good as Wang Zhi Zhi, I played in my first Olympics and saw players even better than him. When he left for the U.S., I had a championship to win.

If a person has a target or a goal, he will run as fast as he can to get to that goal. If there isn't one, he will be a little slower. Watching other players, I can see that not everyone has always had what I had. Wang Zhi Zhi did not have it. Something special always happened to push me to the next level. I don't know what you want to call it—coincidence, luck—but it was there for me. I think that destiny, as much as anything, is why I am where I am today.

Other great Chinese athletes in other sports have left the country or struggled to make decisions for themselves, but none of them ever walked my path, either. Before Wang Zhi Zhi and me, China's top athletes were in sports that are special to China—diving, gymnastics, badminton, table tennis. We've always been good at those sports. Not basketball. It's a Western sport, and we've never been good at it. So it means much more to China to have a star in basketball, because it says that in at least one way we can compete with the West. That's something China has not believed in a long time.

Great Chinese athletes before me have left the country and had success, but people in China haven't always been happy about it. He Zhi Li was a world-champion women's table-tennis player who moved to Japan and became a Japanese citizen because she didn't like how she was treated by China's national table-tennis team. She became a big star and beat a Chinese player to win an Asian Championship, but many people in China still hate her and say she is a traitor.

ERIK ZHANG: *Everything came down to the final few days, which I spent relaying what the Rockets needed in order to draft Yao Ming and what the CBA needed in order to issue his release. Two days before the draft, Goldberg was still saying, "As it stands today, we cannot draft Yao." That was two days before the draft!*

During the day I was explaining Houston's position to the CBA, and at night I was helping Houston understand what the CBA was saying. I helped Goldberg draft the letters he was sending to the CBA, and I was giving advice to the CBA about how to reassure the Rockets that Yao Ming was coming to the NBA. They couldn't afford to have Yao not go number one because of something they did, but as a government organization they also couldn't afford to say OK and later go back on their word to a foreign organization. So their problem was, how do we word a statement that puts the Houston Rockets at ease so they can draft Yao but at the same time protects our interest in further negotiations? Houston had two needs as well—to make sure that if they drafted Yao, he would be able to play that season, but also to not give away so much that he could be called back in the middle of the season for something.

MICHAEL GOLDBERG: *I went up to see Jim Baker, my law partner and the former secretary of state, when all this started. His office is lined with pictures of presidents and prime ministers. It's very impressive. "You've read the papers," I said. "You know I'm going to be negotiating with the Chinese, so give me some clues."*

"They're tough," he said, and he gave me some general tips. Then he added, "Read my book." That would be The Politics of Diplomacy. *That was the extent of Jim's involvement. Bush Sr. was not involved on any level greater than providing the letter of introduction. My connections with these leaders were always there in*

the background, and although I thought about it at one point, I never had to pull those triggers.

With the draft just a few days away, we knew we weren't going to have negotiations with either the Sharks or the CBA completed in time. But we couldn't make Yao the number-one pick and not know if he was going to be available. So the day before the draft I sent a statement for the CBA to sign that would meet the approval of FIBA. It was one sentence: "This will confirm that Yao Ming is not subject to an existing and validly binding player contract to play basketball with the Shanghai Sharks or any other club in the Chinese Basketball Association."

I got this back: "Once we received your letter to ask for the FIBA release, we immediately transferred your letter to the Shanghai Sharks and asked them to reply soon, as we should be honest to you that the Shanghai Sharks still have the existing and valid binding contract with Yao Ming. The NBA draft is coming close, we still hope that Yao will be drafted by the Rockets. What we discussed before regarding Yao are quite effective and constructive with sincerity."

So I send another letter to Commissioner Xin and say, "Guys, if I don't have this, don't count on him being the number-one pick." I quickly got a letter back from Bai Li: "If the Houston Rockets draft Yao Ming number one, I've spoken to Commissioner Xin and there will be no new terms negotiated." I then received a fax from the commissioner at 2 A.M. the morning of the draft. I called Erik as soon as it arrived.

"What's it say?" Erik asked.

"I don't know. It's in Chinese."

I gave it to Erik to translate, as well as a friend in Hong Kong who was helping me. Independently, they both said it basically repeated Bai Li's letter, that we have an understanding and it won't be changed. Was it the one sentence I asked for? No, it was three pages long and that sentence wasn't in there anywhere. But it was enough.

ERIK ZHANG: *One side had to take the greater leap of faith, and I have to credit Houston for that. I credit Goldberg. He put his China hat on rather than sticking to the American way of interpreting things. Events since, of course, prove that he took the right risk.*

In the end, half the credit has to go to the macro environment made possible by the Chinese government's reform movement. Marketization, globalization, integration into the world—all of that made Yao Ming, NBA star, possible. The sentiment was there because of the failure of soccer and the religious following of sport and what sport represents to national pride. Yao was like a boulder sitting right at the edge of a cliff; all you had to do was push it over, and that didn't take much. A single tap and it was rolling down the hill.

Everyone flew from Shanghai to Beijing, where they were putting Yao and his parents in front of a camera for TNT, to show Yao live when he was selected. I decided not to go. I went home and went to bed.

JOHN HUIZINGA: *I went to Beijing, where we were in this really small CNN studio during the draft. There were no monitors, so we couldn't see anything, but we could hear Charles Barkley going on and on about what jerks the Rockets were to draft Yao with the number-one pick. Yao was listening to it all, wearing this Rockets cap that was about six sizes too small. When we got on the bus back to the national team's training center, I asked Yao how he felt. He didn't answer. Instead, he asked,*

"Where is Charles Barkley from? Phoenix?"

"He played there, but he's actually from Alabama."

"Hmmm." That's all he said.

A lot of people asked me, "After the Houston Rockets made you the number-one pick, how did you feel? Were you excited?" Sometimes I would say yes, just to say the right thing. But I wasn't excited. First of all, by then I already knew I would be the number-one pick. Or at least I knew the chance was very high. And second, I had waited too long for it to happen. It didn't feel like a surprise anymore. It felt like a relief.

6

WELCOME TO
THE NBA

fter all that time not knowing if I would be going to the NBA or when I would be going, I was finally on my way to Houston—and I was hurt. A week before I was to leave for the U.S., in the final game of the Asian Games against South Korea, I made a low-post move and stepped on someone's foot with my left foot, injuring my left arch. All my injuries seem to happen that way—nothing big, just one wrong step. What also hurt is that we lost that game and the tournament. It was worse for our coach, Wang Fei; he lost the game and his job.

So now I was in Houston to show my new teammates what I could do, only I couldn't play my normal game. Nothing was broken or torn, but when you hurt your foot, you feel it anytime you run or jump or do anything. I am right-handed, so I use my left foot to pivot, to push off for right-handed layups, jump hooks, everything. It felt like a rock was in that shoe. Anytime I made a move, I felt it.

JOHN HUIZINGA: *Despite having all summer to work on it, we still didn't have Yao Ming's release from the CBA when he ar-*

rived in Houston, in October. Yao had missed training camp be-
cause he was required by the CBA to play in the Asian Games and
now, because he didn't have the release, his contract with the Rock-
ets couldn't be approved by the NBA. This meant Yao had no insur-
ance against getting injured. He was introduced at the Rockets
exhibition game against Orlando and then left at halftime to go to
the hospital to get a physical. The entire first half Goldberg is telling
me how great it is to have him here and finally have him practice.
"He's not going to practice; he doesn't have a contract," I said. It
turned out to be a really unpleasant night, and it should've been a
really happy one.

The Rockets knew about my foot, but I don't know if Team Yao did.
It didn't matter; I had waited so long to put on a Rockets uniform,
even if it was a practice uniform, I wasn't going to wait any longer.

They had TV cameras and reporters in for the first part of practice, but they had to leave after fifteen minutes. They saw me stretch
and warm up, that's it. So they didn't find out about my foot, either.
When the media came back in after practice, Rudy T. and the players said a lot of nice things about how I played, but I only practiced
at maybe 75 percent, and then my foot started to hurt again. I was
on the second team, so I didn't play right away with the team's two
stars, Stevie Francis and Cuttino Mobley. The only player I connected with in that first practice is someone whose name I don't remember because he got released a couple of days later.

After practice, they had a party for season-ticket holders. It was
a lunch party, and then there was a golf tournament. Stevie took
me from practice to the golf course in his Hummer. I've never
played golf. I've never had time. Stevie and I talked for the first
time on the way there.

"Do you have a girlfriend?" he asked.

I said, "Yes, I have."

"Watch out," he said. "They all want your money."

Welcome to the NBA, I thought. You just got your first lesson.

STEVE FRANCIS: *I could tell he was scared in that first practice, that he didn't want all those cameras looking at him. He didn't know how to come talk to the guys. Everybody was basically in a circle, and he was stretching a little ways away. He was just trying to ease in, but you could tell he didn't feel comfortable. So, of course, I went over and said, "C'mon, get in the circle with us." Maybe they do it different in China, but you could tell he didn't know what to do. He was kind of stuck. Then once we got through the stretching, Coach Rudy and Coach Smith went right at him, talking to him about the offense we run. They weren't using the translator, Colin, they were just talking to him in English. You know how some people will try to talk to you loud or slow if they're not speaking to you in your language? Rudy wasn't like that. He was just talking to him like he would anybody. Yao picked everything up pretty quickly, but I don't know how much he actually understood from that first day.*

I gave him a ride from practice at Westside to the Royal Oaks, where the lunch and golf thing was being held for our season-ticket holders. When I told him to be careful about his girlfriend and his money, he was like, "No, no, no, she plays for the Chinese national team." I was like, "All right, that means he has some history with her." I thought maybe he'd just met somebody over here and was in trouble already.

Now I know that he doesn't hit the clubs or hang out, but nobody on the team sweats that. Everybody understands that's just his culture. Nobody pressures him with "Hey, Yao, go out with us." Everybody understands that's how he was raised. There's no need to expose him to that life if he's never lived it. He doesn't need it. Nine times out of ten, bad things happen, anyway.

And, man, being devoted to one girl, that's straight. The only thing that's different about it is, once he starts talking about her, he gets all googly-eyed and his cheeks get all red. Other than that, there's nothing wrong with having only one girlfriend, I don't think. A lot of younger guys would do well to be the same way. Me? I'm an old guy; it doesn't apply.

I talked to Stevie later about the friendship bracelet my girlfriend gave me. It's on my left wrist and it's very loose now, so I'm always pushing it up my arm. People often ask about it. "In China," I told Stevie, "if you have one friendship bracelet, that means you have one girlfriend. You, I think maybe you need ten."

He thought that was funny. It was very important for me that I was OK with Stevie. I felt he was the team's leader, and I wanted to make sure we were OK—and that I was OK with the rest of the team, too. I really didn't want any problems made by people from outside the team. I was especially worried about all the media attention focused on me. I was scared my teammates would feel differently about me because of that.

CARROLL DAWSON: *What I remember most about Yao's arrival was going out to the airport and picking him up for his first press conference. There were hundreds—maybe even thousands— of people out there at the airport to greet him. We hadn't announced it or anything; I guess people were just curious about this guy. There was an hour or so before we had to get him to the press conference, and he spent the entire time taking pictures and signing autographs. Everybody was going nuts. I arranged for ten extra cops to be there for security. I should've had twenty-five extra, but*

I didn't know there were going to be that many people. We finally had to drag him away because we had the media waiting over at our old arena, the Compaq Center. As they were winding up the interview session, someone asked, "Is there anything you can say to the Houston community in English?"

Yao Ming looked at Colin, his interpreter, and thought about it for just a second. "I'm sorry I'm only one person, and I didn't get to sign all the autographs and take all the pictures everybody wanted at the airport," he said, "but if you give me another chance, I promise I will do that."

He won over this community almost instantly. I started getting calls from people who weren't even basketball fans, saying, "I will be a Rockets fan now because of that young man."

I know now that I was lucky to come to the Rockets. They were the right team for me. My mom liked CD right from the start. She told him he was like a grandfather to me. He told her it made him feel old, which isn't always a compliment in America. She told him, that's OK, in China it is.

Another reason I was glad to be in Houston is that Stevie was the right kind of team leader. Some players wouldn't be happy with a rookie getting so much attention, especially one who was still learning how to play at the NBA level. But he helped me. When he said that he might be Stevie "Franchise" but I was the Ming "Dynasty," that made me feel really good. When he said we were the same, the only difference being that I was 7′5″ and Chinese, that made me feel good, too. I know now that wouldn't have happened on every NBA team.

STEVE FRANCIS: *I learned two things from Yao that I now think of as Chinese traits: attention to detail and being generous.*

When Yao and his family first came to Houston, they gave gifts to everybody with the team. Most of us got chopsticks. I can't tell you what makes a good chopstick and what makes a bad one, but these aren't just some wooden ones you'd get at a fast-food joint. They definitely put some thought into what they were buying. I took that as a sign of the Chinese people's heart.

I also learned pretty quickly how hungry he was to get better. The day after we introduced him at the pre-season game, he was ready to work. When we started lifting weights, he wanted to get big and gain weight, and that was definitely a positive from a big man. I'm not saying all big men are lazy, but he had the kind of energy you'd expect to see from a guard.

I became friends with Bostjan Nachbar right away. He's from Slovenia; his nickname is "Boki," and he was a rookie like me. Maybe not all NBA players feel this way, but I think of all the players who came into the league with me as my brothers. That's why, on All-Star Weekend, I wanted to sit on the West team bench during the Rookie Game, even though I couldn't play because I was in the All-Star Game. I just wanted to be with my brothers.

Boki is a typical European player: he passes the ball quick, not a lot of one-on-one dribble, and he's a good shooter. I got to know him in my second preseason game, at home against Philadelphia. The 76ers played zone defense. At that time, the Rockets didn't know how to play against a zone because this was the first year teams were allowed to play it in the NBA. But international players know because we face it all the time. So I went to the free-throw line to catch the ball and then face the basket. That brought the defense to me, and Boki went to an open spot for a 3. I passed it, he made it. Later I told Boki, "Every international player knows how to get a shot against a zone."

My foot was better after about three weeks, and I started playing better when it stopped hurting. That's when I finally had my first big game, against Shawn Bradley and the Dallas Mavericks. But my foot wasn't the only problem in my playing badly at first. The biggest part was still that I was a rookie and a new guy from China and I didn't feel comfortable here. I was very nervous before every game. I couldn't sleep the night before. In warm-ups, I'd run very, very hard. The assistant coaches would tell me, "Take it easy. We have a game for forty-eight minutes. You need to keep a little." But I didn't know how to control it. I was so nervous, I wanted to do everything fast. Then I'd get into the game, and after five minutes I would be so tired, I couldn't catch my breath.

I felt especially nervous before my first regular-season game in the NBA, of course, but even more so because it was in Indianapolis. Yes, I'd played there in the World Championships, but the arena in Indianapolis is very big, and there weren't a lot of people there for the championships. It was like a different place for my first Rockets game: lots of people, lots of media, lots of noise. The locker room and the hallways that go to the floor are all very small. Everything is very close. Then you walk into the arena and it's very big. Lots of space. That wasn't a problem during the World Championships because there weren't very many people there. But this time when I ran out onto the court with the team, all that space was filled up with people yelling. I felt like, Wow! Where am I?

Here's another reason I felt nervous: when I played with the Chinese national team in the World Championships, we had a lot of bad games in Conseco Fieldhouse. China didn't play very many good games in the tournament—we were 1–7—and the one game we won, against Algeria, was in the Fieldhouse, but for some reason I played better in the RCA Dome. I had such a bad feeling about the Fieldhouse that when the team went to watch the tournament final between Yugoslavia and Argentina, I walked in and walked back out. I told the coach that there were too many people who wanted to talk or have me sign an autograph and I couldn't concentrate on the game, but the real reason is I just didn't like being there. I walked back to the hotel and watched the finals on TV.

But I still don't know what happened to me in that first game against the Pacers. I didn't play in the first quarter and then started the second quarter. There was a jump ball; we got it but then gave it away and had to hurry back on defense. They threw the ball to their center right away, and it was one-on-one against me. I just fouled him. It was really stupid. It never got better after that. I never woke up. I played only eleven minutes and missed the only shot I took. It was like when you're in a car. In America you have automatic transmission, right? In China, we have a lot of manual transmission. Sometimes when you're driving your car and you don't change the gear, or you change too slow or too fast, the car suddenly stops. That was me in Indiana. I couldn't find a gear. I told the reporters afterward that everything has to have a start and this was my start in the NBA. But I also was scared it might be my end. I thought the Rockets might just send me back to China the next day.

JOHN HUIZINGA: *I thought, "This poor guy." He played so well with the Chinese national team in Oakland, I thought he was Superman. But after the Indiana game I knew he had to be hurting.*

My wife had baked a box full of chocolate chip cookies and given them to him earlier in the day. "I don't want to take these with me," he said. "Give them to my mom. Wait, I'll take one."

No points, two rebounds, two turnovers in front of all those millions of people watching in China and around the world. But if he was rattled, he sure didn't show it. When I saw him in the locker room afterward, he looked up at me and smiled.

"If I'd eaten two cookies," he said, "I would've played better."

FANG FENG DI: *I was not a strong supporter of Yao's going to the NBA. Having played basketball myself, I knew Yao's strengths and weaknesses. He's not very strong. He's not physically gifted. He has a good shot, good touch, but he uses his brain to play. I didn't think that's what it took to succeed in the NBA, so I wasn't sure he'd make it. I thought he was at a disadvantage compared to most NBA players in speed, strength, and jumping ability. But when a kid has a dream, it's the parents' job not to stop the dream but to allow him to have the opportunity to pursue it. So that's what I did. But I was prepared for disappointment, and the first game confirmed my fears. In that way, it wasn't a shock. I thought that he'd fall apart in the face of such a physical game, and all his bones would be crushed.*

WANG FEI: *Yao looked like a fish out of water, even though he was trying very hard. When the Pacers ran a pick and roll, Yao didn't just try to challenge the guard if he used the screen to take a shot; he tried to block the shot. Now he's smarter. You can see that the Rockets coach told him, "Don't jump. Hands up."*

I wasn't worried, because I know him. He'd watched a lot of NBA games, but he'd never played in one. The one thing about Yao is that he can quickly adapt to different situations.

A lot of players said they were going to play me hard—Ben Wallace on Team USA said he would be physical, and Shaq said he would use his elbow on me—but I was not worried. You know why? There's a better chance of getting hurt in China than in the NBA. In the States, basketball is very professional. In China, some bench players only come in to foul, and they'll hit you in your face or your body or wait for you to jump and put their foot underneath you so you'll land on it. That's why sometimes I'd barely jump in CBA games. Some people still do that, but it's not as bad. But I remember five years ago in the CBA they had a team on which all the players were policemen. It was like the army team, except this was a police team. All the players on that team used their feet, elbows, and knees to try to hurt you. I played against one big guy on their team who tried to stick his knee into the side of my knee. I know that a couple of guys in the NBA do things like that, too, but not as many as in the CBA. That police team, by the way, is not around anymore; it folded, and the basketball court in China is now a safer place.

I didn't have long to think about the Pacers game because we played two nights later in Denver. That's where I scored my first basket. I just hoped it wouldn't be my last one. Right before I scored, the Nuggets rookie, Nene Hilario, had a big block on me. Really big. I had a layup and boom, he sent the ball into our bench. He pissed me off. That made me want to score even more than before. But I thought, am I going to have to have my shot blocked into the bench every time before I can make a shot?

STEVE FRANCIS: *We talked for the first time about basketball after he had that first bad game against Indiana. That was the first real conversation we had. I said, "Don't even worry about it. You're straight." Then we played Denver two nights later and I had a really bad game. It might've been my poorest game of the season. He said, "Don't worry about it. Remember me in Indiana."*

We played our first home game against Toronto the next night. I thought Hakeem Olajuwon, a great center for Houston for many years, would be playing for the Raptors, but he retired right before the season started. I got a chance to meet him later, but that was not the same as playing against him. Instead, that night I made a move that people said reminded them of Hakeem and his Dream Shake. I had the ball on the left block, the same place Hakeem liked to get it, spun to the baseline, and scored with an easy layup. They called it the Shanghai Shake. It was a nice welcome, but this was only one move, one moment in a game.

The best part of those first games at home was playing the Portland Trail Blazers and Arvydas Sabonis, their center from Lithuania. I wanted to play Sabonis more than anybody. More than Michael Jordan or Hakeem. Both were great, great players. Jordan is a basketball god, and Hakeem represents the great center. It's just that Sabonis was a great player, he was from another country, he was big like me, and he showed everybody the art of basketball. He didn't come to the NBA until he was old and hurt, but he could still do everything—shoot, pass, dribble, rebound, block shots. When I was twenty years old in China and just starting to think about the NBA, I used "Sabonis" as my online screen name.

The best part of the Portland game, for me, was that I got a chance to talk to him. He wasn't in the starting five, and of course I wasn't either, but I got into the game before he did. Play had stopped for a free throw, and Dale Davis, the Blazers' starting center, went to the bench. I just stood there waiting, and all of a sudden I felt the light change. That's how big Sabonis is. He walked up next to me, and I knew he was there without looking because the court had suddenly gotten just a little darker.

Sabonis asked me about a guy named Vaidis Jurgilas while we waited for the free throw to be shot. "Vaidis, I know him," I said. He's from Lithuania, a left-handed guard who played one season with the Shanghai Sharks, my rookie year.

"He's my good friend," Arvydas said.

"Oh, really," I said. "We called him Y. Y is a good guy."

I played fifteen minutes that night. I scored 7 points. Rudy T. told me before the game, "Don't let Sabonis catch the ball. He's a great passer. He's strong; he's got good hands. Just front him every time so he can't get to the low post." He was like an elephant, and I felt like a little guy. We are about the same height, but he's bigger, wider, much stronger.

Rudy T. was right. I couldn't just stand behind Sabonis and let him catch the ball. He's too big. Once he has the ball, whatever he wants to do—dribble, shoot, pass—you can't stop him. On offense, I really couldn't play with my back to him, either. I had to face him and use my speed because his knee was hurt.

I scored against Sabonis when we ran a side pick-and-pop play. Steve threw the ball to me, and I made a shot-fake. Sabonis came up and I drove the right side, scored on a layup, and got the extra free throw because he fouled me. Every game my goal was just to score one time, no matter who I was playing, because I didn't want to get another zero like in Indiana. So it felt good, but I also knew I wasn't playing the real Sabonis. I had seen tapes of him playing in Europe before he hurt his Achilles tendon. I couldn't believe it. If he hadn't gotten hurt, he could've been the best NBA center ever. Better than Hakeem, who won two championships. Better than Shaq, who has won three and might not stop there. Maybe Sabonis wasn't stronger than Shaq, but he's the same size, and he can shoot from outside and pass the ball. Sabonis can do everything on the court. He can play point guard to center. The no-look, over-the-head pass in the post that I like to make—I got it from Sabonis.

Mengke Bateer, another Chinese center who came to the NBA, tried that Sabonis pass too, in the national team's training camp. When I defended him, I pushed him out so he wouldn't catch the ball in the low post. Then, when a player cut down the baseline, I stepped back and caught the pass. I knew he was going to throw it. He had done it before, during the CBA season for the Beijing Ducks, so I knew it was coming.

Sabonis retired from the NBA the next year. He went home, played for a team in Lithuania, and spent more time with his family. That made me even happier and more honored to have played against him before his NBA career ended.

As I said, that was the best part of those first home games. The worst might have been hearing the song they wrote for me. The music is from the bullfighting song "Olé, Olé, Olé" only instead of "Olé" they say my name. They played it all season long at every game and sometimes on the radio. Maybe this is bad, because not everybody has a song written about them, but I hated that song. There are other words in it, but all I heard was my name, like fifty times. Do you know what it's like to hear your name like that? It's like your mom calling you when she wants you to do something, only worse. Even my mom never said my name that many times in one breath. Sometimes, when everything was quiet, I would hear "Yao Ming, YaoMingYaoMingYaoMing" in my head. I thought I was going crazy. My second season they still played it, but just the beginning of the song. That was still enough to say my name three or four times. That, I think, is enough.

We were home for almost two weeks, so I heard this song—the whole song—a lot. They play it in China now, too. It's called "Breakfast with Yao" there. I'm not sure why. That song is the only reason I was happy anytime we left Houston. On our second trip of the season we went to Phoenix first, then L.A. In Phoenix I got noticed for another move, only this time it wasn't mine.

GLEN RICE (former Houston Rockets player): *My favorite Yao moment from that first season was when the Suns' Stephon Marbury crossed him over so bad he fell down. It was the seventh game of the season, and we were in Phoenix. After Yao went down, Marbury went right by him. I think just about everybody in the arena was laughing. We ragged on him for a whole week about that. That's when we realized he was all right, because he took it and didn't get mad. If you can get crossed over and fall down and be cool with it, well, that really went a long way with everybody on the team. He wasn't some tall dude from China after that. He was our boy Yao.*

It didn't bother me. Stephon is a very good player. They ran a pick-and-roll play from the top of the key, and I left Jake Tsakalidis to help stop Stephon. We were in the middle of the paint and I tried to step back, but I was already on my heels. I fell on my butt. The way I looked at it, nothing could be worse than my first game in Indianapolis.

We played the Lakers for the first time right after that, and even though I knew Shaq was hurt and wouldn't play, I was feeling a lot of pressure because Charles Barkley had said the night before on TV that I wouldn't score 19 points in a game all season. He made a bet with Kenny Smith, another TNT analyst, that if I did score 19, he would kiss Smith's ass. To me, that meant Charles was pretty confident I couldn't do it. I didn't care about that so much, but I felt as though now everybody would be watching to see how long it took before I did it. I couldn't be sure at that time I would ever do it. But I had fun with it. If I had learned one thing before I left China, it was not to take things too seriously.

"Oh, OK," I said when reporters asked me about what Charles said. "I will only score 18 so I don't make him look bad."

But Charles might not have made that bet if he'd seen the Rockets practice the week before the Lakers game. I started to feel stronger and play more physically, and I had a lot of dunks. I said once that I didn't like to dunk because the Chinese think it's impolite. That was a joke, but everybody thought I was serious. Believe me, a lot of players in China try to dunk on me all the time. It just wasn't something I did. I didn't think it was a very good habit. A lot of times when I dunked the ball, I was fouled before I could jump or my shot was blocked and the ball didn't go in. In the CBA, no one blocked my jump shot or my hook shot, so that seemed to be smarter than dunking.

After two weeks in the NBA, though, I was dunking all the time in practice. You know why? I started to trust myself more. The game is much faster than in the CBA. The players are much bigger, much stronger, and they jump higher. Not too many players could block my layups or stop my jump hooks in the CBA. In the NBA, lots of players can play above the rim, so I learned it was better to dunk. I had to change, but it takes time to make a change.

I didn't plan to make Charles eat his words the very next game, it just happened. My foot was feeling better, I was feeling stronger, and without Shaq the Lakers had no one who could guard me. I had 20 points by making nine of nine shots and two of two free throws. We won, and Charles lost his bet one day after making it.

(Instead of kissing Kenny Smith's ass, Charles had to kiss a donkey Kenny rented, all on national TV. Charles has made other bets since then, but not about me.) In China we say, "A man is truly unlucky when even the water he drinks gets stuck in his teeth." I've never been to Las Vegas, but I hear that Charles goes there a lot. Does the water get stuck in his teeth there, too?

My feelings about Charles have changed a little bit since I came to the NBA. I still like him, but my respect for him has changed. Most people love Charles, and a few don't like him. But nobody really hates him. He's too funny and not serious enough to hate. I don't know how much of what he says is what he really thinks and how much is just to be noticed, but I think it's probably around 50-50.

I respected that in Charles's last contract with the Houston Rockets, he did what Karl Malone did with the Lakers in 2003: he signed up only to try to win a championship ring. Charles was a superstar, but he played for less money than he could've gotten. He was willing to make a sacrifice to win a ring. He was willing to sacrifice for honor. If I could invite any three people in the world to dinner, Charles still would be one of them. Sabonis would be another. My girlfriend would be third. (But if she asks, say I mentioned her first.)

Two nights after that Lakers game we played Cleveland at home, and I caught a rebound with one hand for the first time in the NBA. That was a sign I was finally comfortable. The game was fun and interesting again. In the CBA, I caught a lot of rebounds with one hand. My hands are big enough that I can hold the ball comfortably that way. But in the first eight games I tried to be very careful and take care of the ball, hold it with both hands, not turn it over, and score just once a game if I could. That's all I hoped to do.

I managed to do a lot more than that against Dallas and playing Shawn Bradley for the first time. A lot of attention was focused on this game because we were the two tallest players in the league. Charles said something bad about me before this game, too. He said that, compared to me, Shawn Bradley looked like Bill Russell because I was not ready for the NBA. Even in China we know that Bill Russell won many championships with the Celtics, so I knew what this meant.

Before I came to the NBA, I heard myself compared a lot to Shawn Bradley, but I felt I knew how to beat him: maintain body-to-body contact. Give him space and he can block your shot every time. But keep your body next to his and bump him and he will fall back, and if you are my size, then you can take hook shots and fade-aways and not worry about being blocked. I scored 30 points that night, and he might've blocked my shot once.

MAURICE TAYLOR (Houston Rockets forward): *I had two favorite Yao moments from his first season, and that first Dallas game was one of them. First of all, you just wanted to see those two guys with that phenomenal height going against one another. That, and we weren't quite sure yet exactly what Yao could do. He'd had 20 against the Lakers, but that was without Shaq. Then we sat there on the bench watching him play Shawn Bradley like he was 6'2". That's when we knew Yao was going to be something special.*

We went right to the Dallas airport after the game to fly home. When we started to get off the bus and get on the plane, Stevie gave me the bag with his suit in it. "Here, rookie, take it," he said. "You scored 30, but you're still a rookie." Stevie takes this suit bag everywhere, but he never has anyone carry it for him. "OK," I said. "I'll take it. No problem." Jay Namoc, our equipment manager, saw me taking the suit off the bus and said, "Yeah. Rookie's job."

I carried the suit bag from the bus to the plane. A very short walk. As soon as we were on the plane, Stevie took it back. "Thanks, rookie," he said.

That was the one time all season he ordered me to do something. I know it was just a joke, but I don't believe in older players doing that to younger players. It's not something that happens just in the States; in China I saw older players order younger players around, too. They made them do small things—get them food or do other jobs. I will never do that. I can ask a rookie for help with something, but that's different. As I've said before, I like being equal with my teammates. That's *all* my teammates.

What rookies have to do for the team is different. It's not one player making another player do something; it's something all the rookies do for the team. For example, for every away game, I and the team's other rookies had to go to the equipment manager's room and deliver the practice gear to each player in his room. That meant that if the bus left for shootaround at 9:30, I had to wake up at 8:30. That was the only thing we had to do. I was lucky because there were four rookies—Boki, me, Juaquin Hawkins, and Tito Maddox. So everybody just had to take two or three bags of practice gear.

Our next game after we played Dallas was against Michael Jordan and the Wizards in Houston. I hadn't seen him in person since I played at his basketball camp when I was eighteen. I remember how, at the camp, they offered a pair of Jordan's shoes, autographed, to anyone who hit shots from five different spots on the floor. I was so nervous I could barely walk. These were easy shots, but I missed the third one. What is amazing about Jordan is that every time he shoots, you can tell by his body that he expects the shot to go in. It's magical.

Reporters in China talk about how, if I had been allowed to be in the draft in 2001, maybe I would've been the number-one pick instead of Kwame Brown, who didn't do very well. Not much was known about either Kwame or me then, and no one knows if I would have done better—I would have been a year younger—but the reporters in China believe I would have. Maybe then, they say, Jordan would've made it back to the playoffs and would be playing still. This is not something I can think about; it didn't happen, and too many things would have had to happen differently for it to happen. You can talk about almost anything and say that if the past had been different, then the present and future would be, too.

I wasn't as nervous this time when I saw Jordan. I made my first start, and I scored 18 points, making 7 of 11 shots. We won, 93–86, which I was happy about, but there was something that happened during the game that bothered me. The Rockets mascot ran out wearing my number 11 jersey and waving a Rockets flag. Then an old man wearing Jordan's numer 23 Wizards uniform came out, bent over and walking like someone very, very old. The crowd laughed, but I think it's wrong for anyone to be disrespectful toward Michael Jordan. I especially wouldn't want to be part of something like that.

We were in Seattle when I had my first Thanksgiving and my first turkey leg. The team ate together at the hotel, and I have to say that I gave thanks for the meal being over. The leg was so big, and when I bit into it, it was like biting into wood. I can't understand how Americans eat so much turkey. Be good to yourself. Enjoy the holidays. But I'll have chicken wings or steak.

I can't blame the turkey for our next loss, in Sacramento, to the Kings. If there were a team other than the Rockets that I'd like to play for, it would be the Kings. If you can build team chemistry and cooperation around individual talent, it's a very strong combination. And that's where I think the Kings were my first year.

They are very mature in the way they play. Sometimes our chemistry was good, and sometimes it was not good at all. This was one of those games when it wasn't good at all. We lost by 19 points.

Our next game was against the Spurs and their Twin Towers, Tim Duncan and David Robinson. I had one of my three best games of the season, with 27 points and 18 rebounds. I think because they had two big guys, they didn't double-team me as much as other teams had, so I had a lot of opportunity. It also helped that I had already played against them in a pre-season game. Whenever I have a chance to learn from my mistakes, I usually do better.

I learned in December that joining a team in the NBA doesn't mean you will be with that team forever. That's when the Rockets traded Kenny Thomas to the 76ers. You know what I felt? Scared. A lot of people I talked to said, "Why are you scared? They'll never trade you." It's like this: You go to a hospital and you see a dead guy. You may not be dead, but now you're scared, seeing what it would be like.

I'd never had a teammate traded before. They don't do that in the CBA. If I had stayed in China, I would've been with the Sharks my whole life. Star players never change teams. Second-level players will change teams, but not by trade. If their team doesn't want them, they are free to sign with another team—but only if their team doesn't want them. Otherwise, they have to sign with that team again. I've had teammates go to other teams, but never in the middle of the season. Before Kenny left, they took everything out of his locker. Then he came in and said good-bye to everybody. A few hours later, James Posey came in and said hello. I don't know if I will ever get used to that.

Our rematch against the Pacers was that night. Isiah Thomas was the Pacers coach then. I remember him being a really smart player. People called him the Smiling Assassin. He's always smiling. Before we played them the first time, he shook my hand and said, "Good luck with the season. And every time you play us, play bad." He was smiling when he said it.

I didn't play bad against the Pacers this time. This was another one of my three best games of the season: 29 points, 10 rebounds, 6 blocked shots. We won easily, 95–83. I don't know why it was so different. Maybe I took all the first game's points and got them in the second game. Or maybe it was like the NBA message to kids, "Read to Achieve." I watched the tape and thought about their team play and what their center, Jermaine O'Neal, wanted to do. I studied his moves, his defense, whether he liked to jump or maintain contact. I don't watch a lot of tapes on my own, but I would watch whatever the team gave me, and there's always a tape of the other team's last game on in the locker room before we play them.

I had my first Christmas a week later. That was nice—two days off. I knew a little about Christmas and how Americans celebrate it before I came to Houston, but my family didn't do any of those things. I did send Christmas cards to all the centers I had played up to that point, every GM who came to my pre-draft workout in Chicago, and Michael Jordan. I also gave cards to people who work for the Rockets. Since Rudy T. and CD and Michael Goldberg were so important in getting me to Houston, I gave them silk shirts from China as presents.

Our next road trip was to L.A. to face the Clippers and Wang Zhi Zhi. As you might assume, this game got a lot of attention in China. I had a hard time—4 points on four shots, 7 rebounds, in twenty-eight minutes. This is not just because Wang knows me and how I play better than anyone. He didn't play much, and he played even worse than I did—eleven minutes, no points, no rebounds. The main reason I had trouble is that this was the first time the defense really focused on me—double-teams all the time, putting a man in front of me so I couldn't get the ball. The other reason was their center, Michael Olowokandi. I shook him twice with the same move in five minutes, but he played me very hard. I don't like the way he always uses a hand in my back or how he always attacks me when I am on defense. If I could have picked players I didn't have to play against that first season, the first would have been Shaq and the second Olowokandi.

The L.A. game started another long road trip. Ten of our next sixteen games were away from home. The travel, in the end, is what made me tired, not practice or games—especially the long flights right when the season started. I started off tired and never stopped long enough to recover.

If I had been in China, I would've had a week off for Chinese New Year. That's the biggest holiday in China. It's not on the same day every year because it goes by the moon's calendar, but it's always in January or February. My first year in the NBA it was on February 1. For Chinese New Year, you make a lot of food and give red bags—coins with red paper around them—to the kids. Every kid waits all year for this day. I did, too, but not now. I have money now, so I'm giving bags, not getting them. At midnight of the first night everyone goes outside and yells "Happy New Year!" and shoots off fireworks. Every day has a special meaning. The fourth day, for example, is the birthday of the kitchen god, who sees everything that goes on in the house. You have to prepare a lot of food that day, even if you don't eat it. Many people don't do this anymore, but it's an old tradition. Day Six is the day of the fortune god, and everybody shoots off fireworks that day, too.

COLIN PINE (Yao Ming's translator): *The team surprised Yao with a Chinese New Year's celebration after practice that day. I went to Houston's Chinatown and bought all these decorations and decorated the locker room with Keith Jones, the team trainer and vice president of basketball operations. I bought as many decorative characters as I could, even though I didn't know what all of them meant. Every symbol or character has a special meaning. One of the decorations I bought turned out to be for a wedding. I also bought a tape of Chinese music; it turned out to be in Cantonese and most Chinese people speak Mandarin, so no one understood it. But it still sounded like New Year's music. Then we got a bunch of red envelopes and all the players put two dollars in their envelope and gave it to Yao. Someone—not one of the players, but I can't remember who—made a mistake and gave him a white envelope. That's very bad. White is the color of death in China.*

The locker room party was really a big surprise for me—a nice surprise, except for the white envelope.

Ten days later, I got my first technical, in Atlanta. It cost me $500. I just lost control of myself. Theo Ratliff had made me look bad all game long. I felt I couldn't do anything against him, so I wanted to dunk over him. Just once. He had blocked my shot, he had beat me up and down the floor, he had dunked on me. I couldn't get all that back, so all I wanted was one dunk. My whole game was bad. I missed my first seven shots, including a dunk that no one else touched and a hook shot that Ratliff blocked. I missed three of four free throws. I had no assists.

And then I finally got my one dunk.

It was with about a minute left in the third quarter—a two-handed dunk on Ratliff. I yelled, loud, and shook my fists, letting go of all the frustration. If my teammates liked the dunk and my celebration, they liked it even more when the ref gave me a T. Moochie Norris, one of my teammates, was on the bench, waving a towel. When I came to the bench at the end of the third quarter, even Rudy T. gave me a high five. Cuttino Mobley said, "Now you look like a real NBA player. You've got everything! You can dunk, score, block shots, foul out, turn the ball over, and get T'ed!"

I would tell myself before every game that I can't be like that, but when I got into the game, sometimes I'd forget. I joked with guys who got a lot of Ts, like Eddie Griffin. I'd say, "You just lost $500!" That's still a lot of money to me. Kelvin Cato would tell me, "Hey, you need to get a T because I can't get any more. The next one I get, they'll suspend me." So now I had one.

JUAQUIN HAWKINS (former Houston Rockets forward): *It caught all of us by surprise. We'd all been telling him he should get excited after he dunked, but we'd been telling him that for a while. It got all of us going. I'll take that T any day, I told him. It's weird; he's so different, and he comes from such a unique background, and yet, no matter where you're from, you can relate to him.*

Even though I finished with only 9 points and 6 rebounds and we lost that game to the Hawks, I put it among my best three games of the season. This is why: I learned something from that game and that technical. You have to be tough when the playing is tough. If the other team plays hard, you can play harder.

LI YUANWEI: *I am not concerned that by playing in the NBA Yao Ming will develop a personality that is offensive to Chinese people. People will be able to distinguish his off-court personality and virtue from his on-court personality. In a way, his on-court personality needs more improvement. I still think he's not as aggressive as he could be. He doesn't give people the feeling he wants to dominate and crush his opponent. Some of this, of course, runs counter to Chinese culture. We have a saying: "Always shoot the bird that pops up." But even Mao Tse-tung said, "Physically we want to be a wild man, while spiritually we want to be a civilized man." I think this transformation into being more aggressive is good for Yao Ming and a good example for other Chinese players to follow. In the Chinese leagues they ask players to be aggressive and dominating, but because they've never been told that before— they've actually been told the opposite all their lives—there aren't too many players who play that way.*

One thing I am concerned about is that in developing that aggressive spirit, Yao should not lose his strength, which is the finesse with which he plays the game. His shooting touch and passing shouldn't be sacrificed for the sake of dunking or intimidating his opponent. I don't believe he needs to be more selfish. After all, this is a team sport, and his statistics never should mean more than wins and losses. An assist is just as good as a basket to him and that shouldn't change. He just needs to perfect his decisions on when to go one-on-one and when to pass the ball.

I was ready for players to challenge me when I came to the NBA. I knew everybody would want to try to dunk on me. Every time somebody dunked over me or shook me, like Marbury did, I just wanted to get them back. Maybe not double, but just get them back. After Marbury crossed me over, Stevie threw a nice pass and I dunked at the other end. That's all I'd think about—getting back at someone. Some guys tried to trash-talk me, but I just focused on the game. I just wanted to dunk on them, score on them, block a shot. I wouldn't say anything; I'd just look at the player who did something and I'd do something back. I just wanted them to know that if they did anything to me, there would be a payback.

A week before my first game against Shaq, we played the Denver Nuggets, and I played only eleven minutes after banging my knee into Nene's knee going for a rebound. He beat me to the ball and then dunked on me. I even fouled him.

I could've kept playing, but when our trainer, Keith Jones, asked me how I felt, I said I just wanted to sit down and put some ice or heat or something on the knee. He put ice on it and then talked to Rudy, and they didn't let me play for the rest of the game. I had 6 points and 6 rebounds, and it was only the first quarter. I wanted to keep playing. I had a chance to have a very good game. And with Shaq coming up, I needed one.

7

RACISM AND SHAQ

I know what "nigger" means, and I know it's a bad word. When I first joined the Rockets, my teammates thought they heard Colin and me using it all the time. There is a word in Chinese that sounds a lot like it, but it doesn't mean the same thing at all. It really sounds like "NAY-guh" and it means "that" or "that one" in Mandarin. Colin even told me once, "Don't say that." But it's a habit. We use it the way someone in English would say, "uh-uh-uh" while thinking of what to say next. Everybody would stop anytime they heard Colin or me use that word, especially if we said it more than once. They couldn't understand anything else we were saying, but they thought they understood this one word. One time I was playing and Cuttino Mobley overheard Colin and me talking. Cat—that's what we call Cuttino—said to Colin, "Did you just tell Yao . . ."

"No, no, no!" Colin said.

"OK," Cat said. "Anyway, if you yellow people say that it's not so bad, but if a white guy said it, I'd fight with him."

Before I joined the Rockets, I didn't know how different one black player could be from another. I had played with only a few black players in the CBA, and when I was in the U.S. for the summer, the only teammate I really got to talk to and be around was Teyo. Maybe that's similar to the way Americans see Chinese people: we all look or seem the same. I think it's important to talk to people who don't look or live like you. That way, you can find out that people of one color are not all the same. You can also find out that maybe they're not so different from you. When I went to the Nike camp in France, I had one teammate who was very friendly; I only spoke a little English, but he tried to talk to me almost every day. On the last day we were there, I said, "Maybe one day you'll come visit me in China." He said, "China? I thought you were Japanese!" Maybe someone else would've been bothered by his mistake, but I wasn't. He just didn't know. But that's where misunderstanding is created—between people who don't really know or understand each other.

Race and the color of people's skin is a much bigger thing to worry about in the U.S. than it is in China. Maybe one reason is that we Chinese are mostly of the same race and we don't think about it. We know there are lots of people in the world who look different and have different skin colors, and we've even made war with some of them. But if you're smart, you know there are good and bad people of every type of skin and from every country. I'm not going to like you or hate you just because you look like me or don't look like me. Sometimes those most like you can hurt you the most. Chinese people have learned this lesson, too.

Whatever the reason might be, I was asked a lot of questions about race and racism my rookie year, and not by black and white American reporters as much as by Asian-American reporters. Maybe that shouldn't be a surprise, but I could tell by the way they asked their questions how they wanted me to answer. They wanted me to give the answer they would give. But that's not me.

It all started because, not long after my workout in Chicago, people asked Shaq what he thought about playing me. In an interview before the draft he said he would elbow me in the face. Then in a TV interview after the draft he talked in a fake Chinese accent. He said, "Tell Yao Ming, 'Ching-chong-yang-wah-ah-soh.'"

I heard the U.S. national team also got a lot of questions about me before China played the U.S. in an exhibition game in Oakland a few weeks before the World Championships. I'm sure they had to be tired of being asked about me. They were all great NBA players, getting ready to compete for a world championship, but all the questions being asked were about me, a Chinese player they didn't know much about who never had played in the NBA. The national team players said they would be very physical with me. Some people took this to mean in a dirty way, but I didn't. I was still not very strong, and some of my opponents had success pushing me and keeping a hand on me at all times. I think it started with Richard Anderson, a center for the Canadian national team who is only 6'6" and 260 pounds. We played an exhibition game against Canada, and he did much better than anyone expected by being very physical.

Or maybe they all wanted to be physical with me just as payback for having to talk about me so much.

If the U.S. players were trying to intimidate me, it didn't work—and one reason was the fans in Oakland. They made me feel like I was playing a home game. Some guys painted themselves with the letters of my name on their chest, and there were lots of signs in English and Chinese that said nice things about me. All that made me feel really good.

And, as it turned out, Ben Wallace, on the U.S. team, did land on me when he tried to block my shot. But he fell to the floor after that, and it was much worse for him than me.

GEORGE KARL (2002 Team USA coach): *The guys were impressed. He was much better than any of us expected. We tried to get into him a little bit, and he didn't back down at all. He still needs to get stronger, but there aren't too many guys with that kind of size and touch. There's not a whole lot you can do with that fadeaway jumper. It might not be Kareem Abdul-Jabbar's sky hook, but it's close.*

As for Shaq, I don't know if what he said was worse than what anybody else said. Maybe it was a little worse because Shaq likes to be a little more than everybody else—bigger, louder, stronger, scarier, funnier. But no one really said anything about it until Shaq and I played in January. That was six months later. I thought of the two things he said as the same—Shaq trying to be noticed or maybe trying to be funny. That's Shaq being Shaq.

I don't have a problem with that, but a lot of Asian people in the U.S. didn't like him for talking with a fake accent. They said he was racist. When I said I thought he was joking, they told me, "You can't make a joke like that." All I can tell you is that if you make a joke like that in China, it's OK, no big deal. But in the U.S., there are a lot of different people, a lot of different races, so they think about things like this and talk about them a lot.

The people who were most unhappy with Shaq were American-born Chinese. Maybe Americans don't see a difference, but American-born Chinese are different from Chinese from the People's Republic of China. After the game against the Lakers, in an interview, an Asian reporter asked if I thought what Shaq said was OK. He asked me in Chinese, so I'm not sure where he was from, but I would guess he was an American-born Chinese because of the question. I said I just hoped Shaq was joking. If it's a joke, then it's just a joke. I tried to say that no matter what any of us look like or where we're from, we are all together. When I was asked about this by other reporters, I said to Colin in Chinese, "We're all living on this earth." Colin translated it as we're all living in this "world." I told him, "No, don't say 'world.' The world is big. Say 'earth.' The earth is small."

Racism is not a problem, as far as I know, in China. First of all, as I said, almost everybody is of the same race. There are fifty-five minorities in China, but they are all very small. The majority are Han Chinese, who make up 93 percent of all people in China. (I am Han. So is Wang Zhi Zhi. Mengke Bateer is Mongolian.) That leaves a very small percentage of minorities. Some minorities have maybe 10,000 or 20,000 people—that's out of more than a billion people in China—and almost all of the minorities live in far-western China. We are taught in school that a long time ago there was racism, but it ended with the Communist liberation in 1949. Minorities were given special privileges, like money from the government, and they were allowed to have more than one child. They also had more positions in the national government than their total population would have earned them.

The situation in Tibet is another topic that I feel is talked about more in the U.S. than in China. Most Chinese people think that Tibet has been part of China for a very long time. If a Chinese president were to allow Tibet to go free, I suspect that would be remembered in China as a big sin. It would be looked at as a prize that the leaders gave away for nothing. For people in China, Tibet wanting to break free is like Québec trying to leave Canada.

It will be hard for any Chinese official who has studied Chinese history to let Tibet go. At the end of the Ching dynasty in the nineteenth century, officials gave a lot of land to Russia. That territory still belongs to Russia. It's called Shandong Province and is occupied by Russians and Japanese. The names of the Chinese people who signed that treaty are cursed to this day. Maybe there are things about that time we don't understand. It was a tradition in China long ago that a warlord would give away land in order to get stronger and then he'd take back the land. Maybe that's what the officials back then hoped to do. I've never read or heard an explanation. All I know is that many Chinese still think that those men betrayed the country. Still, the world is changing all the time, so maybe one day people in China will feel differently about giving away land.

I believe that genetics is a part of what makes you the athlete you are. I also believe that only a small percentage of Chinese are built to play basketball. With 1.3 billion people, you can find enough players to make a good team with good coaching, but I don't think a large number of Chinese will suddenly start to jump real high or have long arms or big hands or move very quickly. That's not something you learn; it's given to you at birth. I don't think this will change.

In some ways, there's a bigger problem between Chinese and American-born Chinese than between the Han and any minority in China. People in China call American-born Chinese ABCs and say they are "banana people"—yellow on the outside, white on the inside. When they say "white," they mean American, even though they know Americans are many colors. When I talk with ABCs, they always mix English words with Chinese words, always. I believe they're not sure what they are or what they want to be more—American or Chinese. I sometimes think they cheered for me when I came to the NBA not just because I was Chinese, but because they wanted me to be better than the American players. It was as if they wanted me to punish U.S. players for something some other Americans had done to them. Maybe that was supposed to make them feel good, as though I was getting back something for them.

That's why it was hard for me when ABCs wanted me to attack Shaq for what he said. I was more unhappy with being expected to not like Shaq than I was unhappy about anything he said or did. I understand the ABCs were upset, but I am Chinese, not American-born Chinese. I just don't think people in China are as sensitive about someone making that kind of joke. Don't ask me to hate somebody just because you hate them and you and I have the same skin. I don't like to be forced to do anything, and they tried to make me feel pressured; they seemed to want me to say that what Shaq did was wrong because they thought it was wrong. I worry about my own business, which, first, is basketball. I do what I can on the court. If someone can beat me on the court, I'm not going to complain or say bad things about them afterward. It's the same if I beat someone; I'm not going to talk about how I'm better or how bad they are. The competition between players or teams should be just about being the better team or player, not about who said something or what someone believes. I think this is where the focus on something Shaq said off the court was wrong. That shouldn't be the reason I want to beat Shaq, and some people tried to put the focus on that.

I also think you have to understand what you need to take seriously and what you shouldn't. I'm very careful about what I say now. But sometimes you can be too concerned about people looking down on you or saying something about you. You create a problem that is not there. Did Shaq say what he said because he wanted to look down on me? I don't think so. Maybe it didn't make people laugh the way he wanted, but everybody makes mistakes. If you only look for mistakes, you are always going to find them.

Maybe I will change; maybe I will become more American. Maybe there will be a day when something like what Shaq did will feel different to me. But that's not the way I feel now. All I can say is that I never heard anybody say anything bad to me about being Chinese, and I don't think it's because I am deaf in one ear.

There were other times during my first year when people in the NBA tried to do something that looked or sounded Chinese. At some games they had dragon dances or martial arts shows, or they passed out gifts they thought were Chinese. Some of the things they did were very close to how they would do them in China, but not everything. When they gave away fortune cookies in Miami, I tried to tell the players the fortune cookie is not from China. The NBA even had me doing tai chi in a commercial, but the truth is that was the first and only time I've ever done tai chi.

It's like this: Everything has an outside and an inside. Everybody studies the outside but doesn't always know the inside. Dancers in China on the outside look like they're just having fun, but on the inside everything they do means something. It might mean giving thanks to God or being happy for getting married or saying that someone is dead. You feel these dances with your heart. The dragon dances I saw here had no meaning for me; all I saw were what Americans saw—something that looked like it was from China but didn't mean anything beyond that.

This is how I felt about what Shaq said—it sounded a little like Chinese, but it had no meaning. I did not feel it in my heart. And maybe, to some people, what Shaq did sounded or looked bad on the outside. But I don't think the inside, the reason he did it, was meant to be bad.

Of course, feelings are not good among all Asians. Some Chinese do not like the Japanese because of what they did when they invaded our country. A lot of Chinese don't like the fact that I am playing in the Toyota Center, an arena named after a Japanese car company. People even said bad things about me when they found out I have a Japanese car. Just so you know, I tried many different cars and SUVs—American, English, German. The first car I bought, a Toyota SUV, had the most space inside and was the one that was most comfortable. That's the reason I bought it.

The first time I met Shaq was in L.A. after we played the Lakers. He didn't play because of a foot surgery, but we talked for just a minute after the game. It was the game when I made Charles Barkley look bad for saying I wouldn't score 19 points in a game all season. But I know it would have been different if Shaq had been playing.

"Nice to meet you. How's your foot?" I said to Shaq. Inside, of course, I'm thinking, "I hope you're always hurt. Just so I don't have to play you."

"You played very well," he said.

"Thanks," I said. That was it. It was nice. In the Christmas card I sent him, I wrote, "Thanks for the encouragement. You're the only one I look up to—be like Shaq!" I sent the card to his home in Florida. His stepfather drove all night to see the first game Shaq and I played, and he brought the card with him. He came to the morning shootaround before the game, walked right onto the court while we were shooting, and asked if I had sent the card. I'd written my name in English and Chinese, but I guess he still didn't believe it. Erik told me sending Christmas cards was something good to do in America, so that's what I did. When Shaq's stepdad found out it was really from me, he said he was going to have the card framed. Maybe if I ever get a card from Shaq, I'll do that, too.

Another thing happened right before we played that first time: Phil Jackson, the Lakers coach, told reporters that I invited Shaq to my house for dinner. I think he did that for Shaq, so people would believe I wasn't mad at him or that I didn't think he was racist. Maybe Jackson thought it would help Shaq if everybody knew this. It might have been good strategy, but it wasn't exactly true.

Jackson makes me think of an army strategist from ancient China named Sima Yi. He lived at the same time as Zhuge Liang, only he was not quite as good or smart. He could never beat Zhuge Liang until finally Zhuge got too old. In China, most people didn't like Sima Yi. Most people liked Zhuge Liang, and then Sima Yi stopped Zhuge Liang, and that's why most people hated him. Jackson makes me think of Sima Yi. I'm not saying they are exactly alike, but it seems people don't like Jackson as much as they should for as many championships as he has won. He also doesn't seem aggressive in the way he approaches the game. It's almost as though he outwaits everyone and then comes out on top. He doesn't attack; he waits for you to go first and then counterattacks. That's how Sima Yi was. He knew he couldn't beat Zhuge Liang, so he just held his ground. Whatever Zhuge Liang did, he wouldn't respond. Then Zhuge Liang finally got sick from old age, and that's when Sima Yi attacked. Once he had Zhuge Liang out of the way, there was nobody who could stop him.

The truth is that Shaq and I never talked about having dinner. Someone who works for him called someone with Team Yao and said Shaq would like to have dinner with me before the game. I think he wanted to show he hadn't meant anything bad by what he said. When reporters asked me about it, I told them it would be OK with me to have dinner with Shaq and that he could come to my house and my mom would cook for him. Going to a restaurant for Shaq and me would be hard, especially before that first big game. And maybe at home I could get him to eat something very Chinese, like snake. But it's not as though I said, "Shaq, come to my house for dinner." That, I think, is what people thought happened. It wasn't like that.

Anyway, after all the talk, we never had dinner. Someone who works for Shaq called and said Shaq has a daughter who lives in

Houston with her mother, and he wanted to see her instead. He didn't say no, it just never got to where we were really going to have dinner. "OK, no problem," I said. If Shaq still wants to have dinner, that would be fine. If we don't have dinner, that's OK, too.

In our last practice before the game, Rudy talked to me about playing Shaq. He stood in the middle of the paint and said, "If you let him get here, he's going to dunk on you. If he gets here, you're dead." It was good to know, but what would have been more helpful is if he had told me how to stop him from getting to the middle of the paint. I know now that you don't stop Shaq; you just try to slow him down.

After practice there were maybe 100 reporters waiting. I didn't stop to count, but there were so many that Colin had to stand on a ladder 10 feet away from me so he could translate and everyone could hear him. Some people think I didn't really need Colin, that I knew enough English to understand a question right away but used Colin so I would have more time to think of an answer. Not true. I could understand maybe 20 percent of the questions; by the end of the season I understood more because I'd heard many of the questions before. Maybe people thought I wanted the extra time because sometimes I try to give funny answers, but that's something I got from my dad. Ask him a question, especially a serious question, and he'll usually make a joke first.

I think my dad might have answered the question about Shaq and his elbows the same way I did. I said I just hoped he had a lot of meat on them so maybe they wouldn't hurt as much.

After talking to that many reporters, I wanted to do something to relax, so when we walked out to the parking lot, I said to Colin, "Give me the keys." I tried to drive the first time I came to the U.S., and I tried it again when I was in Denver the summer before my rookie year, practicing with the Chinese national team for the World Championships. And I had started to practice driving a couple months after I joined the Rockets with the idea that I could get my driver's license. At first I would just take the car around our neighborhood at night; the streets are very wide, and there are no parked cars or traffic. Then I started driving around the parking lot where the Rockets practiced.

We had to wait for Bill Sanders from Team Yao to show up so we could meet with the China Unicom people and talk about a commercial, so while we waited, I drove, all alone, in a circle. It was nice to be by myself, even for a few minutes. Juaquin Hawkins was getting ready to leave but rolled down his window and said, "I'm calling the police to report a 7-foot-10 man on the loose!"

There were a couple of reporters standing in the parking lot watching me. When I went past them, I took my hands off the wheel and gave them a big smile. Then I parked, but a woman reporter from a Beijing newspaper looked in the window and said in Mandarin, "You can't really drive. You just go around in circles."

"Oh, really?" I said. "Get in. I'll show you."

I'm not sure what happened right after that. She got in and closed the door, and I backed up. I wasn't going that fast, and I had backed up lots of times. But this time I went too far and bumped into another SUV parked behind me. I didn't even know what had happened, so I kept trying to back up until I heard Colin yelling to stop.

He told me to pull back into my parking spot and get out. The other car's left fender was dented. I had a dent in the left fender of my car, too. Colin ran inside to find out whose car it was and promise we'd pay for the damage. The other car belonged to Kelley Gibson, a player on Houston's WNBA team, the Comets. I was a little nervous because I didn't have a driver's license or insurance, and I didn't know what would happen to me. If you crashed your car in China and didn't have a license or insurance, you'd be in big trouble. I was nervous but also excited. I'd never crashed a car before, ever. This was something new! Colin was very nervous because, well, first, because he's Colin. Second, because he thought he'd be in trouble with Team Yao for letting something happen. That's why I called Erik right away and told him, first, that what had happened wasn't Colin's fault. Then I told him what had happened.

When Bill Sanders showed up, he looked at the dent and smiled. "Welcome to America!" he said. Then we all got into my car. I couldn't complain when Colin said he would drive. To show you how tired I was already feeling at that point of the season: even with all the excitement, I had no trouble falling asleep once we got on the highway.

The pressure before the Lakers game was also building with reports that I was leading Shaq in All-Star votes. I knew Shaq was the best center in the league, not me. But the reports would give him more reason to be mad and play hard against me. But even with all that, I don't know who was more nervous in the days and hours leading up to the game, me or everybody around me. My dad was nervous, Bill Duffy was nervous, and my mom was really nervous. I could tell the Rockets were nervous, too. I was scared just because I had not been playing well for more than two weeks. In the Nuggets game, six days earlier, I had sprained my left knee against Nene, the Nuggets' power forward, who was a rookie like me. He's big and strong, but only half as big and strong as Shaq, and the Nuggets are not as good as the Lakers. Now my mom was very worried about me. She didn't want me to get hurt even more against Shaq. My dad wasn't worried about who would win the game; he was also just worried about me.

Bill Duffy had sent me a DVD of Sacramento Kings center Vlade Divac to help me. Vlade had played very well against Shaq in a game on Christmas, and the Kings had won. Duffy thought if I saw Vlade play, I might learn something or not be as nervous, seeing that Shaq could be beaten. But I didn't want to watch it. I know Vlade's ideas. He's from Yugoslavia, so he plays like a European center. I played against a lot of them in the CBA. He uses a lot of fakes and tries to surprise you by never doing the same thing twice. But he doesn't push on defense or try to go through you on offense. I like playing against Vlade, because I always play well against him. Maybe that's because a lot of people play basketball like him in China, so I'm used to it. Don't get me wrong; he's bigger and better than all of them. I just mean that for me it's very comfortable to play against someone like that. There's no one like Shaq in China or anywhere else in the world, so there was nothing comfortable about the idea of playing him.

One thing about my mom: she never gives up. The night before the game, I was at home in my office playing video games, and she brought in the DVD from Duffy.

"Do you want to watch it?" she said.

"Put it on the table," I said. "I'll watch it." But when I finished playing video games, I was tired and went to bed instead.

The next morning she said, "Did you watch it?"

I said, "No, I forgot."

"Why not? Why not watch it?"

"I have to go to shootaround now. I'll watch it after lunch."

When I got home, I had lunch. She said, "You want to watch it now?"

"Forget it for now; I have to take a nap," I said. "I'll watch it when you wake me up."

After I woke up, she said, "You must watch it."

So I put it in. I watched it for five minutes. I hit fast-forward a lot. "OK," I said. "I'm ready. Let's go."

You know another reason why I didn't want to watch it? Because I just wanted to make myself feel quiet. I thought that was more important. I just told myself, whatever happens, the game is only forty-eight minutes. Shaq can break me, he can beat me, he can do anything, but only for forty-eight minutes. My job is to try my best to stop him and push him out if I can. But after the game—he scored 31 points—I knew how strong he was. That's why the next game we played, he scored even more. I knew then I wasn't strong enough to push him out.

MAURICE TAYLOR: *The beginning of that first game against Shaq was unbelievable. Yao stopped him enough for one of our other guys to block his shot from behind, and then Yao scored at the other end. Shaq tried to get him back, but this time Yao blocked his shot. Then Yao scored again. Then he blocked Shaq one more time and scored one more time. None of us expected that. It lasted only a couple of minutes, but it let you look into the future. No one had done that to Shaq since Hakeem was in his prime. Shaq kept coming and eventually took over the game, but Yao never backed down, and he never looked to us for help. Whatever he gave to Shaq in the first five minutes, Shaq gave to him for the next forty, and he just took it. I think he won as much respect for that as for the way he started.*

Of course, a coach will say, "Don't worry, your teammates will help you." But sometimes you must tell yourself, nobody can help—like my first game, when I didn't score and had two rebounds and two turnovers. I told myself, "No one can help you. There's only one way to go."

Shaq came to me right before the game started and whispered in my ear. He told people that he had been learning to say "I'm sorry" in Chinese. At first, he was learning to say it in Cantonese, which sounds like "Toy in-chee." I don't speak Cantonese. Someone must have told him that, because then he learned to say it in Mandarin, which sounds like "Dwee bu-chee." But he didn't say that to me before the game, either.

"I love you; we're friends," he said. It was so nice I wanted to remind him that he had just gotten married, but I didn't. I wasn't sure he'd get my joke. "Thanks," I said.

I played well at the start of the game, but only for the first couple of minutes. Then I got tired very quickly. If I hadn't known it before, I knew it then: there is nobody like Shaq. The only way for me to score was to run fast and beat him to the other end of the floor and go to the basket before he could get ready. But trying to keep him from the basket is very hard work. Just trying not to fall over when Shaq leans on you can make you tired. I could only fight him and then run hard to the other end for so long. When I had to choose between trying to score and trying to stop him, I chose trying to stop him.

I'm taller than Shaq, but he still looks bigger, maybe because he weighs so much more. A basketball looks like a Ping-Pong ball in his hands. The scouting report said he weighed only 325 pounds. That's about thirty pounds more than me. But after playing him, I knew he had to weigh much more. When I went to the bench for my first break, I told Juaquin Hawkins and Boki, "He's 350 pounds."

"That's OK, just stay aggressive," Hawkins said. "Just make him guard you."

I thought maybe they didn't hear me. "He's *350 pounds*," I said.

I still tried to shoot the ball against the Lakers, but not much.

When I started missing jump shots I usually make, a lot of people thought it was because I was tired, that I didn't have enough strength left in my legs to get the ball to the basket. My shots kept hitting the front of the rim. I felt tired almost right away, but the biggest reason my shots fell short was that I hurt the first finger on my shooting hand early in the game. I went to catch a rebound and hit that finger on the glass. After that, I couldn't shoot; that finger felt weak. My first jump shot after that was an airball. I tried to shoot harder, but the ball would barely make it to the rim. Then I hurt my right wrist when I fell to the floor, and my shot really got bad. If you were watching closely, you might have noticed that I started trying to score with my left hand, shooting jump hooks or driving for layups.

We had worked on a play the day before the game that we had not used much before. This was a play that Coach Rudy T. used for Hakeem Olajuwon a lot. It's for a center who can shoot jump shots from 15 to 18 feet. Shaq doesn't like to go that far away from the basket, so we thought this would get me some easy shots. But we ran it only once because I was not making very many jump shots and Stevie was making everything. Everyone talked about me and Shaq, but the battle that won the game was between Stevie and Kobe, and Stevie won. I had 10 points and 10 rebounds and 6 blocked shots, but 6 points and 3 blocked shots were in the first three minutes and 8 points came in the first quarter. Shaq had 31 points and 16 rebounds. I beat him at the start, but a game is forty-eight minutes—this one was fifty-three minutes, with overtime—and he was better than me the rest of the game. I didn't score again until the final seconds of overtime, when Shaq came over to stop Stevie and he gave me the ball for a dunk. It felt like I hadn't scored in a long, long time. We won, 108–104, and I did just enough so that no one talked bad about me after the game. Stevie had 44 points, but nobody talked about him as much as they should have. I didn't really know how well he had played until after the game. I knew he had played well, but I didn't know how well. After the game I saw a stat sheet. During the game I was like, "Oh, he scored. Oh, he scored again. Oh, he scored again." I knew a lot of his shots were going in, but I didn't think he had more than 30 points. I was too busy concentrating on Shaq.

After the game, in the locker room, Rudy said, "That was a great game. I'm very happy for you guys. I'm very honored to be with you." Then we came together and said, "One-two-three, Rockets!" I sat in my chair and watched everyone walk to the showers. I watched the trainers take the jerseys and put them away. I just sat there and tried to catch my breath.

Did you see the movie *Black Hawk Down*? At the end, the soldiers run real hard. They see the gate and look back and see all the people running after them. Then they get through the gate and they sit down and can't move. They look around and watch everything and they want to move, but they can't. I felt like that.

Team Yao came in to see me after the game and I told them that Shaq "is like a meat wall." They went out to eat after the game, but I didn't go. I just went home, played video games for a while, and went to bed. The last time I felt that tired was the first time I played the Chinese army team with the Shanghai Sharks. We lost by 40 points. That's four-zero. I remember the day—December 11, 1997.

Usually after a game I like to talk about what happened. It's always interesting to think about what happened and what could have been different. Talking is a way to relax, too. But after playing Shaq that first time, I had no breath left, and I didn't want to think about anything. But then when I went to bed, I couldn't stop thinking. The game had been so exciting, and I knew then exactly how strong Shaq was. I kept playing the game over in my mind. Not even video games could make me tired.

The Rockets had the next day off, but I didn't. I did an interview every Saturday morning for a Houston Mandarin radio station; then there were photos to be taken for a magazine cover and a commercial to be made for China Unicom. I still can't believe how long it takes to make a thirty-second commercial. We started around two o'clock in the afternoon and were supposed to be done by ten. Between takes, I watched an entire movie about China's first emperor, *The Emperor and the Assassin.*

They also gave me lots of different food—chicken wings, barbecued ribs, sandwiches, water, soft drinks, doughnuts, cookies, and potato chips—which was good because I had trouble keeping up my weight all season long, and I knew I had lost a lot of weight playing Shaq. I usually couldn't find a lot of food I liked, other than the food my mom made me, so I ate a lot of chicken wings. A few places in California had Chinese food close to what I'm used to eating; there was almost no difference. But it's difficult to make Chinese food here taste the same as at home, even for my mom. If there's just a little bit of difference in the soy sauce or the beef or pork or chicken, it changes the flavor. They also cook many things in China that you never would eat here—mice and birds and snakes. Some people believe if it has four legs and it isn't a table or a chair, you can eat it. They basically will eat anything that walks or flies that they can catch. Cat, rat, scorpion—if you can think of it, they probably will eat it. As with everything, though, that's changing. These days you can find a pizza almost anywhere in China.

We still weren't finished shooting the commercial at eleven.

Then it was midnight. We finally finished just before 1 A.M. I thought playing Shaq was bad, but at least that was only thirty-eight minutes. That's why I don't ever want to make a movie; I must not be very good if it takes that long.

I made another China Unicom commercial in the summer. I held this kid up to dunk the basketball, and he was really heavy. The first time I lifted him up, he hit his nose on the rim and started crying. The director was calling him "Little Fatty," but that's not what made him cry. We couldn't do anything until the kid stopped crying. It took a while.

We played the Lakers again almost a month later, but Shaq's toe was hurting him, so he didn't play. I first heard I wouldn't face Shaq when I got on the team bus to go to the Staples Center in L.A. I felt one thing: relief. I had 24 points and 14 rebounds that night, but we lost in double overtime, and I fouled out. I will remember that game for two things: Mark Madsen faked a foul to give me my sixth and make me leave the game, and Kobe Bryant had the best dunk of the season on me—or the worst dunk, if you look at it the way I do. There was no contact between us. He drove down the left baseline, and I went up to block his shot, and our bodies did not touch, which is unusual. I touched the ball with my fingers, but only a little. It was a really clean dunk even though I was right there.

After the game, an ABC reporter asked me how I felt about that dunk. He was smiling when he asked. I know it's his job to ask questions, but having someone dunk on me like that was humiliating, and I was still upset about Madsen and how we had lost. It would be obvious how anyone would feel about a play like that. I hope I would never ask someone that question and be happy asking it, or expect the player to be happy answering it. I don't think they would ask me a question like that in China. But then nobody ever dunked on me like that in China, either.

The second time we played the Lakers, in L.A., there also were a lot more boos from the crowd than the first time I played there. Someone told me one guy went to the Chinese department at UCLA to learn how to yell in Mandarin, "Yao, go home!" and "Yao, miss!" He supposedly sat about 30 feet from the court, but I never heard him. I'm sorry he went to such trouble, and it didn't do any good.

I don't take talk like that personally. It would be a lot worse if fans in other cities were happy to see me, because it would mean they weren't worried I could beat their team. When I played my first game in the U.S., the exhibition game in Oakland against the U.S. national team, a few people shouted things at me, too—mostly good, but some bad. I heard a few kids yelling, "Yao, go home!" Only they were saying it in English, not Chinese.

"You bought a ticket to come see me play," I said to them. "If I go home, what are you going to watch?"

When I finally played Shaq again, it was in late March and a lot had changed. The first time we had played, everyone on the Rockets thought for sure we were going to the playoffs. When we won, it put us eight games over .500. But that would be our best record all season.

By early March we were 30–30. By late March Coach Rudy T. had gotten sick and was in the hospital for bladder cancer. We could see our chance to make the playoffs slipping away. And although I felt that I was working just as hard, other teams were concentrating on me more, and I had trouble getting the same high-percentage shots. We lost 96–93 to the Lakers this time, and I made only three of 13 shots for 6 points to go with 10 rebounds.

Shaq had 39 points—18 in the fourth quarter—and 5 rebounds. Glen Rice missed a last-second shot that could have tied it, but the Lakers looked like a team getting ready for the playoffs, while we looked like a team getting ready to go home.

Facing Shaq again, I felt even more tired than the first time I played him. Just looking at him tells you how much work you have to do. The first game I didn't know how strong he was. Sometimes it's better not to know. The second time we played, I knew. I think about it like this: playing against Shaq makes the rest of the games seem easy. It's like with dessert. If you eat something you don't like first, dessert tastes even better.

8

STRUGGLING HOME

The voting on All-Star Game starters ends almost two weeks before the game is played. That worried me. Voting started right around when I began playing better, but I thought, "What happens if I start playing badly between being selected and the All-Star Game?" I felt that, on top of what the dreams in China were for me, now everybody in America looked to me to play at a certain level, too. Being selected was an honor, and it meant that a lot of fans liked me, which is always good, but it also meant more pressure not to make mistakes on the court. When I first came to the NBA, not everyone had high expectations for me. Or, at least, I didn't think they did. Certainly nobody talked about my being an All-Star my first year. Now that a lot of people were saying I was an All-Star by voting for me, I felt I'd be letting them down anytime I didn't play like one.

For a while, it looked as if my fears were coming true. Playing Shaq took something out of me, and being beaten by the Lakers took something out of the Rockets. For the next two weeks, I was really bad. We lost four games in a row, and I had two of my worst games of the season back to back against the Mavericks in Dallas and then Detroit at home.

It was a surprise to me that I played so badly against those two teams. I had played well in my first game against Dallas, so I expected to have a good game again. Looking back, I thought the game was going to be too easy, and I didn't play hard enough. Also, Mavericks center Raef LaFrentz was hurt in the first game. He played in the second game and did very well, but I can't give him all the credit; I was mostly stopping myself. It was the first time Rudy didn't play me very much—twenty-two minutes— when I wasn't in foul trouble. I finished with 6 points, 5 rebounds, and 5 turnovers, and we lost 107–86.

As bad as that was, the game three nights later against Ben Wallace and the Pistons was worse—4 points and 6 rebounds in twenty-three minutes. Sometimes your statistics don't show just how badly you played. Those numbers are bad, but I played even worse. Wallace, the NBA's two-time Defensive Player of the Year, was the reason.

I had played well against him with the Chinese national team both in Oakland and again in Indianapolis, but that was a different Ben Wallace. I mean he even looked different to me than when I had seen him with Team USA. It wasn't just the uniform. Everything about him scared me—his face, his body, his hair, his shot-blocking, everything. He was much more aggressive for the Pistons than he had been in the World Championships. He was so scary, he made me forget how to play basketball.

STEVE FRANCIS: *I saw the fatigue hit Yao after that Lakers game. He just started to get tired, and he stayed tired. It was so bad that I was getting tired for him. I don't think it was just playing Shaq. It was all the off-the-court stuff he was doing that I thought really took it out of him. I said to our media relations director, Nelson Luis, "Can't we slow this stuff down?" But we weren't doing so well attendance-wise, and they were looking out for the Rockets, knowing that all the media attention would bring ticket sales and this and that. About a week after that Lakers game, though, Yao just went downhill.*

A lot of people tried to help me before the All-Star break. Rudy T. was one. He was a very good player in his day—the Rockets retired his number 45 jersey—and he said everybody gets tired trying to play eighty-two games, especially rookies. One thing he did, he said, was think of places that made him feel quiet. So I thought about being a boy back in Shanghai, back before anybody knew who I was or there was anybody like Shaq in my life. I don't know if that helped, but I started playing better, so it certainly didn't hurt.

Or at least I shot better. Over the five games before the All-Star break, I made at least 50 percent of my shots or more. But this is where our team not being mature began to show. We played two of our best games of the season to beat Minnesota and Sacramento at home, but then we lost the next three games, first to Dallas at home and on the road in Minnesota and Cleveland. Stevie and I did not look like All-Stars in the game against Cleveland, at least not at the end. We were down by one and had a chance to win the game in the final seconds, but when Stevie tried to pass me the ball, the Cavaliers stole it.

But I didn't have much time to think about that because next came my first All-Star weekend. It was an honor to be voted an All-Star, as I said, but it's also our job to make the game and the weekend fun for the fans. The All-Star break might seem like one long weekend of parties, music, and entertainment, but it's not

like that for the players. It's taking care of friends and family, interviews, meetings, appearances, and practice. That means it's
work. For fans, it's all fun. For us, it's a little bit of fun and a lot of
work. If you're a player and want to go to the parties, that means
no sleep. Me, I needed rest.

I met a lot of famous people but the best part of the weekend,
for me, was being in my room by myself watching TV and playing
video games and being very quiet. It would be better for me to
have the weekend off, but being an All-Star my first year means I
must try to be an All-Star every year. Again, anything less will feel
like failure.

Not everything about the weekend has to do with basketball.
A lot of business takes place. I actually started taking care of business on Thursday, when I made a Gatorade commercial in Orlando. That meant I got to Atlanta late Thursday night and had to
be up early the next morning to go to a "technology summit" for
businesspeople talking about Internet commerce. I like anything
new when it comes to technology—cell phones, computers—but
I like to sleep, too. The businesspeople noticed me when I walked
in, but then went right back to talking about business.

I don't care too much about what I wear—and you can tell by
looking in my closet. I have maybe nine or ten pairs of regular
pants, and of those I have a pair of brown corduroys that I wear
the most. When I got a hole in them, I was upset—but it didn't
stop me from wearing them. Warm-up suits, basketball shoes or
slippers, and T-shirts and shorts—that's my style. But clothes are
a big part of All-Star weekend, and Team Yao was sure I'd be playing in at least the Rookie Challenge—the game between rookies
and second-year players—so Team Yao tried to get me something
I could wear. Nothing worked. At the start of the season they
had three big boxes of shoes sent to my house from Friedman's,

a famous Atlanta shoe store that has lots of shoes in big sizes; it's a place where a lot of NBA players shop. But I have very high arches and the shoes they sent were not good for them. Then they had some suits custom made by a company in L.A., but my mom didn't like them, so we sent them all back except for a dark gray one. Then they had a shoemaker in Houston order a custom-made pair of shoes from Brazil to match the suit, but they got stuck in L.A. going through customs. I wanted to wear the suit to the summit to try it out, but I had only my Doc Martens that I had bought in China. They wouldn't have looked right with the gray suit, but they looked OK with the corduroy one I had from China, so that's what I wore. That suit is like an old friend to me, although sometimes it looks like it. Fashion is not important to me, but I understand that it's important to Team Yao for business. I think of it like this: if everybody is wearing suits and nice clothes, then I should, too. I don't think it should be different for me because I'm Chinese or 7'6".

I was surprised to see basketball commissioner David Stern as I walked into the tech summit. Since I couldn't be at the draft, this was the first time I'd seen him since the 2000 Olympics, and I hadn't been able to talk much with him then because I was looking for a bathroom when he said hello. I wanted to be nice, but I didn't want to talk to him too long, if you know what I mean. Of course, he didn't have a lot of time, either. I don't know anyone who does as much in one day as he does. He's everywhere.

DAVID STERN (NBA commissioner): *We really didn't have much time to talk, either at the Olympics or the All-Star Game in Atlanta. We had a nice lunch in New York later on that first season, and I got to discover what a lot of people have learned: Yao is good company. But even in Atlanta I sensed he enjoyed being here and*

wanted to play as hard as he possibly could. Now that he's begin-
ning to speak English, we're getting to know his fun sense of humor
and that he has a very good perspective for someone so young and
so famous.

Having international players is interesting to our fans because
they get to know people from other countries through that player.
There's a certain demystification that goes on. Sarunas Marciulio-
nis, playing for Golden State, helped us understand the difference
between being Russian and being Lithuanian. We've learned about
Croats not speaking to the Serbs and the Yugoslavian national team
breaking up. There's a real-time history lesson going on all the time,
and what could be more historic than somebody coming from the
most populous country in the world that, nevertheless, we know al-
most nothing about? So you have this smiling, gentle athlete who is
clearly defined as world class because a team took him with the
first pick in the draft. Suddenly, here he is. He's huge, he shoots,
he's talented. That has to be intriguing for our fans.

After the tech summit I had to hurry to the All-Star media session.
I had been around reporters all season, especially the first time I
played Shaq, but that day there were more reporters than I'd ever
seen before. Colin was lucky; he didn't have to face them. Now
that I think about it, Colin got more time off on All-Star weekend
than I did. To save time, the NBA had a translator from the United
Nations work with me because he could translate as I was talking;
with Colin, I would talk and then he would repeat what I said in
English.

Stevie had the table next to mine, but there were so many reporters, I couldn't even see him. They tell me there were thirty reporters just from China. Most of the questions I'd heard already
many times that season, but since I was working with a new trans-

lator, I had to answer all of them so he'd know what to say. (With Colin, after a while I could just look at him or say, "You know the answer," and he'd answer it.) When a reporter asked me what I looked forward to most on All-Star weekend, I said, "Leaving this room." I said it with a smile.

On Saturday, before the All-Star practice, the NBA wanted me to be part of a "Read to Achieve" program for local schoolkids. I was happy to do it, but I would guess the kids could read English better than I could. LL Cool J was there, along with some other rappers. I have to admit that I didn't know any of them. I don't listen to rap; it's too loud and doesn't sound like music to me, and I don't understand the words. I like to listen to Asian female singers because I can understand the words and their voices calm me down. I hope that doesn't get me into trouble with my girlfriend.

I went from the reading program to the All-Star team practice. Well, "practice" probably isn't the right word. We talked and laughed and took a few shots. Shaq and I compared shoe sizes; his feet are 3 inches bigger than mine. I didn't see this, but I heard later that Shaq saw my parents on his way to the locker room and was very friendly, taking pictures with them, hugging both of them and kissing my mom. Strangers in China don't kiss the first time they meet, but then again, by that point Shaq wasn't exactly a stranger in my life.

My mom went to Friedman's while I was at the tech summit and found a black pair of size 18s I could wear with the new suit. I really liked those shoes, but I lost them somewhere in Beijing the summer after my rookie year. I was not happy about that.

Anyway, I didn't have to go to the Rookie Challenge that first year because I was playing on Sunday, but I asked if I could sit on the bench with the Western Conference rookies. I wanted to be with the team because I felt that, as rookies in the same year, we were a little like friends or brothers. If I had had a choice, I would have worn warm-ups instead of a suit, but you can't do that on All-Star weekend. That's OK; I can do it once a year. (I hope I get to do it once a year.) But you won't see me in one much more than that.

Warm-ups would have been more comfortable for getting to the arena, too, after our van had a flat tire. The traffic in Atlanta was very bad—worse than in Houston—and so the driver of our van had tried to drive on the sidewalk to get us to the arena, but one of the tires went flat when he hit the curb. Team Yao didn't want me to get out of the van, but I wanted to walk. I don't like having to do things differently than a normal person. If you're late for an appointment and your car has a flat tire, you would probably get out and walk, right? Me, too. I didn't think it would be a problem. But there were lots of cars and lots of people, and they started honking their horns and leaving their cars to ask me for an autograph. Their cars weren't going anywhere because of the traffic, anyway, but I wasn't getting far on foot, either. A security guard stopped a bus going to the arena for us. When I got on, the people gave me high fives and chanted, "Yao Ming! Yao Ming!" That was fun. And riding on a public bus felt like being back in Shanghai.

Maybe it was good that I didn't play in the Rookie Challenge. No one slowed down the whole game. No zigzags, all straight lines, up and down. And there weren't very many passes before someone took a shot. For me, it would've been like running sprints without the ball. Even though I wasn't playing, the coach, Cotton Fitzsimmons, talked about me when I went into the locker room at halftime.

"You guys don't have pressure," he said. Then he pointed to me. "That guy has pressure. He has big pressure tomorrow. You guys just keep playing. Have fun."

I wanted to say, "Thanks for reminding me, Coach," but I didn't.

With all the foreign players in the NBA, you can learn a lot about other places. After the game I went into the locker room again. There's always food there, and even though I didn't play, I was hungry. I waited until the players who did play had taken their food before getting some for myself. I took a bite of fried chicken, but it didn't taste very good, so I went to throw it out. Marko Jaric, who plays for the Clippers and is from Yugoslavia, saw me walking with my chicken to the trash. With all the war in Yugoslavia, life is hard, and there isn't much food. I knew that, but Marko reminded me.

"No, no," he said. "In Yugoslavia, you must eat it all."

"OK," I said. "My bad."

In the media interviews on Friday, Stevie had joked that he was going to help me win game MVP, and I joked about us only passing to each other. We said it just for fun. The All-Star Game doesn't fit my style. I tried to get Tim Duncan or Kevin Garnett to jump center for the tipoff, but they made me do it. I thought about getting a rebound, dribbling down the court by myself, and shooting a 3, but I couldn't do something just for myself like that in my first All-Star Game.

Stevie did get the assist on my first basket, throwing an alley-oop that I dunked sixty-five seconds into the game. What I didn't know is that would be my only shot of the game. I could've had more shots, but I didn't look to shoot. I feel that the game is for fans to see incredible things, and while I sometimes can do things like that, I don't plan for them, they just happen.

Coach Rick Adelman made sure, though, that I was part of at least one incredible thing: he had me play with Shaquille O'Neal, Tim Duncan, Dirk Nowitzki, and Steve. That's four guys 7 feet or taller on the floor at the same time. Imagine a team with Tim

Duncan as small forward and Nowitzki as a shooting guard! I told Steve he was really our center, the smallest big man I've ever seen. Sometimes I really think he thinks of himself that way.

I played seventeen minutes, the fewest of any starter, but that was OK. I knew Shaq deserved to play more minutes, and I was happy to watch. I had a front-row seat to see some of the greatest basketball players in the world, and I got to be part of saying good-bye to Michael Jordan. For someone who couldn't be sure he was even going to play in the NBA a year earlier, it was a great honor just to be part of everything.

I also got to know some of the great players in the league better. Stevie helped me with that. When we went into the locker room at halftime, he asked me to do my Rudy T. impression for everybody. So I looked at a halftime stat sheet and pointed at the turnovers and said, "What the f——!" Then I crumpled the sheet, threw it on the floor, and walked across the room as if I was mad. Everybody laughed, which made me feel good. I don't know if everybody thought I belonged there or that I was really an All-Star, but their laughter said to me that it was OK that I was there.

The only real rest I got was after the game. The next morning Stevie and I flew back to Houston in time for practice. I was happy to have been part of All-Star weekend, and I was just as happy it was over, but I have to say I was more tired when the weekend was over than when it started.

My first All-Star Game in China wasn't that much different. In the U.S., the All-Star games are between East and West. In China, we usually had them between North and South. But that year the people in Shenyang, the host city, wanted it to be different, so they made it between the Chinese and foreign All-Stars. How many players in the CBA do you think are from Europe or outside of China? Two at the most per team, and not every team had foreign players. So they had barely enough foreign players to make a team. It looked like the Chinese national team playing a practice game against a visiting team. We should have won the game, but you know what? We lost. At halftime, we led by 10. We were up by 2 points with five seconds left, and the foreign All-Stars made a 3-point shot from half-court. The fans threw all their bottles of water onto the floor. The court looked like a swimming pool.

The older players on my team weren't happy with me because I played really hard for the five minutes I got into the game. I wasn't trying to make them look lazy, it was just my first time playing in an All-Star Game. Even if someone told you to take it easy, do you think you're going to play that way? I don't think so. You want to show you can play. It felt a little like my first year in the NBA—pressure to play well. I guess the foreign All-Stars felt the same way. I still didn't do that much—2 points on one-for-two shooting, 2 rebounds, and 1 steal, just like my first NBA All-Star Game.

Nothing changed for the Rockets during the All-Star break, either. We continued not only to play well one night and badly the next, but we'd be good when no one expected and lose when we should have won. Our first two games after All-Star weekend were both against the Utah Jazz. We lost the first one in overtime on our home court. Then we flew to Utah and beat the same team on its home court by 30 points the next night. Then, two nights later, we played the Miami Heat at home and lost by 12. The Heat was one of the toughest teams for me to play. They were like a pack of wolves.

When we lost the next game in double overtime to the Lakers—with no Shaq—the Rockets no longer had a playoff spot. That was hard to accept. Just one month earlier, we had beaten the Lakers, with Shaq, and were certain we'd be in the playoffs.

186 YAO: LIFE IN TWO WORLDS

Now we were going to have to fight the rest of the way, and I looked more tired every week.

I say "looked" tired because there were games I really didn't feel tired but played that way. Reporters were asking me about hitting the "rookie wall." There were times I did feel very, very tired, but to me hitting a wall means I stop and can't start again. I didn't feel like that. I'd say I hit very tall bumps in the road, slowing down every time I did. But in watching game film or seeing my shot fall short a lot, I could also see that I looked tired even when I didn't feel tired. I just kept hoping that, with Team Yao not having me do any more commercials or big interviews, I would find a way to rest and improve. But it didn't happen.

I won't take you through every game for the rest of the season; it might make you sick to your stomach because the Rockets went up and down so much. I will say that although I thought I had a chance to win Rookie of the Year, I can see why Amare Stoudamire won it. I've never seen an eighteen-year-old with a body like that. The way he runs reminds me of R2D2 from *Star Wars,* or Arnold Schwarzenegger in *Terminator;* he's like a machine.

But he's not a machine. First of all, he's always smiling. Even when he's angry, he looks like he's smiling. Second, when I touched him on the stomach one time during a game, he pretended like I hurt him. "Agggh," he said. "C'mon, man," I said, "you're stronger than me!"

Individual talent is the start of everything in the NBA; that's different from China, where everything starts with teamwork. I can't say one style is better than the other, or that I like one more than the other; they're just different, and I like that I get to play them both. I do think that if you can build team chemistry and co-operation around individual talent, it's a very strong combination. That's where I think the Kings are: they're a mature team.

The Rockets' youth showed in our play. Sometimes the chemistry was good, and sometimes it was not very good at all. We should have made the playoffs, but it also was pretty obvious we had some problems.

By the end of the season, some critics were saying the Rockets should give me the ball more. I had a problem showing what I could do and playing within the team sometimes, but I'd never want my play to be more than what the team is doing. I think like this: whatever the team needs, that's what I want to do. The games that I was happiest about were not the ones you might think; they weren't always games in which I scored or rebounded the most. Of course those games with the individual performances made me very happy, but they only made me personally happy. It's always more fun to make your teammates happy. The team played well in three of the four games against the Kings, and we had a collective happiness. That's the feeling I like the best. From a technical standpoint, if I play very well and we win, the next team will make adjustments and can take away what I am doing. But if we all play well together, that's something that can't be stopped.

I could feel the new pressure of being an All-Star and my role with the team changing in New York when I played at Madison Square Garden against the Knicks for the first time. If I could live in any city in the U.S., it would be New York, because it reminds me a lot of Shanghai—lots of tall buildings, lots of interesting things to see, lots of people from different countries. A very busy place. Even Madison Square Garden reminds me a little of the Sharks' arena, in that both are very old.

Like Shanghai, New York is also very expensive.

Anyway, I had 24 points and 6 rebounds against the Knicks, and everybody talked about how well I played. But I turned the ball over twice at the end of the game, and I thought that's why we lost, 102–95. The team was looking to me not just to help but to win games. That's something I wanted to do and something I wanted them to do, but I wasn't doing it. That's another reason I never would complain that I wasn't getting the ball enough. Sometimes when I did get the ball, I couldn't do the right thing with it.

From the beginning of the year to the end, I didn't really see a difference in how the team used me, only when they used me and how much. I didn't get the ball more because I was a rookie. If I had been getting the ball a lot, what I did would affect how everybody else played. I understand it's hard to make everybody play off a rookie. I don't think the second half of the season would have been any better if I had gotten the ball more in the first half, because by then I had taken a lot of blows to my confidence. I kept playing worse. We kept losing. A bigger worry, though, was that it seemed that the players on the team didn't really trust one another. It seemed that we all were on different paths, that we couldn't find each other. At the end of the year, if Steve scored, he would keep shooting. If he missed, then we'd give it to the next guy to shoot. If he made a couple shots, we'd keep giving it to him. If he missed, we'd go to the next guy and the next guy.

I had a few small individual victories after the All-Star break. I played much better against Ben Wallace and the Pistons the second time around because I knew how to face him, and we won. The first game I had used a lot of turnaround fadeaway shots; I played very soft, and he was very aggressive. The second game I knew he liked to jump and block shots, so I used a lot of pump fakes and got him to foul me. One time I had him one-on-one and dunked over him. My performance was so different the second time that I joked I had taken his picture and put it next to my bed the night before the game. It scared me all night, so by the time I got to the game, I wasn't scared anymore. What can I say? I like to make jokes.

Another good development in the second half was the return of our best shooter, Glen Rice. Glen had hurt his left shoulder and couldn't play for most of the season. Having an outside shooter is really important because then defenses can't just collapse on me. Nobody in the league wants to leave Glen open, no matter how far from the basket he is. When we won five in a row, Glen made 14 of 27 three-pointers in those five games. That says everything.

But just when we thought we were ready to start winning the way we did early in the season, Rudy T. got sick, and that changed everything. We learned about it after beating the team fighting us for the eighth playoff spot, the Suns. That meant that if we both had the same record at the end of the season, we would go to the playoffs because we had beaten them more times face to face. Rudy congratulated us in the locker room and told us how proud he was of us. Then he told us he had bladder cancer and wouldn't be with us for a couple of games. That meant Larry Smith, his first assistant, would run the team until Rudy came back.

STEVE FRANCIS: *Everybody sat back when Rudy told us. We had just won a big game. We were in the locker room, all hyped. He was just sitting there. "Nice game," he said. I'd never seen him take his tie off until we were leaving the locker room. We came in, and his tie was all jacked up. Then he told us. And once he told us, everybody looked around, thinking, "What does this mean?" He said he'd be away for a couple of days. So I guess everybody just thought, not that we'd run over Coach Smith, but that if Coach was off for a couple of days, we could screw around. You know, go out and be a little more free with our shots and not have to come out of the game. But*

then those days turned into weeks and weeks into months, and we
never picked up where we had been when Rudy left.

I didn't lose faith in Yao down the stretch, because I knew how
it was being a rookie. I remember times when I couldn't throw the
ball in the ocean. Honestly, he didn't play that badly down the
stretch. The coaching change had the biggest effect on him. Look at
the stats. The numbers changed dramatically for me, Yao, and Cut-
tino. Everything went down for the three main guys. It wasn't that
we changed a lot strategically from Rudy to Coach Smith. And I'm
not blaming our not making the playoffs on Coach Smith, but
that's when the production of our big three stopped. It definitely
hurt us.

But I never lost confidence in Yao. I was force-feeding him the
ball even in the last game of the season, at Denver, during what-
ever minutes he did play. I told him to keep playing hard so he
could build for next season.

News like that from any coach would be hard to hear, but it was
especially hard to hear from Rudy. Some people think he is soft as
a coach, but I can tell you that he yells as much as any coach I've
had. What makes Rudy special is that he talks to you as one person to another, not as coach to player. I remember when he and
CD came to see me practice in Beijing before the draft; that was
the first time we had met. CD said very quietly, "Hello, Yao Ming."
But Rudy said, "Hey, how ya doin', Yao?" in this big, happy voice,
as though we had been friends for years. Maybe it wouldn't have
been so hard for the team if he wasn't going to be with us for a
while but we knew he was going to be all right. But when you
hear someone has cancer, you think about that person and if
they're going to live. From that point on in the season, we were
never thinking about the game 100 percent. If you were a Rocket

and thought about playing an NBA game, you couldn't help but think of Rudy.

That was the emotional part. The technical part is that I, along with everybody else on the team, had to start adjusting to a new coach. When some assistant coaches take over, they don't change anything; they have the players do everything as if the head coach were watching. They don't say too much, and they use the team's best players or leaders a little more than the head coach might. Coach Smith wasn't like that. He didn't change our plays, but he did change how he used us. One mistake and you were on the bench. Now that I think about it, he reminded me of Wang Fei coaching the Chinese national team in practice.

Coach Smith was strict as an assistant coach, and that didn't change once he became the head coach. But taking over a team at the end of the season—a team trying to make the playoffs, not knowing when the head coach will be back—is a big challenge. Not every player trusted him. When Rudy was there, every player was like part of a machine. Rudy told the machine what to do. Then Rudy left, and the machine had no one to tell it what to do. Or everyone had their own idea of what needed to be done, so the machine wasn't listening. Everybody wanted to go to the playoffs, but we all saw a different path to get there. We were 35–30 before Rudy left the team; we were 8–9 without him.

At the beginning of the season, I set an NBA record by making 31 of 35 shots over six games. That's 88.5 percent. I led the league in field-goal shooting percentage at that time, shooting better than 60 percent. I wasn't doing anything like that at the end of the season, especially after Coach Smith took over. I made 28 of my last 70 shots, or 40 percent.

We had a five-game road trip right after Rudy told us he wouldn't be with us for a while. We lost four of the five games. I think we all hoped he'd be waiting for us when we got back from the trip, but we didn't see him, and we didn't really know how he was feeling. Then we played the Lakers again on our home court, and this time they had Shaq. He did whatever he wanted against me, scoring 39 points. I outrebounded him, 10–5, but I missed 10 of 13 shots and had only 6 points. The Lakers won, 96–93, and it seemed as if Shaq dunked the ball every time he touched it. This time he went slower, backing me down until he was under the basket. The last time, he had tried to go faster and shoot from a little farther away, which allowed me to be more effective. The worst was when Shaq dunked, I fouled him, he shot a free throw, missed, got the rebound, and dunked that.

The Lakers' Rick Fox actually hurt me more than Shaq in one way: I missed a shot and went for the rebound and hit my jaw on his head. Normally I can't hear out of one ear, but after that I couldn't hear at all for a few minutes. I tried not to let it bother me, but every time I went to the basket it was another thing to think about or block out.

I can't blame everything on Rudy getting sick. My shooting already was getting worse and worse before that. Halfway through the season, as I said, sometimes I looked tired on the court even if I didn't feel tired. Well, now I looked and felt tired all the time. How many games did the Spurs play to win the championship— 110 or more, counting regular season and playoffs? If you count the Asian Games, NBA regular season, World Championships, and exhibition games for the Chinese national team, I played 107 during almost the same time. And that's not counting the months of two-a-day practices with the Chinese national team. I'm not saying I didn't want to play all those games—although nine exhibitions with the national team was a lot—but I think there was a good reason for my feeling tired. It's not just because I'm Chinese or because I didn't train enough or in the right way. Anybody would've been tired playing that many games.

Being tired meant I couldn't get good position near the basket, because that takes strength and energy. Another reason my shooting percentage dropped is that I wasn't as careful about taking only high-percentage shots as I was at the beginning of the season. Back then I never wanted my teammates to think I was forcing shots, that I had learned too well my first summer in the U.S. to "look for your own shot." But at the end of the season the team wanted me shooting more. I did, but that meant not waiting for a high-percentage shot.

Rudy told everyone on April 1 that he was out and might not come back for the rest of the season. A week later we had our worst offensive game of the year, losing to Portland at home, 81–66. If there was a game all season that made me feel like I just wanted to get on a plane and go back to Shanghai, that was it. The 66 points was a Rockets' franchise record for fewest points in a game. We played great defense; we just couldn't score. I missed 11 of 13 shots, and as a team we shot 29.5 percent. It wasn't one of my worst games only because I had 12 rebounds, but in the last few minutes I felt no hope. I'd never felt that way before.

Two nights before the game, Eddie Griffin, our second-year power forward, was arrested for speeding and having drugs (possession of marijuana). A lot of people thought that was why we played so badly against the Blazers, but I don't believe that. Maybe it bothered Eddie, but the rest of us didn't really think about it. Not knowing what might happen to Rudy made everything else seem like no problem. But the basic reason we lost to Portland is that we just couldn't shoot straight.

We weren't much better the next night, shooting 31.5 percent and losing 94–73 in Salt Lake City to the Utah Jazz. We still had a chance to make the playoffs after those two losses, but I think a lot of players already believed we wouldn't because the Suns would've had to lose all their games and we would've had to win all of ours for that to happen. When the Suns beat the San Antonio Spurs, it was over. The Rockets were not going to the playoffs. That meant I was free to go home once the regular season was over. I didn't know how to feel about that; I really wanted to make the playoffs and thought we should have, but now I knew I could go home earlier, and I liked that feeling.

We won our last three games, and I learned one more lesson before the season ended. We played Seattle and beat them easily, but I didn't play very hard. I played twenty-two minutes and had only 3 rebounds, along with 10 points. After the game Cat got mad at me. "The season ain't over," he said. "You can't stop playing." Nobody likes to get yelled at, but it was good that he said that. Later, on the bus, I went to him and said, "Cat, you're right. Thank you for saying that."

I played only twenty-one minutes against Memphis but had twice as many rebounds, 6, and 3 blocked shots. And in the final game against Denver, I had 16 rebounds, 5 blocked shots, and 13 points for my twenty-seventh double-double of the season. I played hard, thanks to Cuttino, and I got the ball a lot, thanks to Stevie. It was disappointing that the season was over, but that last game gave me hope there were better times ahead.

However tired I felt after playing Shaq or that last Portland game, none of it was equal to when we got off the plane in Houston after finishing the season in Denver. Before then, I had always had my mind on the next game or the next practice. I had to stay focused, and I always felt a little nervous, which gave me energy. But now there were no more games, no more reasons to be nervous or stay focused.

"OK," I said to myself. "I've seen it now. Here's the end." I had finally reached the end of the highway. I almost always want to drive when I have the chance, but as we walked to the car, I told Colin, "You can drive home. I want to take a nap." I was asleep before we reached the highway.

It wasn't until the end of the year that I learned that some of my teammates didn't want the Rockets to take me with the number-one pick. They thought the team should trade the pick for a veteran player who could help them right away. I didn't know anybody felt that way until I read it on a message board online, because nobody made me feel that way or said anything in the locker room. It didn't bother me to read that. Everybody has their opinions. I would've felt much worse if my teammates had been saying that at the end of the season, not before it started.

STEVE FRANCIS: *I never ever came out and said, "Don't take Yao." I said, "I haven't seen the kid play." I didn't know. So what they did, of course, was rush me a highlight tape. But anybody can look good on a highlight tape. I can make a tape of anyone and make them look like they could be the number-one pick. Quentin Richardson of the Clippers went to his Chicago workout and said they'd be dunking on Yao all day long, but I took that as just being immature. Honestly, it was that I didn't know. Were we getting a Shawn Bradley type? Were we getting a Gheorghe Muresan, who just stood there? Or were we getting, maybe not a Shaq, but somebody who could at least move? Until I saw the tape, I'd heard so many different things, I wasn't sure. Obviously Rudy and CD had their minds made up from Day One. I was suggesting we trade the pick for some other players. I didn't have anybody in mind, but I thought we could explore it. We needed some veterans at that time.*

Once I thought about the pros and cons and all the players who were in the draft, I came around on Yao. Chris Wilcox from Maryland was one of my closest friends. He came and worked out in Houston. I saw some of the guys they were working out and said to myself, "This ain't going to make it." I knew Wilcox wasn't the number-one pick, even though he's my boy. I can't give you a date that I was cool with taking Yao, but it was before we actually drafted him.

Since I had a chance of winning Rookie of the Year, the NBA didn't want me to go back to China right away. At first I wanted to stay because my girlfriend, Ye Li, was supposed to come to the U.S. with the Chinese women's national team to play against Houston's WNBA team, the Comets, the first week in May. But when that trip was canceled because of the SARS problem in China, I wanted to go home right away. Team Yao also didn't want me to go back right away because of the SARS outbreak, but that's one reason I wanted to go—to show people that they shouldn't be afraid.

I don't know if the NBA did me a favor, but Rookie of the Year was the first award announced, a week after the regular season ended. I went home the next day.

I wasn't that worried about getting SARS before I got back to China, and I can't really tell you why. Maybe I just wanted to go home and didn't want to let anything stop me. Maybe, as a professional athlete, I'm used to thinking that I can overcome any physical problem. It was a little more real once I was back in Shanghai, but I can tell you that, even though everybody felt they were in danger, life went on. Maybe some people stayed at home more or washed their hands every thirty minutes, but life went on. You do what you can do not to get it, and that's it. If you still get it, you get it. You're unlucky. Hey, how many people got SARS in China? Three thousand? How many people are in China? One point three billion. That's what percent? Point zero, zero, zero, zero. . . .

SARS also gave everyone a chance to help someone they didn't know, not because they were getting money or because someone ordered them to, but because it was the right thing to do. Sometimes it takes big things that scare us for us to remember that it's important not just to take care of yourself, but to help take care of society. If you take care of society, I believe, there will come a day when society will take care of you.

When Bai Li, the director of the Shanghai Media Group, asked me to host a SARS telethon, I was happy to help. It was the first telethon ever in China. The belief in China for a long time was that there was no need for telethons or anything like that because the government took care of everything. I might have been the host, but I didn't really do more than anybody else; I was just part of it. A lot of people from the NBA helped, too. Steve Francis, Rockets owner Les Alexander, Shaq, Magic Johnson, and Steve Nash were all in a video shown as part of the three-hour telethon, and Michael Jordan and Tiger Woods donated autographed items to sell to raise money. Steve also donated a check for $10,000, showing how big his heart is, but I already knew that from playing with him.

Making as much money as I do in the NBA makes me think I can do a lot of things to help other people, and we can't always wait for something like SARS before we act. Even the idea of helping build a hospital is attacking a problem after it already exists. Giving money to research is one way to get ahead of problems;

donations to education or building schools is another. People's minds are the first place you can help. Before I give money to anything like that, though, I will want to see the plan and the schedule. I want to know that I'm helping and not just spending money. More than anything, I want to do that for China. I'd like to see all the money I am making by being in the NBA—both for myself and the league—go back home. China is a big country with a lot of resources, but I think my help is needed there more than in the U.S.

As you know, I didn't win NBA Rookie of the Year; Amare Stoudamire of the Suns got it. I wanted to win it to prove the Rockets were right to make me the number-one pick, but I think I showed that without getting the award. The NBA Rookie of the Year is picked by the media, so maybe I shouldn't have made so many jokes about reporters. A vote by the league's coaches for the All-Rookie team tied me with Amare, and a vote by the league's GMs for *Sporting News* picked me over Amare. If I impressed the GMs and coaches in the league, that means the most to me.

Besides, I didn't win Rookie of the Year in the CBA, either, and went on to win a championship. If that's what I have to trade for an NBA championship, I'd be happy to do it again.

The day before I flew back to Shanghai, Team Yao asked me what I'd like to do. I said I wanted to go fishing. It's one of my favorite things to do. I was staying near Bill Duffy's house in the San Francisco Bay area, so they made reservations to take me deep-sea fishing. We ended up not going because it was raining and too windy. I went to a video arcade instead. Team Yao arranged it so I could go for a couple of hours before the place opened.

Erik told me later that the boat we were supposed to take fishing looked just like the one in the movie *The Perfect Storm*.

"Don't say that!" I told him. After all the things that had happened my first year in the NBA, if we had gone out in the wind and the rain, a perfect storm would have been a perfect ending.

9

CULTURE CLASH

I f you've been to China, you know that everything doesn't always go the way it's planned. Sometimes it looks as if there is no plan. If you are Chinese, learning how to stay calm when you don't know what will happen next is important. In that way, I am happy to say, I am still very Chinese, because a lot happened during my first year that was not planned.

First Impression

MICHAEL GOLDBERG: *We couldn't get anything done in time for Yao to fly to New York and be part of the draft festivities, so they arranged a satellite feed from China to get him in front of a camera. They showed him sitting on a couch with his parents, which made it look as though he was at home. I flew into New York the next morning on other business, and when I landed, I turned on my phone and it rang. It was Nelson Luis, our media relations director. There was an uproar. On the front page of the* Houston Chronicle *is a photo off the feed from China, and behind Yao there's*

a poster that says in Chinese, clear as day: "Down with U.S. Impe-
rialism!" People in Houston who could read Chinese were going
nuts that Yao had this in his house. I frantically made some calls
and found out that he had been in a CNN studio where old posters
from the '40s and '50s decorated the walls. He just happened to be
sitting in front of one of them. We got the word out pretty quickly,
but for that night there was an uproar.

Lost Luggage, Stolen Uniform

The first thing to go wrong in the U.S. happened when I came over with the Chinese national team for the 2002 World Championships. *Sports Illustrated* wanted to take my photo in a Rockets uniform to put on the cover before the season started. The Rockets sent me my uniform so the photo could be taken in Indianapolis in between games. I had to take the photo then because no one knew when I'd be coming back to the U.S., or even if I'd be back before the season started.

That's when things started to go wrong. On the day of the photo shoot, the national team officials decided I couldn't go. Then on the second day of the tournament, after our morning practice, I came back to find my room cleaned and the uniform gone. I remember leaving it out on a table in my room. I didn't think that much about it, because in China you would just make a call and whoever made the uniform would give you another one. That's what is nice about so many companies making their shoes and clothes and other things in China: you never have to worry if you need to replace something. Everything is there and it's very inexpensive. I've learned it's not like that in the U.S. The Rockets wanted me to pay for the uniform, and it was very expensive.

I will say this: whoever took it has a good collector's item, because it was one of two uniforms with both my first and last name on it. I also wore one like that in our first pre-season game, before the NBA made me change. The NBA doesn't allow two names on a uniform, so I had to switch to just Yao.

Sports Illustrated still put me on their cover. I snuck out of my room and had my picture taken in my China national team uniform. Then *SI* used their computers to turn it into the Houston Rockets uniform. Technology is a great thing.

No Credit, No Purchase

The next thing happened after I went back to China for the Asian Games. My mom came to Houston early to find a house. But the person selling the first one she found didn't really own it. And then, because I signed with the Rockets only after I arrived in the U.S. in October, I didn't have money yet to buy a house. And because I am Chinese and had no financial history in the U.S., the banks here didn't want to lend me money.

BILL DUFFY: *We were all ready to rock and roll and then when we started trying to facilitate a loan, we found out the first house his mom liked was in foreclosure. His mom found another house, but now we had to find a way to buy it, because he didn't have the basic financial structure to even attempt to qualify for a loan. No bank account, no social security number, no identification card, nothing. Even his immigration status hadn't been finalized yet. All he could prove was his address in Shanghai, and that's not going to buy a house in Houston. The only money he had at that point was from a trading-card deal we did before he came over. (We told the trading-card companies it was a likelihood he'd be coming over.) I ended up buying his house for him. We've transferred it to his name now, but his entire first season the house was in my name. I knew, though, that this would be the last time he'd ever have trouble qualifying for a loan.*

Drinking on the Job

I know New Year's Eve is a popular time for people in America to get into trouble drinking, but my first New Year's Eve was different. Well, maybe not that different. After beating the Milwaukee Bucks on New Year's Eve in Houston, I went straight to the airport to fly to Los Angeles to shoot my first commercial. Team Yao had a rule to keep me from doing too much off the court: I shot commercials only when I had two days off in a row. The commercials still meant more time flying somewhere, and they still made me tired, but the rule helped.

We arrived in L.A. at two o'clock in the morning, maybe later. There was no food on the plane, only soft drinks. I had slept only four hours before someone from Team Yao woke me up for breakfast.

A limo took us to the studio. Team Yao also had me taking a lot of vitamins to keep my strength up, but sometimes I'd forget. Bill Sanders asked if I had taken my vitamins that morning, and I said no. They had a glass container in the limo that looked like it had water in it. So I took out my vitamins and asked Colin to pour me a glass. "OK," he said. He poured a big glass.

I was tired, so I drank it all at once. Straight down. No stopping. I thought, "That's how water feels? The water in Houston and Los Angeles is different?" And then my face got hot. I was coughing. "Colin," I said in a choked voice, "that's not water!"

BILL DUFFY: *It was straight gin. He just chugged the whole thing. Now he's turning red and gagging. I'm thinking, this guy is about to do a major commercial shoot, and he just took the biggest shot of gin in his life! It's a little after six in the morning, and we were about ten minutes away from the studio. He had to be made up and get prepped, so we figured we had an hour to get him in shape. But I'm thinking, "If he stays red all day, we're dead."*

I can remember all the times I've had too much to drink—maybe five or six times my whole life. The last time before this had been after we won the CBA championship. The time before that was in 1998, when we had a Russian player on the Sharks. He liked to drink vodka. On his birthday, the whole team had vodka with him. That was the first and only time for me with vodka. Now, thanks to Hollywood and Colin, I can also put gin on my list.

I felt funny right away, and I was still red in the face when we arrived at the studio. "You need sleep?" someone asked. "I think so," I said. "Colin can shoot the commercial for me, because it was his fault."

But everything turned out OK. It was a couple of hours before we began shooting the commercial. It was for Apple computers, with me and Mini-Me. A lot of people saw it, but no one's ever asked if I was drunk. Maybe that means I'm a better actor than I think.

JOHN HUIZINGA: *We had turned down ads that just emphasized Yao's height; he has many appealing attributes we wanted to*

establish. So when Bill Sanders told me Apple wanted to do some-
thing, I said, "Great, as long as they don't want to pair him with a
midget." Sanders paused and said, "Well, actually . . ." But once we
saw the script, we could see the reason. The ad was for their biggest
and smallest notebook computers, and they had Yao Ming sitting
down. If they'd gone for the gag angle, they would've had Yao
standing up. I think the ad did a great job of letting people get a
glimpse of Yao's personality. We had initial doubts about the "Yo,
Yao" Visa commercial, too. He goes into a souvenir store in Man-
hattan to buy a miniature Statue of Liberty and asks if he can write
a check. The young woman at the counter points to a sign that
reads "No Checks" and says in classic New Yawkese, "Yo." Yao
points to himself and says, "No, Yao." Then they go back and forth
with the "Yo" and "Yao" exchange. It was tricky, because we didn't
want it to make Yao look ridiculous or ignorant. I think the ad
worked well, however, and "Yo, Yao!" has become a signature line.
It's amazing how many fans use "Yo, Yao" to greet him with genuine
affection.

Blue Suede Shoes

The 2003 NBA All-Star Game was the first one I've played in, but I've watched others in China, so I know wearing shoes with bright colors or new designs is something a lot of players do. But that wasn't why I wore powder blue Nike shoes in my first All-Star Game in Atlanta. Those shoes were a big mistake. At first I wanted to wear white shoes with a small Chinese national flag on them, but I had to forget that after I checked with a Chinese basketball official. He said it wouldn't be a problem, but he would check to make sure. That's when he found out it would be a problem.

Other CBA officials thought it would be disrespectful to have a flag on my shoes.

I thought, OK, then I'll just wear white shoes with a little bit of light blue trim. I like that color, and the Rockets' uniforms we wore my rookie year had just a little bit of this light blue in them. I thought it would look nice. But I wasn't thinking of a shoe that was all light blue, which is what I found when I opened my Nike shoebox in Atlanta.

COLIN PINE: *I would've sworn he said light blue shoes with a little white trim. I'd also swear I showed him an artist's drawing of what the shoes would look like that Nike sent me to show him. I can't be as sure that I showed him the photo of the demo model Nike sent me. Someone asked after the game if he wore North Carolina blue shoes in honor of Michael Jordan, the former Tar Heel, and this being his last All-Star Game. That sounded good, so we went with it and said yes, we wanted to wear the old Nike Air Flight model to honor Jordan, but we couldn't find any in his size. Now the truth can be told. In any case, you never saw those shoes again.*

STEVE FRANCIS: *Nobody among the West All-Stars cracked on him until I did. I told him they were the worst ever. When I saw them, I said, "What the hell . . ." He said the colors were supposed to be reversed or something. I said, "I hope that's why you left Nike." As bad as they looked in person, they really looked crazy on TV.*

I joke with Colin now that maybe he was paid off by Reebok not to show me the photos of the shoe. All I know is I had to wear some ugly shoes that you could see from far, far away. I will say, in Colin's defense, that the drawings of the shoe didn't look that bad. I would've worn another pair of shoes, but I didn't have any with me that fit, and it's not like you can go to any store and buy a pair of size 18s. It's one thing if you are an All-Star and you choose to wear a crazy-looking shoe, like Jermaine O'Neal did with his bright yellow shoes or Chris Webber did the year before with his silver-plated Dada shoes. During warm-ups, someone told me the camera would focus on my shoes and they would play Elvis Presley's song "Blue Suede Shoes." But I didn't hear that. Sometimes not being able to hear in one ear is helpful. Maybe I should be happy I didn't play much. If I had, there would've been more questions about my shoes. Or maybe that's why I didn't play more; TNT may have been worried the shoes would keep people from watching the game.

Behind the Wheel

I didn't grow up driving a car or even thinking of driving a car. Besides, it's very hard to find a car that is comfortable for someone as tall as I am. Imagine driving a go-cart at 60 miles an hour; that's what it's like for me to drive most cars.

I drove a car only once in China before I came to the U.S., but I wouldn't say I knew how to drive. Even if I had learned to drive in China, I don't know if that would have helped me when I started driving in the U.S. If you go to China and watch the traffic, you might think there are no rules, that it's just crazy driving. People drive on the wrong side of the street and go while the light is still red and cross the double yellow line to pass all the time. There are rules; they're just very different from in the U.S., and there aren't enough police to enforce them. If two cars are going in the same direction, and the car on your right decides to turn left in front of you, if you hit him, it's your fault. Even if there's no way you could've stopped, it's your fault.

BOSTJAN NACHBAR (Houston Rockets forward): *I was at the DMV office getting my license the same day Yao Ming got his. I'd already had one in Europe for four years, so taking and passing the test was no problem. But I knew it was a big day for Yao. He was more nervous than he is before a game. When he passed the test, he was so happy he looked like a little baby. I think he was happier that day than the night we beat the Lakers. But know this: he's still a very shaky driver. I'm still not sure he knows what all the signs mean or what a red light is. He followed me from the arena to the airport one time. It usually takes fifteen minutes, but it took thirty this time, with no traffic, because I didn't want to lose him. He drove verrrrrry slowly, but that's probably better for everyone. Sometimes Colin would come to practice shaking, and I'd ask, "Did Yao drive?" Colin would just nod his head and look for some place quiet to sit and calm down.*

I drove once when I came to the U.S. in '98. When we were in San Diego, I drove a minivan around the courtyard of our hotel. I really started learning how to drive late at night in my Houston neighborhood. I had a rental car, a big Mercury something.

When I was first learning to drive, Colin told me about the school bus. We have school buses in China, but I don't remember cars being careful around them.

But Colin said if I saw a school bus here, I couldn't pass it. And if a school bus stops, I must wait 15 feet behind it. When I took my driver's test, I remember him telling me something like that, but I wasn't sure exactly what he told me. Anyway, when I took the test, I was sitting at a stop in my car. The examiner just had me driving on neighborhood streets. We'd get to a corner, and he would just say, "Turn left," or "Turn right." The test was almost over when I came up behind a school bus. It was going slower and slower. It was like a bad dream: I'd forgotten if I could pass him or not, so I said, "OK, whatever he does, I'm just going to follow him." No matter what the bus did, I just followed. I couldn't remember what the specific law was. I passed the test, but I was very nervous about that school bus.

Parallel parking was the hardest part. It was hard to tell the distance from the safety cones. Even now I sometimes have to ask Colin to park my car for me. I touched one of the cones on the parking test the first time. The second time I passed. The written part was easy. I was allowed to have a friend translate. I wasn't sure if I would pass the test when I went to take it, but I thought I'd give it a try. The worst that could have happened was that I'd have to do it again. I was prepared to have to do it again. When I didn't, Boki says I was happier than when we beat the Lakers. To this I say: beating the Lakers took teamwork, but getting my driver's license was completely me.

When the team went on a three-game road trip to New Jersey, Milwaukee, and Philadelphia in April, Colin went to New York instead of coming home on the team plane. That's the first time I drove back from the airport myself. I was on the plane when I realized that I had never paid attention when Colin was driving, so I didn't know the way home. I knew part of the way, but not all the way. Moochie Norris lived on my street, so I asked, "Can you take me to the highway? That's all I need, I can go the rest of the way myself."

"OK," he said. "Just follow me." Jim Boylen, one of the assistant coaches, waited until Moochie walked away. Then he said, "Yao, watch out. Don't follow him all the way. He may not be going home." What he meant was that Moochie might be going to see a girlfriend or going out to a club.

MOOCHIE NORRIS (former Houston Rockets point guard, now with the New York Knicks): *He tried to fit into my car one day. He did it, but his knees were up by his chin and he had to look straight down at his lap. No way he could have driven it. I agreed to let him follow me home, but every time we came to a stop I'd veer into the other lane to give him more room to stop. I was thinking about that truck he had backed into and didn't want to take any chances.*

I didn't have to worry about following Moochie for long. As soon as we got to the highway, he took off—*ssssshhhhhwwwsshhhh!* He has a two-door Mercedes sports car. His car was better than mine at the time. His sports car versus my SUV—I had no chance. But that's OK. I knew how to make my car feel the same as any other car. I turned up the music as loud as I could and rolled down the windows. It was two o'clock in the morning. There were a couple of cars on the road, but not many. It felt really good.

There's not much chance for me to do that in China, even if I had a car. When I went back for the summer, I didn't work out for almost three weeks and got fat—well, fat for me. My weight got up to 315. After everybody telling me all year to gain weight, they now wanted me to lose some. So I decided to go to the Sharks' training camp before reporting to the Chinese national team in Beijing. I needed to get used to playing again. Now that so many people know me in China, I couldn't ride my bike or take a bus, so I borrowed the car of my Chinese agent, Lu Hao, to get to practice. It was a compact car, and I could barely fit in it. I didn't have a Chinese driver's license or insurance, and I was very scared about hitting somebody or something, so every second I was hitting the brake. I barely touched the gas. The police stopped me once, but then they recognized me and let me go.

Meeting Women

If you're a young guy in the NBA, you usually have a fast car, and lots of girls want to meet you. It doesn't matter what you look like. For some players in China, it's like that, too—but not for me, in China or in the U.S. I didn't have a fast car as a rookie, and only one girl tried to talk to me. I was in Seattle, in the hotel lobby. I don't think she was a fan of mine. She wanted to convert me to Christianity. She was pretty cute. I wanted to be nice, so I couldn't say no. I didn't talk to her because she was cute—but she was cute. There also was one girl in China, back in 2001, who wanted to be friends with me. It was before Wang went to the U.S. and before anyone knew I was going to the NBA. I don't know where she got my cell phone number, but she got it. So I changed my number.

Maybe one reason I don't meet more girls is that I don't go out to clubs or bars. When I do go out, I'm in the car and the windows are dark; nobody knows it's me. I think maybe 60 percent of the players in the NBA go out two or three times a week. I went out twice my first season. One time was to a disco in Houston's Chinatown. That was the day I got my driver's license, so I could finally drive by myself. I didn't go alone, though; I went with Colin and a couple of friends. I had heard this was a really good place to go, but we went on a Sunday, and there weren't a lot of people there.

The other time I went out was in L.A. Wang Zhi Zhi took me

out for Korean food. That's it. No club, no disco. In Houston, I didn't go out more because I was living with my mom and dad. And after away games I was tired. Do other players live with their moms? I don't think very many do. Tell David Stern he doesn't have to give orientation to rookies; he should just tell them to bring their moms and live with them.

The Family Yao

There are some good and bad things about living with my parents in the U.S. One good thing is that home feels like home, even if it's in a different country. Our house is very quiet, and not many people know where we live. If anything on the outside hurts me, like somebody yelling, "Yao sucks," when I get home, I can close the door, and everything from outside stops. My parents have made it that way. They won't allow outside problems to enter our home.

But I understand it's hard for them to live in America. They had lived in China all their lives, and had friends and jobs that they enjoyed. I sometimes joke that the NBA created a job for one Chinese person (me) but forced two (my parents) to lose theirs. Coming to the U.S. also was easier for me because I'd been here several times before. But it was the first time for my parents. They had been to Europe a couple of times to play basketball, but only for a week or two. In the process of living here and making this our home, they've had to learn a different way of life.

I don't worry about them when I'm in Houston. I worry when I'm on a long road trip to the West Coast or the East Coast and they have to stay there alone. They only go out to go shopping for food; the rest of the time they stay in the house with nothing to do. I'm not happy about that, but they don't understand English, so it's hard for them to go out alone. They only can say, "How much is that?" or "How many pounds?" or "Get gas" or "Good morning" or "Good-bye." You can't get very far in Texas if that's all you can say.

Living with your parents when you are twenty-three also is a learning experience. I have a friend who says that sometimes you have to flatter your parents. At home, when they are bringing you up, obviously you have to be respectful and listen to what they have to say. But when you go out in the world, sometimes you have to do what you think is right, even if it goes against their thinking. You may not be always right, but at least you have the experience of trying something out, and if you're wrong, you can adjust to that. But there's a way to listen to yourself and still respect your parents. No matter what, you always have to respect them.

The nice part is that I can see now what I have from each of them. My mother is a serious person. Sometimes I think she doesn't know how to joke around. There are times when I joke with her that I think she thinks I'm serious. My dad is a little more laid back. I get from my mother the desire to completely understand a situation, to leave nothing uncertain at all. From my dad I get my humor, especially when I really can't figure something out. His philosophy is to kick back a little, give yourself time to rest, and then try again. You have to figure out the puzzle eventually, but there's nothing wrong with a little rest in the meantime.

I've always talked to my parents a lot about basketball—basically, after every game. We talk about how the game is played, not about certain players or plays. I don't think it's helpful to talk about the mistakes players make or about how they should change. We talk about the overall game, whether we need to go faster or slow down or work harder on offense or defense. Because my parents are at most of my games and see them live, they see situations very clearly. They'll talk to me about the other team's defense, where the other team is coming from when they double-team me, and where I could get fastbreak baskets.

Obviously, there were a lot of conflicts during my first year between how my parents and the Rockets viewed basketball. The game is different in China. Teamwork always comes first. You don't look for your shot first, and you don't take low-percentage shots, especially if there's time to find a teammate. You also don't try to make your opponent look bad. It's not like that in the NBA. That doesn't make either side right or wrong. But I will always listen to what my coach says, because in the game everyone must play with the same mind-set. It does no good for me to play the way my parents think if no one else is playing that way. The same is true when I play for the Chinese national team. It does no good for me to play an NBA style if that isn't good for the rest of the team.

That said, I'd say I felt more pressure my first year in the NBA than when I was trying to win a championship with the Sharks— and I couldn't be sure the Sharks would let me leave unless we won. It's not that I thought a championship was less important. But winning the championship always seemed to be something I knew I could do.

That's not how I felt at all when I got to the NBA. Everything was new. I didn't know if I would survive even one season. I didn't know how my teammates would be. I didn't know how other teams were going to defend me. Because I missed almost all of training camp, I didn't know anything.

Super-sized Hospitality

I also had to adjust to all the traveling in the NBA. I've played in a lot of countries with the Chinese national team, but in most places we were there for a tournament. That meant we spent a week in one city, staying in one room in one hotel. A hotel can prepare a room for someone big like me if I'm staying that long. In the NBA, we stay at a lot of nice hotels, and they give their best rooms to NBA players, but that still doesn't mean that the bed or the doors will be big enough for someone like me. We almost never stay in a hotel for more than one night, so I understand why they can't worry too much about making a room comfortable just for me.

But some did. Most hotels would put a bench at the end of a regular king-size bed so my feet would have a place to rest. Then there were places that tried too hard. We got into our Washington, D.C., hotel very late, around 2 A.M., after playing in New York. When I walked into my room, I found two beds—not side by side, but end to end. Mo Taylor was going to his room and looked in. "Oh my God," he said. "Everybody, come see this!" So I had the whole team in my room to see my two beds. There was so much room our little point guard, Moochie Norris, could have slept at one end and I could have stretched out at the other, and we never would have known the other one was there.

Ink Blots

A lot of NBA players have tattoos, and some have tattoos of Chinese letters. I can tell you they don't understand what those letters really mean, or whoever told them what they mean doesn't know Chinese. A single character in Chinese sometimes can mean something by itself, but some don't make sense unless they appear with another character. Allen Iverson's tattoo on his neck means "loyalty." That's the only good one I can remember seeing. Moochie's tattoo on his forearm makes no sense. Marcus Camby of the Nuggets has some Chinese letters on his arm that could mean a lot of different things, because they are characters that you wouldn't normally put together. His tattoo could mean "encourage" or "force" or "reluctant." Whoever put on Kenyon Martin's tattoo must not have been a Nets fan. His letters mean "not aggressive" or "indecisive." Anybody who has seen Kenyon play knows he isn't like that.

Terence Morris, a forward who played for the Rockets my rookie year, had a tattoo that said in Chinese, "I'm a bad guy." I don't know if that's what he wanted it to say or knew that's what it said. I never asked him.

I don't have any tattoos. No earrings or anything else, either. Well, I have scars now, after playing a season in the NBA. Shawn Kemp put one on my back and Jamal Magloire of the Hornets put one underneath my left arm. I think of scars as being a man's badge of honor.

But scars aren't something you try to get; they just happen. In China, we believe that your parents gave you your body, so you shouldn't change or hurt it. Centuries ago you weren't even supposed to cut your hair; that's why some Chinese men wore long braids down their back. I don't go that far.

Now some young people in China are getting tattoos, too, but not me. I'm an old man when it comes to that.

Eastern and Western Medicine

The Chinese concept of medicine is very different from the Western world's ideas. Chinese, for example, do not believe in using ice. When we played in the 2003 Asian Championships in Harbin, China, all the games were in an Olympic sports complex with a speed-skating rink. But the rink was about the only place in Harbin you'd ever find ice, at least during the summer. (It gets very cold there in the winter.) I sprained my ankle stepping off the bus early in the tournament. When Team Yao came to see me and saw how big my ankle was, they asked if I was putting ice on it. I said no. I was getting acupuncture instead. Even if I wanted to put ice on it, I'd have to wait until we got back to the hotel and ask for room service.

The Chinese believe that balance is the way to good health. There are certain foods that are cold (yin), while others are hot (yang). There are neutral foods, too. Ice, believe it or not, is considered hot, or yang, so you can see why you wouldn't want to put it on something already sore, like an ankle. Whether the food is considered hot, cold, or neutral has nothing to do with the temperature of the food; it's what the food does inside your body when you eat it. Fish and seafood are yin, or cold, while meat and alcohol—except for beer—are yang, or hot. Beer is yin. Most spices are yang, but soy sauce and salt are yin. Most fruits are cold, but apples, cherries, dates, mangoes, and tangerines are hot. A lot of vegetables are cold, too, but chives, leeks, and green onions are hot. Rice is neutral or yin, depending on how it's cooked.

There also are nineteen types of food that can be yin, yang, or neutral—like soybeans. Basic soybeans are yin, fresh soybean curd is neutral, and dried soybean curd is yang.

One time before practice with the Chinese national team, I ate an apple. For the whole practice I felt as though my stomach was filled with a lot of air that wanted out. An apple is yang, or hot. Maybe I was confused, thinking hot food would be good to warm up. (That's my yin-yang joke.)

I know a little about both Chinese and Western medicine, and I believe in using whatever works. I had high blood pressure after I went back to China for the summer, and I used Chinese medicine to bring it down. I took a medicine made of dried grass, which tastes like vanilla. I don't have high blood pressure now, so I have to believe it helped. I do believe in Western thinking more when it comes to sports medicine, but the important part is having a good doctor. The medicine, or the method, is just a tool. The doctor has to correctly decide what the problem is.

The Chinese Capitalist

This is my philosophy about everything: the most important thing is to live your life the way you want it. I don't believe in a certain way of thinking for everybody. As long as you're comfortable with the way you live and don't feel that something has been taken from you, your life should be OK. Of course, I still feel the differences between how I grew up thinking and living and the life I have now.

There's an expression in Chinese that says when you go somewhere, you must adopt the customs. If you have money, you're a capitalist—that's the way some people think. So, OK, I'm a capitalist. But I still feel as though whatever money I have in my pocket—the money I can see and use—is what I have. And it's definitely all I need. The money I can't see, the money in the bank or the numbers on a check, just gives me a feeling of success. I think most people with a lot of money are like that. No one making millions can say he really needs that money to live. That's not what it means. It is a way to measure your worth in your job. If my next

contract with the Rockets is for more money than what I'm making now, it's because I'm worth more to them.

I still think of myself as a blue-collar worker. I sweat for my pay-
check. If that makes me the best-known capitalist in China today, I
don't have a problem with that.

10
LITTLE GIANT AND LONG LEGS

A lot of people think that I almost didn't get to the NBA because of Wang Zhi Zhi, but I don't believe that. They think that his decision not to go back and train with the national team after his first year with the Dallas Mavericks made the CBA more cautious about letting me go. I know they were concerned, but I think they would have been careful about letting me go no matter what had happened. That's how China has been for a long time.

Whatever Wang Zhi Zhi's decision did to me, I will never think of him as having hurt my career. The way I see it is that if it weren't for him, maybe I wouldn't be as good as I am, because from the time I started playing, it was my goal to be as good as he is. Even though I owe my country for giving me the chance to play and teaching me how, a big reason for my being where I am is timing and coincidence. One thing after another happened to help me when I needed it or made me want to work to get to the next level. From the time I started, catching Wang Zhi Zhi was my goal.

My dream at first was not to be better than him but just to be good enough to be his teammate. I was close to his level when we went to the 2000 Olympics, but then I saw there was an even higher level when I played against the best players from other countries. That's what I mean by coincidence. That was great timing for me. Just when I needed a new goal, I had one.

The truth is, in one way, I never will be able to pass Wang Zhi Zhi in the hearts of the Chinese people, because he was the first center from our country who could run and jump, shoot, block shots, and be part of the fast break. He also became a star in China before me and was the first Chinese player to play in the NBA, which was a historic moment, but that doesn't mean as much in my country as being the first center who could do everything. People had never seen this kind of big man before. Chinese centers before Wang Zhi Zhi had all been the kind that were very big and very slow; they couldn't dribble and couldn't jump. They would just stand in the paint and that's it.

There's a Chinese expression: "The first to arrive is the most important." That was Wang Zhi Zhi. I was the second who could do all that, but I will always be just one of the people who came after him. In this respect, nobody can ever move above him. Wang Zhi Zhi also became a star about three years earlier than I did. Nobody even knew who I was then. So he already had a place in people's minds as a great player before I came along. It's almost impossible to change the order in someone's head after it has been set.

That goes for Mengke Bateer, too. He's been first in some things ahead of both Wang and myself, but some Chinese fans question how important those firsts were. He was the first Chinese center to play in an NBA starting five, which he did for the 2001–2002 Denver Nuggets, and the first to win a championship ring, which he did with the 2002–2003 San Antonio Spurs, but he's still more like the old-style Chinese center. There's a lot of talk in China about how much credit Bateer deserves for those accomplishments. He has a ring, but he played forty-five minutes in eighty-two games during the Spurs' regular season and didn't play a minute in the playoffs; still, you could say he was part of the effort because he was with them all season. I don't think you should look down on someone because they didn't do a lot for their ring. That sounds like jealousy—as though someone wishes they had that person's ring. Personally, though, I just don't want to win a ring that way. I would think to myself, "That's not my championship ring."

I first saw Wang Zhi Zhi play in 1995 when I went to see the Bayi Rockets, the army team, play the Sharks in Shanghai. I couldn't believe someone that big could be that quick. He was a center and taller than me at that time, but he ran like a small forward. I was on the Sharks' junior team then. We passed each other in a hallway after the game, but we didn't stop and talk. We just looked at each other.

Two years later, we said hello for the first time. Well, I said hello. We were playing in an arena just outside Shanghai in the eighth Chinese national championships. This tournament is different from the CBA, where foreigners can play, or national-team competition, of course, which is against other countries. The national championships are strictly for Chinese players representing their city, province, or profession; for example, there are teams made up of players who don't all live in the same place but they do all work for the railroad or the post office or the police. A player can decide if he wants to play for the team where he lives or the one representing his profession. There are so many teams that games are played from early afternoon through the night every day. The arena for the eighth championship was so small that the teams had to warm up in the parking lot outside. The tournament is always in the summer, so it could have been worse.

I played for the Shanghai team, of course, and we were getting ready to play Wang Zhi Zhi's army team. Both teams were stretching outside in the same area. A friend of mine, who used to play for the Sharks but played for the army team in the national championships, saw me. "Take it easy on us," he said. "Don't beat us up too badly." Wang was right there, so my friend said to him, "Wang, watch out for this Yao Ming." I said hello, but Wang didn't say anything. He just smiled and jogged the other way.

I knew my friend was just joking. I wasn't very strong back then, and I'd broken my foot for the first time four months earlier. I could block shots, but that was about it. They beat us easily that game and won the championship. We finished seventh. But I did make Wang Zhi Zhi look bad in that game. I blocked his shot, and I wanted to smile, but I knew he was right behind me, so I held it in. The second time I blocked his shot, I also tried not to show anything, but I couldn't keep from smiling.

In the ninth national championship we went to the finals, where we lost to Wang and the army team by 3 points.

The first time we actually talked was about seven months later, at the CBA All-Star Game, which was in Shenyang, a city in northern China. Well, I tried to talk and he answered me. Nike did something special for this All-Star Game by giving a prize to a few lucky fans—a free trip to Shenyang, tickets to the game, and lunch with Wang, who had a Nike contract then, and me (I was about to sign with Nike).

At the lunch, Wang still wouldn't talk to me, but I felt that I had to say something. So I said, "Hey, Wang, I hear you like to play video games." I just wanted to say something, anything.

"No," he said. "I don't play video games."

"Oh," I said. "Maybe they were talking about somebody else." And that was it. For a whole hour. In a room by ourselves with three or four fans.

I don't blame Wang Zhi Zhi for not talking to me, because a lot of Chinese are like that. He's naturally very quiet and keeps a small circle around him, which makes him stay even more to himself. He's also stubborn. It seems very easy just to say hello, I know, but Chinese kids grow up being quiet like that. I went to a school in Houston with Calvin Murphy, a former Rocket who works for the team on TV now, and I saw a lot of American kids there. Anything Calvin Murphy asked—"How tall is the basket?" or "How far is the free-throw line?"—all the kids would shout out the answer. But if you asked a bunch of kids in China those questions, only a few would say anything. They would know the answers, but they wouldn't want to be the first to say anything.

I was quiet like that as a kid, too. I wouldn't say anything, either, even if I knew the answer. When I went to school, I wasn't a top-level student. My self-confidence wasn't very high. Now I think about how much better I could have done. Maybe I didn't do as well because I went to school a year early. Most kids in China start school when they're seven years old, but I started when I was six. One reason I started early was because I was so tall. The other reason is that, in China, as soon as you turn seven, you start school the next September. (July and August are the summer break.) My birthday is September 12, so if I had waited until I was seven to start school, I would've had to wait a whole year after my birthday. I would've been almost eight years old when I started. My parents and I didn't want to wait just because of twelve days.

I'll tell you a funny story about that. In China, you have to take a test before you can start school. It's very short, very easy, and they ask you the questions. You're supposed to be seven years old, so they can't ask any hard questions. I remember when I took the test, one of the questions they asked me was, "When is your birthday?"

"I don't know," I said.

"You don't know your birthday?"

"No," I said.

"Well, what day were you born?"

"Oh," I said. "September 12, 1980."

I knew when I was born, but I didn't know the meaning of "birthday." Sounds weird, I know, but, hey, I was six years old. Maybe if I were seven, I would've known better.

Nobody in China knew the Mavericks were going to pick Wang Zhi Zhi in the 1999 draft. I think Wang Zhi Zhi knew, but in keeping with his personality, he didn't tell anybody. When it was announced, the national team was practicing in a camp that really sucked. CBA officials were worried that it was too hot to practice at our training center in Beijing, so they looked for someplace cooler. They picked Kowloon Lake in northern China. They said, "It's nice. There's a lake." It didn't look bad when we first got there, but there was nothing to do other than practice. And it was hard to talk to anybody back home because it's the kind of place where the most you can get is one bar on your cell phone service. I'd walk around looking at my phone until I found a spot where it would have that bar. I'd sound like that commercial: "Hello? Can you hear me now?"

So we went there because it was supposed to be cool, and for ten days in a row it was very, very hot. Over 100 degrees. Hotter than Beijing. And because all year it's normally so quiet and cool at this lake—no one even goes there in the winter because it's too cold—there was no air-conditioning in the rooms or the gym. It was so bad I wanted to sleep in the swimming pool.

Then we found out that Wang Zhi Zhi had been drafted by the Mavericks. Nobody in China even knew when the NBA draft was held. I mean nobody. When we saw the report on TV—"The Dallas Mavericks, with the thirty-sixth pick, have taken the first Asian player in NBA history, China's Wang Zhi Zhi"—Wang immediately switched off his cell phone. We must've been where there was one bar on all of our cell phones, because a minute later, they all started ringing. Reporters were calling to find out where Wang was because his phone was off. They'd ask, "Is Wang Zhi Zhi there? Can I talk to him? What's he saying?"

The coach of the national team at that time didn't want any superstar players. Or he didn't want anybody to feel that they were a superstar. So after it was announced that Wang Zhi Zhi had been drafted, anytime Wang would shoot in practice or do anything, the coach would say, "That's a bad shot!" or "Why did you do that?"

That's how I got my chance. Before the draft, I sat on the bench a lot. I didn't play much at all. But after the draft, the coach started letting me play more and more to show Wang Zhi Zhi that someone was right behind him. The coach never said it, but everybody knew that's what he was doing.

I didn't care why the coach was playing me. It was my first chance to play a lot. If Wang Zhi Zhi had not been drafted, I still would've played ahead of Mengke Bateer, but never more than

Wang Zhi Zhi. Some games the coach even put me in the starting five. That happened only because Wang Zhi Zhi had been drafted.

I have to admit that I was jealous when I first heard that Wang Zhi Zhi had been picked by an NBA team. It was like when Liu Wei went to the junior national team and showed me his jersey, saying, "This is niiiiccce." I just wanted to rip that jersey apart.

I don't think there's anything wrong with feeling that way. It's how you act that matters. If you don't like a person because they have something you want, that's wrong. If you treat someone badly or get angry because someone has something you want, that's wrong, too. The important part is how you use that feeling. You can use it as motivation to work harder and get whatever that person has for yourself. There's always a way to do that without hurting others. I didn't care if Wang Zhi Zhi went to the NBA and became a big star. In a way, I hoped that would happen because it would be better for me and all of China.

I learned a lot about how to play against Wang Zhi Zhi from Fan Bin, a point guard on the Chinese national team. Fan Bin does not look like a good basketball player; he looks more like a wrestler, except he's not that strong. He doesn't have long legs or arms; he's maybe 6' tall with a buzz cut, and he wears big goggles when he plays. But he is a very, very smart player, and he taught me a lot about playing in the paint. Both of his knees have been badly injured, and he can't jump anymore, but he's still on the national team, and he was a big reason we beat South Korea to win the 2003 Asian Championship. Korea has a very good full-court press, and Liu Wei picked up four fouls in the first half and fouled out early in the second half. We tried another point guard, but he turned the ball over three or four times before the national team coach put in Fan Bin. He had a couple of turnovers, too, but he got the ball over midcourt enough for us to win. He even made a big 3-pointer, and he's not a good 3-point shooter.

When I first went to the national team I was very young, only eighteen years old. My second year with the team, Fan Bin was my roommate. Point guards, I have learned, know everything about the court. Maybe that's why I always had one as my room-mate with the national team—first Fan Bin and now Liu Wei.

Fan Bin taught me how I should position myself, how to keep that position, and how to protect the ball from a defender when I'm catching it or shooting it. What was most important, though, is that he told me I needed to play against Mengke Bateer and Wang Zhi Zhi as much as I could. At that time I wasn't very strong, so I didn't really want to play against them. But Fan Bin told me, "The first time you play them, they will kick your ass. The second time, maybe they kick your ass, but it will be harder for them to do. The third time, maybe you can kick their ass a little. But just do it. Play them hard every time. Every time it will get better."

Wang Zhi Zhi never had to go through that process. He grew up as the favorite, always, and never failed. He was picked for the national junior team when he was fourteen years old. He went to the national team when he was sixteen years old. He did all these things very young, very quickly. He was on the army team and won five championships in a row. They'd beat every team by 20 points.

I'm the opposite. I came out of failure. I don't think I have nat-ural talent; I had to work to learn how to do everything. I'm still like that. My first game in the NBA showed how much I had to learn. So, when I beat Wang once or twice in China, I think it had an effect on him and his NBA career. I don't think he was used to failure or that he took my beating him seriously, and maybe he thought it was just an accident. Anyway, he was always on the highest level, but I started at the bottom and had to climb to get to the top level. When we came to the NBA, we both had to start at the bottom. But for me it was starting at the bottom again. For him it might have been the first time. I think it helped me that I'm a little more used to the process.

Our nicknames sound different, but they're very similar. In China, they give my nickname, Little Giant, to every big guy. The "little" means in age, not size. It's more like Young Giant. I got the nickname from the older players in the CBA because I was seventeen when I started playing for the Sharks, yet when I'm forty years old, they will still call me by this nickname. They call Wang Zhi Zhi Little Long Legs, which is almost the same as Little Giant. It basically means the same thing.

Most NBA fans probably don't believe there's a rivalry between Wang Zhi Zhi and me, but in China there is a lot of talk about who is better. From ancient times, China has always had only one emperor. If there had been two, they would always have been fighting, and there would never have been peace between them. There's only one person who can be at the top. That's why Wang Zhi Zhi's fans don't like me and my fans don't like him. He and I don't think this way, but plenty of other people do. There is competition between us, and we like to challenge each other, but that's only on the basketball court.

LI YUANWEI: *If there's one big cultural difference that's important to understand, it's that America is a society that reveres individual effort and glory. In China, as with a lot of Eastern civilization, the focus is on how something benefits the nation—not just yourself, but the people around you. That's why it is so important that Yao fulfill his national-team obligation. It is for his own good, basically. This is where he can gain the biggest benefit, as Chinese people see it. Being an NBA star is all well and good, and that has its benefits for China as a whole as well, but Yao Ming is doing far more for himself, overall, in helping the national team to greater glory. Look at Wang Zhi Zhi. At one point he was a much more revered figure than Yao Ming. His reputation, in the eyes of the Chinese people, has just dropped off a cliff because of what he's done. In American society, that probably wouldn't happen as dramatically to a player who refused to play for his country. At least some people would say there's nothing wrong with that. But in China it's a big issue.*

You must also remember that China is not a wealthy nation. So the government and taxpayer money spent on developing a player is much more substantial than it is in the States. Yao's becoming a player is not just due to his own effort and his parents' upbringing; there's also the element of government support—in his training and in the opportunity to play against international competition.

There is a cultural lesson to be learned in what has happened to Yao Ming and Wang Zhi Zhi. It is a lesson in the balance an individual must strike between himself and his interests and those of his country. He has to make the relationship work. The biggest problem with Wang Zhi Zhi is that he went back on his own promise. He promised that he would play for the national team before he left, and it hurt a lot of fans' feelings when he didn't come back. Sports in China is an enterprise that involves a lot of national pride. There is a lot of national support for the country to realize its potential. The country puts a lot of money into developing athletes, with the intention of having these government-sponsored athletes achieve glory for the society. Right or wrong, that's the exchange offered to an athlete in China.

WANG FEI: *The difference between Yao Ming and Wang Zhi Zhi is not really physical. I think it's in their attitudes and how hard they play the game. Yao is the hardest-working player I've ever coached. There was a game when Yao and Wang Zhi Zhi played each other in the CBA. I was coaching Wang and the Bayi Rockets then. It was the first game of the 2000 season. I was back from studying basketball in the U.S. for a year, and I had changed the way we did a lot of things with the Bayi Rockets. We lost that first game against the Sharks. Wang Zhi Zhi was 0 for 11. Yao Ming did everything. He hit threes, twos, in the post, midrange jumpers, but maybe most important, he was diving for loose balls. There was one loose ball that Yao went after, and Wang Zhi Zhi didn't even bother to bend over. That was pretty standard. If the ball was on the floor, Yao, at 7'6", always would go down and get it, while Wang Zhi Zhi would stand and watch. If Yao could do that, every Chinese player should be able to do that. My other frustration was that the players, in general, would not practice hard. Yao was the exception. He might not have agreed with or understood everything I asked him to do, but he always tried his best to do it.*

I can't really say what more Wang Zhi Zhi can do on the court now in the NBA. He's not playing much, and on the bench these days he looks more like a spectator than a player. When Yao and Bateer are sitting on the bench, and a teammate makes a good play, when that player comes to the bench they will applaud and stand up and give him high fives. Wang Zhi Zhi has this detachment from all of it. In a way, he's losing his fighting spirit. And when that happens, it's over.

I spend a lot of time on the Internet reading what fans say about me. I want to know what people are thinking, even if it's bad or puts pressure on me to do more. The Internet is a different world. In the regular world, maybe someone wants to say something bad about me, but they won't say it if they know me. On the Internet people say what they really think about you. Nobody knows who the person writing or talking is, so the person says whatever they want. I sometimes think the Internet is where the truth is. I go to the message boards, where people write what they have to say about a particular subject. Some people will write "Yao Ming is bad" or "Yao Ming is stupid." Nothing else. That's it. And that's OK. That's life.

What I don't like is that people who like me talk bad about Wang Zhi Zhi and people who like him talk bad about me. Wang Zhi Zhi likes to play, and not just basketball. He likes to go to clubs. I'm not like that, but that doesn't mean Wang Zhi Zhi isn't smart. He's very smart. Maybe too smart, even. He's more Chinese than I am, too. Remember how I told you I like to say what I'm going to do? Wang Zhi Zhi isn't like that. He will try to accomplish his goal first without telling anyone what it is.

But no matter how we are different, we are both NBA players, and that means we are together. We are different people, but we come from the same place and we are doing the same thing. A lot of people hate him because he left China and won't come back. His fans don't like me because they think he's the better player. Maybe they like the fact that he does what he wants, that he was not afraid to make the Chinese officials mad. Or maybe they blame his agent or the people around him, not Wang Zhi Zhi, for his decision not to come back. But if you want to say something good about me, you don't have to say something bad about him.

WANG FEI: *One impact of Wang's decision is obviously on the national team's performance. I believe that with Wang we could've made it to the top eight in the World Championships. The second, and more important impact, is that a lot of doors of exchange with U.S. basketball were closed as a result of Wang Zhi Zhi's actions. I was invited to work at Pete Newell's camp the summer after Yao's rookie year, but with Wang not coming back, the CBA wouldn't allow anyone to go anywhere outside the country, especially to the U.S.*

The sad truth is that Wang is very easily satisfied. In China, he's plenty good enough to be a star. Wang Zhi Zhi has long been a great player in China, even if he's no longer the best Chinese player. With the Bayi Rockets, he was on a team that won the championship every year. Sometimes I think that maybe Wang Zhi Zhi pays too much attention to media hype and the newspapers. He competes with many different players, but it seems that psychologically he's not in the best shape when he plays Yao. If he does well in the first few minutes, he'll continue to do well in that particular game. But if he doesn't do well, he'll be a total waste for the rest of the game. And that only seems to happen with Yao. He doesn't seem to be able to look at playing Yao as just another game. He always has something to prove. They played each other in one game after the 2000 Olympics, and there was a lot of hype about who the best center in China was. At the start of the game, the Sharks ran a pick-and-roll play in which Wang Zhi Zhi, instead of sliding over to help cut off the guard driving off the pick, just stayed with Yao. I yelled at him that he had to help. The next time they ran the play, he did the same thing. I yelled at him again. The third time, no difference. I knew then that it was no accident and sat him down for the rest of the first half and didn't play him at all in the second half. The Sharks won that game by 3, and Yao Ming had two very important free throws in the final minute. The idea that the first is always the best may be traditional Chinese thinking, but it also can be a reason why you can't make progress.

The CBA still wants Wang Zhi Zhi to come back, and he still wants to play for the national team, but now there's a rice-paper wall between them. They know where the other side is, but no one will reach around the wall or pull it down. I wish he would come back to the national team, too, because it would make it easier on me, but I don't think it's just up to him to make this happen.

The CBA still has some control over me, but not too much. If I wanted to, I could be like Wang Zhi Zhi. But I don't want to do that because I feel very comfortable playing for the national team. I like playing in the Olympics. I don't want to do anything that would keep me from doing that. To me, just being asked to try out for the national team is the biggest honor I've ever received.

I was a rookie playing in the CBA All-Star Game when I first heard that the national team might want me. Before the game a reporter told me, "This year the national team wants you to go to training camp with them." I didn't believe that at the time. They had a lot of players in their prime on that team, all under thirty years old. I thought, "They won't pick me. I'm too young. I'm seventeen years old." Of course, they cut me on the last day of training camp before the games started. But when I got my practice jersey and it said "China" on it, that, as Liu Wei would say, felt niiiiccce.

There's no bigger honor I can think of than playing for my country and maybe winning a medal in the Olympic Games or the World Championships. It would be a very difficult decision, and luckily I don't have to make it, but if I could only play for either the Rockets or China, I would have to choose the national team. Maybe that's left over from my idea as a kid that there was no bigger achievement than winning a gold medal. Or maybe it's from my mom, since she was the captain of the women's national team. In China, a lot of people say that if the parents do something, the children must follow them.

The reason for Wang's failure in the NBA so far, I think, is that he has tried to become too much of an all-around player. I have just concentrated on doing what a center should do—block shots, rebound, and score in the paint—because I think I can be more useful to my team that way. Wang Zhi Zhi likes to shoot 3s and face the basket and drive. His defense also has caused problems for him. Starting from the 2000 Olympics, I could tell his defense was suffering. I could still play defense and do some things on offense. But his defense was not the same as it had been when he first joined the national team.

There's another important difference. When Wang Zhi Zhi and Mengke Bateer came to the NBA, they were not in the same position as I am. Wang Zhi Zhi was a second-round pick by the Dallas Mavericks in 1999 and then waited two years before he left China. Mengke Bateer went to the Denver Nuggets as a free agent. Both teams already had big stars, so Wang Zhi Zhi and Bateer had to make themselves fit into the team. Now they are both with different teams, and again it's up to them to find their purpose for the team. The Rockets wanted me enough to make me the number-one pick, so they are committed to making me a success. They have made a place for me in the team and are building the team to help make me better. If you look at the changes the team made from my first year to my second, you can see that.

Wang Zhi Zhi and I never have been close friends, but I will always like and respect him because he wanted to play in the NBA. He had a dream, and he worked hard to reach it. Most Chinese players have no chance to play in the NBA. That's OK. But some don't even set that as a goal, or if they do and then find out it's not possible, they don't set any new goals. That's too bad. What is it you say in America? Be all that you can be.

11

YE LI

My girlfriend is the only woman I've ever dated, so I'm in no way an expert on relationships. Coming to the NBA, though, has certainly been an education. A Chinese newspaper interviewed Moochie Norris and me and asked us if we had any kids. They asked him first, but I answered for him. "Of course not," I said. "He's not married."

"Actually," Moochie said, looking at me with a half-smile, "I have two."

I was very surprised to hear that. I'd never known anyone who was a father who wasn't married. For a long time in China, if you had a baby and you weren't married, you didn't tell anybody. Now it's a little different; young people don't look at it as being bad and are less afraid to tell somebody. But the rule still is that every family is allowed only one child. Well, now you are allowed two if you live in Beijing or Shanghai and both you and your wife are only children. But a Moochie is hard to find in China.

I think I'd like to have five kids, one a year for five years. On second thought, no; that would be too tiring.

It would be too tiring to have more than one girlfriend, too. I don't think there's anything wrong with the NBA players who do have more than one. This country is different from China, with different people who live in a different way. I don't want to live that way, but it's not up to me to say what other people should and shouldn't do.

From what I can tell, the usual dating process for most people isn't too different in the U.S. than it is in China: you ask a girl for her number or you ask if you can bring her a drink if you're in a club or you ask if you can have dinner with her. It's the same in the U.S., no? The difference between a regular guy trying to get a date and a sports star is also the same in China as in the U.S. Chinese national team players are all superstars in China. Girls are waiting for them. They don't have to ask. Just like in the NBA.

I don't have a lot of women ask me out because I've always made it known I have a girlfriend. Some NBA players don't want anybody to know they have a girlfriend so they can look for a better one, or have more than one. But not me. That's why I wear a red friendship bracelet on my left wrist. I've never told anyone about it until now, other than to say it was from my girlfriend, Ye Li. This is also the first time I've talked about Ye Li. I like keeping a little of my life private, and I'd like to protect her privacy. But I'm afraid refusing to talk about my friendship bracelet and our relationship has created more interest than any of it deserves. So I want to tell you a little about us in the hope that, maybe, the interest will fade away.

I first saw Ye Li when I was seventeen. She was practicing with the women's national team. At that time, I didn't try to talk to her. I didn't want to ask her out until I was on the national team, too. But whenever I could, I'd ask the newspaper photographers for their extra photos of the women's team. There are other girlfriends

I could have had, but there was only one I wanted. When I finally made the national team in 1999, I asked Ye Li to go out with me.

She said no.

That didn't stop me. It's always like that with Chinese girls. They can't just say, "Yes." Nothing ever has come quickly to me, so I thought, "This is no different. I know how to do this. I can wait."

For one year she said no, real quick, like this:

"Will you go out with—" "No."

After about a year, I noticed something change. For the next six months, she still said no, but she didn't say it as fast. When she started to say "no" more slowly, I said to myself, "Something has changed. I have a chance now! I'll still wait."

I thought about a lot of things during that year and a half. You may not believe me, but it was a good thing. I wasn't always asking her out. There are only so many times a day you want to hear "no." I didn't call her every day, but sometimes I'd send text messages to her phone, asking how she was doing or saying hello or telling a joke.

I didn't give up because I had a feeling she was the one. In Chinese, we say if you believe "She's the one," no one can ever say you're wrong because only you know that. You could be lying, but only you would know if you are.

Now, looking back, I think I know why something changed after that first year. It started with the Olympics in Sydney, Australia. Memo to David Stern: Have the American basketball team live in the Olympic village. It's so much fun, being in one place with athletes from so many different countries. The NBA players are missing out on something by not living in the village. Because the Sydney Olympics were my first, I took lots of team pins to exchange. I went to trainers and players from every team and country and traded with them. I probably collected 200 pins, all from different countries and different sports.

Then I put together fifty of the best and gave them to Ye Li for her nineteenth birthday. I think that's why she finally turned soft on me. After that, she'd at least hesitate about going out with me before saying no. I saved the other 150 pins in case nothing changed and I had to try with her again. But it's nice to have them; when I'm tired, I look at the ones I kept and think about how interesting that Olympic experience was. Somehow, it makes me feel less tired. I'm looking forward to the next Olympics, because Ye Li and I both will be going and can collect pins together.

Ye Li finally went out with me after a dinner given by the Shanghai Media Group for all its teams—men's and women's basketball, soccer, all of them. There were maybe sixty people there. Ye Li played for the women's team, and I was there with the Sharks. The dinner was at the top of the OTV building in Shanghai, in an area of the city called Pu Dong. The building's top floor is a revolving restaurant with lots of windows. You can see all of Shanghai from up there. I promised everyone at that dinner that the next season we would win the championship. After dinner I talked to Ye Li and we went out to a club. It was a good night.

She gave me my friendship bracelet at the start of my last CBA season, on February 14, Valentine's Day. When it was new, it was deep, deep red. She has one, too. She made both of them. Hers looks better than mine because I've played more games. More games means more sweat, more showers. I wear mine on my left wrist and she wears hers on her right. This is a Chinese custom. In China, we say the man is the left hand and the woman is the right hand. So anything like this a man will put on his left hand or arm and a woman will put on her right hand or arm.

Luckily, other players have never gotten a hand or fingers

caught on my bracelet, even though it's loose. Well, it happened once. Someone's finger caught it in a game. I don't remember who it was, I just remember a quick tug on it. That's why I always push it up my arm. Some people believe it's bad luck if a friendship bracelet is broken, but I don't believe that. One day it will break because I can already see where it's getting worn. When that happens, we'll just change to new ones, but we will pick a special time to do that together.

One reason I've played more games than Ye Li is because she hurt her right knee a couple of years ago and needed surgery. A lot of people told Ye Li she should stop playing, but she doesn't always listen to what people tell her to do. It might mean trouble for me later, but I like that about her. Team Yao flew her to northern California to have the surgery performed by a famous sports surgeon, Dr. Art Ting. I didn't have to ask; they just did it.

One nice thing is that I've never had to wonder if Ye Li was with me because I'm famous or because I have a lot of money. We've known each other since we were teenagers—even if she was saying no back then.

The bracelet isn't the only way I let people know I have a girl-friend. A photo of Ye Li is the screensaver on my cell phone. When Boki saw the picture, he said, "The boy is bad." I know that means good.

After my rookie year in the NBA, Ye Li also gave me a tiny dog to hang on my phone. The dog has a magnet inside. She has a dog just like it with a piece of metal inside; put them close and they stick together. I didn't really like people seeing me with it because a man with a toy dog doesn't look right, so when I would make a call, I would hide it between my hand and the phone. Then I took the dog off before I went back to the U.S. because I knew Boki and my other teammates would kill me for it.

What they don't know is that I picked my uniform number, 11, for Ye Li, too. I wore number 15 with the Sharks and I wear number 13 with the Chinese national team. Some numbers have special meanings that everybody in China knows. Fifteen doesn't have a special meaning for anyone except me. I wore it because that was my dad's number when he played for the Shanghai team. Thirteen means "stupid" in Chinese, but it's the number most often worn by centers in the Olympics. I don't know how to explain that. Nine is an emperor's number. Eight and six are good numbers, too. Four is a bad number; it means death. When China Unicom gave Team Yao and me our cell phone numbers, they made sure there were a lot of eights and nines in them.

A lot of reporters wanted to know why I picked number 11 to wear with the Rockets since I wore 15 with the Sharks and no one was wearing 15 for Houston when I got there. Erik told everyone I wore it for its feng shui qualities, the two lines pointing up meaning that everything is looking up. But the truth is I picked it because it's the number that most looks like two Ys, as in Yao and Ye. You can tell which car is mine because I have my number and two Ys on the back and woven into the carpets. I used to say that if you ever saw me change uniform numbers, you'd know I changed girlfriends. But now I'd have to change cars, too.

Ye Li wears number 11, too, for both the Chinese national team and the Shanghai Octopus. She's only 6'3", but she also plays center and likes to say she has better low-post moves than I do. Sometimes, I think, it's better not to argue.

Based on my first year in the NBA, I can tell you that a lot of women want to be a player's girlfriend. They will look for any chance to meet a player. When I was at the All-Star Game in Atlanta, they had a couple of bars where women would pay security to introduce them to a player. My Rockets teammate, Kelvin Cato, is from Atlanta. "Watch out, boy," he told me. "You better be careful. There are a lot of nightclubs in Atlanta, and you're an All-Star now."

The All-Star Game is almost as much about women as it is about basketball. I remember after the game a reporter asked me in an interview, "Did you find a girl this weekend?" I said, "No, I have a girlfriend in China." He seemed disappointed. I feel that a lot—that people think I'm doing something wrong by not taking everything I can get as an NBA player. I like to look at the girls, but Ye Li is enough for me.

Bill Walton talked to me about girls, too. Walton is a funny guy. We talked more than once, and every time Colin would say to me, "I don't know how to translate for him. I'm not sure what he's saying."

One time Walton asked if I had tried to find some girls in the United States. Like dancing girls. He was joking, but Erik and John Huizinga were standing right there, so I couldn't speak in English or Mandarin without someone knowing what I said. So I told him, in English, "Yeah, I tried, but they all said they wanted you."

As I've said, I really thought I had a chance to go to the NBA in the 2001 draft. But I also said that I believed the result was already in place and all I needed to do was work toward it. I can see now that maybe I was moving toward a bigger goal than just playing in the NBA—a goal that included Ye Li. Life is not all basketball. When the 2001 draft was held, she and I had been together only two or three months. Since I had waited so long for her to go out with me, I wasn't ready to give up the relationship, especially

244 YAO: LIFE IN TWO WORLDS

after finding out how nice that was. An extra year with Ye Li was a gift. My first year in Houston was also a lot easier because I could call and talk to her and hear about Shanghai or how her team was playing. So it was good that everything happened the way it did. I can say that now, even if I didn't think it then.

12

THE PRICE OF FAME

When I went back to China after my rookie year, I forgot to take my computer games with me. Erik had come back with me to Shanghai, and I kept telling him I needed to go to a computer store. He thought it was a bad idea because a lot of people would show up. I told him I had gone there before, after I was drafted by the Rockets, and that it had been OK. I kept talking about it until I finally convinced him it wouldn't be a problem. Or maybe he just got tired of me bugging him.

Anyway, he was right; it was a bad idea. After only a few minutes the store was filled with people who wanted an autograph or a picture. Erik called six security guards, who helped me get out of there.

Maybe I should have known it would be that way in my hometown in China because a similar thing happened in my first NBA season when the Rockets stopped at a fast-food place in California. It was about a month before the end of the season, and we were going from Oakland to Sacramento. It's a short trip, so the team took a bus; the drive is maybe two hours. A lot of teams do the same thing, and part of the trip is to stop at a burger place on the way. I don't know if they all get off the bus or send someone in to get the food, but we thought it would be OK for all of us to go in and order. The Rockets are a little bit known around the country, but it wasn't like the L.A. Lakers all showing up at McDonald's.

The people already in the restaurant started chanting, "Yao Ming! Yao Ming!" and crowded around asking for autographs. Even the people working there stopped what they were doing to get autographs. I didn't want to make it hard for the rest of the team, so I went back to the bus, and Colin brought me my double cheeseburgers.

In China, when I'm in an airport, I can keep to myself as long as I'm sitting down; people don't notice me. But if I stand up, it's hard to miss me. I can't go to a store or restaurant like I could before. That's one thing I love about America: when I ask fans to let me finish eating before I sign autographs or if I tell them I'm in a rush and can't stop, they respect that. In China, sometimes it's not that way. But in America I also have more commitments. What I love about basketball is playing, whether it's in practice or games. Signing jerseys and balls and posters, taking promotion photos— that's just part of the job. In China, because they don't do all that business, I am free of it. In either country, though, I'm careful about when I go out in public. Sometimes I miss having to stand in line like everybody else. Because of my height, I've always stood out, especially in China, where there aren't as many tall people. But I've always wanted to fit in, to be just another kid, or just another teenager, or just another person on the street going to a movie or shopping or playing video games. Before people came to know me as a basketball player, I still had that most of the time. I always wanted to be famous, but I saw only the things being famous gives you; I never thought about what it takes away.

I can give you an example of how I've changed, or how attention has changed me. In 1997 I was with the junior national team on a trip to Taiwan. I was the tallest player on the team, so when we first got there, all the cameras were on me anytime we went anywhere. But I had broken my foot and was still waiting for it to heal, so I wasn't playing. After the first game, all the reporters and media people saw me on the bench and the cameras were never on me again. I have to be honest: at that time I missed the attention. Of course, I would be OK with less attention now. It's like anything: if you eat steak every day, it can be the best steak in the world, but after a while you are going to get tired of it. Anything that is the same every day, I think, can be tiring after a while.

I remember when I signed my first autograph. It was 1995. I was playing for the first time for the all-China junior team. At that time I didn't think anybody knew who I was. I wasn't a bad player, but at that time I didn't know how to shoot or play offense. I just had about twelve blocked shots every game.

A guy who was twenty-one, maybe twenty-two—older than me—asked me to sign his notebook. I was surprised. I wrote my full Chinese name in complete characters, very carefully. I was so excited. Someone wanted my autograph! I went home and told my mom, "I signed my first autograph!" And I showed her how I did it. She said, "How are you going to sign like that all the time?" So she showed me how to write it faster. But then for two years, nobody asked for my autograph again. Not until I turned professional.

One night after my first season in the NBA, I was in Jianjing, not far from Beijing, with the Chinese national team. We had just played nine games in two weeks. These were exhibition games to get ready for the 2003 Asian Championships. The national team

was not ready for the number of fans who wanted to see me, and
there was no security. When we were walking through airports or
walking from the bus to the hotel or even when we were in the
arena getting ready to play, fans came from everywhere to get autographs and photos. The fans in China have always supported
me, so I feel I owe them something; nevertheless, it is tiring to sign
autographs and have cameras pointed at you everywhere you go.
If I walk through an airport, people working for the airlines or for
security will stop me for autographs. Some even have me sign their
uniforms. If I stay in a hotel, the people who work there will come
to my room looking for an autograph. If I'm on a bus and we stop
to pay a toll, the guards will get on the bus and ask for an autograph and a photo. It's amazing. I still think of myself as a private
person, so I'm not entirely comfortable with all the attention.

What was also difficult was that the Chinese national team
wasn't ready for how popular the team had become when we traveled around the country before the Asian Championships. They
hadn't prepared for the crowds at our hotels or at our games. After the last game of the exhibition tour, we went back to the hotel
and the players could barely get on the elevators because of all the
people in the lobby. I signed as many pieces of paper as I could,
but when it's that crowded, someone is going to be left out. Two
fans who wanted a photo and an autograph followed me off the
elevator and all the way into my room. I didn't know what to
think. It was late, long after midnight, and I was sharing a room
with Liu Wei. I understand that sometimes I have to give up my
privacy, but I never like it when other people lose theirs because
of me. A team official saw the fans go into my room and tried to
talk to them, but they didn't listen to him, either.

I was tired and made the mistake of saying I wouldn't take a
photo with them. Twenty minutes later, they were back, ringing

my doorbell, asking once more for a photo and an autograph. I went into the hallway and gave them what they wanted. They were determined, and I probably should have recognized that right away. Liu Wei has been my friend for a long time, so I'm sure he wasn't too angry at me.

ERIK ZHANG: *There is a lot of national pride and emotion in China, even from a historical perspective, attached to Yao making the NBA. There are certain burdens that Chinese athletes will always carry for a long time—maybe for this generation, the next generation, and the generation after that. From the early 1800s until today, China has been pretty backward, a relatively weak nation. The hope now is that it is on the right path to glory, and that's part of the interest in Yao. He is the perfect example of individual achievement in an increasingly individualistic Chinese society. There are people in their early thirties doing things their parents never would have done, going from inland, backward regions to coastal regions and exploring their opportunities and status in society, working hard, taking big risks, and being rewarded for their individual effort. Yao is a hero for those people because no one said to him at seventeen years old, "We're going to give you a job as the starting center for the Houston Rockets." He did that by choice and by fighting a lot of resistance.*

A decade ago Chinese university students, upon graduation, didn't look for a job; they were assigned one. The only choice you had was selecting your major; you had to do that before you matriculated, and you couldn't change it. After graduation the government assigned you to whatever company in whichever region of the country they wanted you to work. And that job was for life, basically. But ever since the '90s, young Chinese students have had a choice. They can find their own place in the world.

FANG FENG DI: *Yao's father and I were famous as players in China in our day, so what has happened to Yao is not such a big surprise. We're used to being in situations like his. The only surprise is that it happened so quickly in the United States.*

YAO ZHI YUAN: *If there's a difference, it's that before, if they mentioned Yao Ming, it would be that he's the son of Yao Zhi Yuan and Fang Feng Di. Now if anyone mentions us, they simply say, "Yao's parents." Of course, even if Yao Ming is as well known as, say, Michael Jordan, it's not because he's as great a player as Jordan was. We think Yao is popular because he's Chinese, and Americans know there are a billion Chinese people, so he has a lot of people behind him. He also is part of a new generation of Chinese that is so different from the old generation. I think Western countries, especially the U.S., don't know much more about China than the Chinese know about America. They don't know the modern culture of China, so Yao Ming comes as a big surprise to everyone here.*

The worst part about being known as Yao's parents is you can't bargain for anything. Everybody knows we can afford to pay full price.

The media in China and the U.S. are different. In the NBA, after a game the media will ask me a specific question, like, "In tonight's game, why didn't your team get more rebounds?" It will have to do with a problem. In China they will ask, "How do you feel about tonight's game?" They give you a big question and let you say what the problem was. Chinese reporters also never stop reporting. In the NBA, after the game we stay in the locker room, and sports reporters ask questions, and that's where it ends. In China, they will follow you home or back to the hotel.

By the end of my first NBA season, my English had improved

enough that I recognized certain questions, either because they used words I knew or I'd heard the question so many times before. When I started playing for the Rockets, if a reporter asked a question, I could understand maybe 20 percent of what was said. But even later in the season I still used a translator because I knew I needed to be very careful and accurate with everything when talking to the media.

I wasn't always that way. When I was seventeen, I played for the Shanghai team in the Chinese national championships. Our team finished seventh, but this was the first time reporters began to ask for interviews and talk about me as a player. The reporters asked me questions after one game but used my answers in a different way than I meant them. They asked how good I wanted to be, if I wanted to be better than Wang Zhi Zhi. Their stories made it sound as though I was disrespectful of Wang and the other national team players, as though I thought I was already better than they were. People who read the reports from that game saw a new me. That's how I learned to be careful.

That's why I want my English to be really good before I start talking to reporters without a translator. I want my English to get better so I can talk better trash, too. In the Asian Championships against South Korea, I blocked a 3-point attempt right in front of their bench and yelled in English, "Get out of my way!" I know that's not very good trash-talking, but I'm not sure if the South Korean players understood me, anyway. Like every young Chinese player, I was taught not to use trash talk on the court, not to get mad, not to do anything except play basketball. In China, we don't really understand what trash talk is. We're not even supposed to curse. Now I think that's impossible for me. I really like talking on the court. When I played in exhibition games against the Melbourne Tigers from Australia before the 2003 Asian

Championships, I talked a lot to the Tigers center, Mark Bradtke. We kept challenging each other, talking about who would have the most offensive rebounds, who would make more jump shots, things like that. My girlfriend watched the first game of the Asian Championships on TV in 2003. We played Syria, and when I missed my first shot, I cursed in English. She told me all of China heard that because there was a TV microphone under the backboard. I wish I could tell you that will never happen again, but I can't.

Regardless of whether I'm in China or the U.S., I'm going to be talking on the court from now on. I won't ever stop talking to reporters, either. It would feel impolite not to answer their questions, because I know those questions are not just from the reporters, they are also from the fans. No matter what happens, I feel I will always owe it to the fans to answer their questions and let them know what I'm thinking when I play.

13
CHINESE BASKETBALL

Professional basketball in China already has changed a lot from the time I started playing for the Sharks' junior team in 1994. When Liu Wei and I first played, the conditions were not the best. The shoes, especially, were really bad. Think about that: some of the best basketball shoes in the world are made in China, but ours were made by a Chinese company, which was a big difference from shoes made by Nike and Reebok.

These shoes were very thin on the bottom and very uncomfortable. They looked like the old, old all-white Converse shoes, except not that good. We had no practice shirts, shorts, or socks. You wore whatever workout clothes you could find. In the gym there was no heat in the winter and no air-conditioning in the summer. The players lived and practiced together all week, and six of us slept in a single room. We had wooden backboards, and there was no skin on the basketballs. Now they use breakaway rims, good basketballs, and good shoes. Every junior player has all that *and* elbow guards, knee pads, and sweatbands.

The old days sound terrible, right? I only think of them that way now. At the time, I felt lucky that I had the chance to play for the junior Sharks, because that meant I had a chance to play for China's junior national team—which meant I might one day have a chance to play for the men's national team.

Going through hard times can be good for you. Back then, I wanted to make the Sharks' first team just so I could have good shoes. I wasn't the only one. Wang Zhi Zhi, Liu Wei, and players on every junior team wanted that. I'm not saying today's players are less motivated because they've had it easier. Maybe if I had had what the junior players have now, my goal would have been different. Maybe I would've thought about the NBA right away instead of after I went to the U.S. for the first time. As it turned out, I got a good pair of shoes about six months before I went to the Sharks' first team, anyway. My mom got them for me. She called Chen Dechun, the assistant coach of the national team. He was the head coach of the Sharks when I first joined their junior team and a friend of my parents. He had two pairs of size-18 Adidas for Zheng Hai-Xia, the 6'8" center for the Chinese women's national team who later played for the L.A. Sparks, and gave me one of them.

What's hard now is playing for the Rockets, going back to play for China's national team, and then going back again to the Rockets. Conditions in the two places are very different. There are so many people involved in preparing the Rockets to play—coaches, trainers, assistant coaches, a strength and conditioning coach, an equipment manager, assistant equipment manager, media relations director, team doctor, security chief. Chinese people believe this is how it always is with Americans. During the Korean War, they would say that for every U.S. soldier on the field there were two or three providing support. So for 10,000 soldiers, there would be 30,000 people providing medicine and food and fuel and ammunition. In comparison, if the Chinese had 10,000 soldiers, they had maybe 5,000 people in support.

That's how it feels in basketball today. In China, for a long time we washed our own uniforms, and we still carry our own shoes and tape our own ankles. We have twelve players, one head coach, one assistant coach, a team doctor, and a team manager. Four people—that's it. They take care of everything—game, hotel, travel, security, media, injuries, training. We fly on regular airplanes, and we stand in line to get our tickets, put our bags through the X-ray machines, walk through metal detectors, and sit in coach. You know how on some planes there are six seats together in the middle? When the national team went to Dallas to train in 2001, Wang Zhi Zhi, Bateer, myself, and three other guys who were 6'7" or taller all sat together in those six seats from Beijing to L.A. and then from L.A. to Dallas. That's sixteen hours of sitting like that! Now they let Mengke Bateer and me sit with the head coach in first class because there's more room for our legs. Maybe they should tell Wang Zhi Zhi that and he'll come back to the national team.

With the Rockets, we have our own plane. We don't have to go through security or buy tickets, and every seat is a first-class seat. There's always lots of food, you don't have to use the seat belt, and you can use your computer the whole time. The only difficult part is finding out where everybody likes to sit. Every player has his favorite seat, and you don't want to sit in the wrong one. Other than that, I never knew traveling could be so nice. When I went back to China after my rookie year and traveled with the national team, the thing I missed most was the Rockets' team plane.

NBA players don't have to think about any of this. Even those who play for Team USA stay in nice hotels and travel on charter planes. I have to believe a player good enough to play for Team

USA has had everything taken care of for him his whole career. If you grow up in a bad neighborhood with no money, it might take you some time to adjust when you move to a nice neighborhood and get a job that pays a lot of money. Once you get used to the change, though, it's easy. But think about having money and living well, then going back to living badly with no money, then being rich and in a nice house again—back and forth, every year. Or if you're working at a job and your boss gives you a raise, you're happy about that, and you get used to earning that much money. If they take that money away and give you what you were making before, life feels harder, even though you have lived like that before.

I know, I really sound like a capitalist now.

The facilities in the U.S. are a lot better than in China, too, but I don't want to complain too much about what China doesn't have. Playing on the national team always has been an honor and always will be. I just don't think everybody involved with the Chinese national team is thinking about honor or making decisions for honor. The summer after my first year in the NBA, the national team played nine exhibition games all over the country. These games did not make us better. They just made money.

WANG FEI: *The struggles Yao went through in his first few years playing in China were totally normal. Yao has met many more hardships—the physical and aggressive play of the NBA—and will meet still more, such as learning to adapt his personality to the team and how to become a leader. I can't pinpoint one thing in particular that poses the biggest challenge, but I can say I don't think anything will stop him. He will continue to progress and overcome every obstacle.*

I also believe that balancing Yao's time between the NBA and the national team is very important. The national team needs Yao for only one month of training. That's enough. The CBA needs to learn from its past experiences with Wang Zhi Zhi and Yao Ming and make arrangements so that Yao can fully develop his skills. If it were up to me, if it were best for Yao to spend more time in the summer in the U.S., then he should do that.

But let's not forget what he already has accomplished. I never could have imagined anyone like what he's become emerging from the Chinese basketball system. Even when I saw him early on, I couldn't have predicted he'd be what he is today. For a long time, China has been at a physical disadvantage competing in international basketball. For a long, long time, China was always weak at center. Its strength was its guards. Now it's reversed. Yao is the main reason for that. He's the type of player who keeps improving in rather dramatic fashion. Before the 2000 Olympics, both Bateer and Wang Zhi Zhi could eat Yao up one-on-one. But by the time we got to Sydney, they were having real difficulties with him. We can't be satisfied, though, with just having produced Yao or believing that our system is good enough because he came from it. Who Yao is as an individual is a big part of why he has become a success. If we want to produce more players of his caliber, we have to continue improving and developing basketball in China overall.

LI YUANWEI: *I would only stress this: China is changing and very quickly. In America, individuals effect change. In China, the country effects change and individuals follow. So I can have ideas about how things should be or what is best, but I can't implement them on my own. Everything I do has to reflect the country's environment. I may think a certain way, but I also have to represent the CBA and the Chinese Sports Administration.*

But I don't think this poses a problem as it once might have.

China is becoming more and more market-oriented. There's more and more transparency. This is the trend that I see, and you can extrapolate it to predict how the next player to go from China to the NBA will be handled. We're not going to take the previous view that the country is all-important or the CBA is all-important or any one thing is all-important. It has to be a balanced view, in which the individual's interest, the country's interest, and the CBA's interest are all considered.

When I first became a professional player, the Sharks paid me 500 RMB a month and another 5,000 RMB every time we won. In American money, that's about $70 a month and $700 for every win. The second year they paid me 2,500 RMB a month and 5,000 RMB for a win. My last year they paid me 5,500 RMB a month and 6,000 RMB for every win. Then we won the championship, and they gave me another 400,000 RMB for that. That's about $50,000 US.

As you can see, there was a lot of pressure to win. You didn't make much money unless you won.

My rookie year with the Shanghai Sharks we won only thirteen games. That's better than it sounds, because in the CBA the regular season is only twenty-four games, so we were better than .500. I got 65,000 RMB for the thirteen wins. We played only one playoff game and lost, but they gave me another 70,000 RMB for the season because, altogether, we had played better than anyone thought we would. The team had just moved up from the second division, so winning against the best in the CBA was something very new.

The next year I played only twelve games, but we still reached the CBA finals. That's when I broke my foot—for the second time—in a practice game before the season started. I played in only the last few games.

After the 2000 Olympics we had eighteen regular-season wins. The last year we won twenty-three games in the regular season and nine in the playoffs, and made it to the finals. We lost only two games until the finals. Both losses were to the army team. No matter how many games you win, you can be sure pro athletes in China aren't paid the way they are in the U.S.

I know a lot of fans think NBA players make too much money, but I don't think the game would be better if they had to win to get paid. It's one thing to do that in China, where we grow up with the idea that we are all equal and must work together, but in the U.S. it would be very bad for team chemistry. Players would play harder, of course, but the game wouldn't be better. Players would be very careful. Turnovers would be down, but there would be a lot of pressure. Every miss would make a player afraid to shoot again. No one wants to watch a game like that.

Basketball salaries in China aren't going to change soon, but other things about the sport could. In the summer of 2003, I talked to the new CBA director, Li Yuanwei. He *wants* to talk with players and coaches about what we think needs to change. I think that's good. The old director never talked to anyone. I told Li Yuanwei two things: we must do more for reporters, and we should get more attention for all national-team players. If you've seen the national team Web site, you know what I mean. There are reports on only a couple of players—the starting five or maybe top six. But the national team has twelve guys. That's twelve from all of China. Twelve players from a country with four times more people than the U.S. It's like the NBA All-Star team: every player who makes the team deserves attention. Even if they are rookies or bench players, they are on the national team, which means they're very good. They deserve to be stars, and making them stars would be good for basketball in China because the better it is to be on the national team, no matter what number you are on the roster, the harder younger players all over the country will play and practice to make the team.

But in China we also must change how we put together the national team. Right now we pick only players who can score. If you score a lot of points in the CBA, you have a chance to be picked. They don't look at anything else. I think we need rebounders, passers, and guys who just play defense. Now, every player on the national team is the top scorer on his CBA team. His only job is to score. I've joked about this. I like to say, "Our players on the national team only know how to catch the ball, not pass it."

It's more important, though, that we make the CBA's professional league better. It's like a pyramid: the CBA is the base, and the national team is at the top. A good base makes a good top. But everyone must understand that it takes time. The national team practices together all year long, and the CBA season is only four months long. The regular season is only twenty-four games. The playoffs are maybe ten games long, at most. So some teams play only twenty-five games, counting one playoff game, each year. It's impossible for players to get better playing only that many games.

The problem with making the season longer is travel. There is one CBA team in western China, the Urumqi White Bengal Tigers. They have to fly six hours to get to the next-closest CBA city. Remember, CBA teams don't have their own planes. They can't even afford to fly first-class. That's six hours for guys 6'7" or bigger sitting in coach seats. There aren't a lot of flights going to and from Urumqi, either. I'd still make the season at least thirty games long, maybe thirty-five, but until it's easier for CBA teams to travel, it will be hard to play more games than that.

A lot of people get excited about college basketball in the U.S. It's the same in China with CUBA, the Chinese University Basketball Association. The difference is that only one player has ever gone from the CUBA to the CBA. The CUBA is very, very hot, and all the players are heroes in college. But they also are students who have decided they want an education more than a basketball career. Their focus is different. After they leave college, no one hears about them anymore. At least not as basketball players.

CUBA, by the way, has a very strange playoff system. It used to be that the two teams that make it to the finals played two games. If one team won the first game and lost the second game, no matter what the score of the second game was, there would be five minutes of overtime. The team that won the overtime won the championship. That was the way they did it at first. Now they've changed it, but I don't think they've made it any better. Now it's more like soccer—instead of overtime, the championship is decided by free throws. Every player shoots one. The team that makes the most wins. Shaq would want to make sure to win both games.

I sometimes wonder if the Chinese way of thinking is wrong for the way you must think to play basketball. On a personal level, it has helped me that Chinese are taught to think things through. I don't believe it's always a good thing to take a long time to make every decision, but it helped me in coming to the NBA to have been trained to examine everything very closely. The problem is that Chinese people often end up being too careful, and in basketball that's not always wise. You need to go forward, go forward, and go forward again. You need to take chances and react quickly, to act almost without thinking. For Chinese people that's not a comfortable way to act. Americans seem to react and make decisions much more quickly and simply, an approach that is especially well suited to basketball.

A lot of people also look at Chinese players and say they're too slow or too small or not strong enough to make a world-class team, that China's winning a medal in international competition is impossible. Maybe this is true, but we can be much better than we are now if we find better coaches. There are maybe four or five coaches qualified to be the national team coach in China. I'm not saying qualified to be a good coach, but five who know enough to coach a national team, because you must know how to pick players and you must know the game. Five people in all of China! That's why I think it's good that they hired Del Harris, the Mavericks' assistant coach, as the head coach for the 2004 Olympics. I was a little bit surprised when that happened; I thought they would go to a European or American coach before the 2008 Olympics, but not this soon. But Del Harris will face the same things with the national team that Jeff Van Gundy did when he took over the Rockets for the 2003–2004 season. He will have to teach a whole new way of playing to a team used to playing only one way. I just worry about how much time they will give him. If he doesn't win right away, I think they will be reluctant to use outside help again.

Coaching is something I might be interested in after I retire, though it's too early to talk about it. I might like to come back and work in the CBA or in Chinese basketball, but I want to do something else first. I just want a change of life, a different life, for a while.

Besides, my experience in the NBA doesn't mean I'd be a good Chinese national team coach. You know why? Sometimes I think U.S.-style basketball is not the best way for Chinese players to play. U.S. players are faster and stronger, and they can jump higher. Chinese players can run fast and some can jump high, but there's one big difference: they can't take contact. If they get bumped, they don't jump as high. If you put a body on them, they can't move as fast. Touch them at all while they're shooting and they will miss. I think this is how a lot of players in the world are. But other countries—Yugoslavia, Lithuania, Spain, Italy, even South Korea—have learned how to make good teams, teams that can beat the U.S., with players who don't like contact.

The problem is that a lot of Chinese are afraid to ask for help. Some people think that if they learn something from someone else, it means that person is better than they are, and they don't like feeling inferior. Hiring Del Harris suggests that is beginning to change. I hoped that everyone in Chinese basketball would have learned something from losing to South Korea in the Asian Games, or almost losing to them in the 2003 Asian Championships. Korea doesn't look like a European team or an NBA team. They don't play like anybody else. They have made their own style. We can do the same in China.

The first step is to improve the CBA itself. Make the arenas more accommodating for the media, so they will want to come to CBA games and cover the teams. Pay more attention to every club's junior team. Give them more games and more coaching. The players don't need more money, but maybe more shoes, more basketballs. Pay the national team more money, and let all the junior players know how much money. Then they will all work harder playing for their teams and trying to make the national team.

LI YUANWEI: *The mission and position of the NBA and the CBA are very different. Not everything about the NBA fits the basketball environment in China. If we want to learn from the NBA,*

it's only in how the game is organized, how the games are pro-
moted, and how the teams are organized. But the NBA is a league
trying to combine global resources into a global entertainment busi-
ness. The CBA is trying promote basketball in China—not just at
the professional level but at every level—youth, senior, junior pro-
gram, both men and women.

The confusion for a lot of people is that the CBA, in one respect,
refers to the basketball federation of China. But people also say CBA
to refer to the top men's professional league. In China, they are
treated as one and the same. Think of the CBA as USA Basketball
running both the NBA and the U.S. national-team programs. The
CBA's main function is broken down into five categories. Number 1
is the selection, training, and managing of the national team. Num-
ber 2 is improving the level of competition throughout basketball in
China. That includes the CBA's highest level, 1A, then 1B, 2, and
the junior and youth programs. We're not going to abandon all those
programs just so the top level can become more like the NBA. Num-
ber 3 is grass-roots promotion: different types of tournaments and
activities for amateur basketball players or other nonprofessional
interests in the game. Number 4: managing the network of organi-
zations so that basketball on all levels is working together. Number
5: improving the business operational side. The CBA's first division
is the flagship, with its ability to sell merchandise, but that needs to
be developed on every level.

Although the function of the CBA is more as a federation of all
basketball in China than just a men's professional league, we'd still
like to see the men's league become more independent. It just has to
grow within the macro sports-entertainment industry and the
framework of basketball as a whole in China. It can't grow at the
expense of it. If the business side of things has grown to where it
can become an NBA-like entity, then we would want to make it

more of a business. But it's not there yet, and getting it there is not our first concern.

Li Yuanwei became the new head of the CBA in 2003, and I think he will stay at least four years. I believe he will do a lot of good things, but he needs time. This is true of everything; you need time. Wang Fei, the former national team coach, went to the U.S. and studied how NBA teams play. Then he tried to teach the national team what he had learned. But he had only two years to change how the national team plays. When there are so many good teams in the world, that's not enough time. He had to work much too fast. The biggest change he tried to make is going full speed in transition. That shouldn't be a surprise since he spent most of his time in Dallas watching and listening to Don Nelson.

During a practice he would say, "You, go there. You, go there." Like that, real quick. If you made a mistake, he'd say, "You, out." The next guy would come in, but he wouldn't be 100 percent ready. If he made a mistake—and the chance was always very good he would, because he wasn't loose—Wang Fei would say, "You, out." And he'd bring back the guy he just replaced. At that time, every player on the national team also was a big superstar in China. You couldn't talk to them like that. It was even worse with the rookie players. They'd feel very tight and nervous whenever he'd say, "You, out, move your ass, next!" or anything like that.

But the biggest thing I think Wang Fei did wrong is that he had a lot of older players on the team, players whom he had played with when he was still playing. For example, he had played with Fan Bin, the point guard who taught me so much about playing in the paint and not being afraid of Wang Zhi Zhi. What Wang Fei did wrong was to treat the older players he'd played with differently. They were better than the younger players, so there was reason for him to treat them a little bit differently on the court. But off the court, like when we were eating all together in the team cafeteria, Wang Fei would sit and joke with the older players and all the younger players would sit at a table on the other side of the room. I don't know if he knows it, but he split the team in two by doing that.

Wang Fei tried to change the way the Bayi Rockets played, too. On the army team at that time, all the players were thirty years old or older. They had played their way for many, many years. Anyone who would want to change them would need time, too. The season Wang Fei put in his new ideas, the Sharks beat the army team by 5 points the first time they played because the army team was still learning how to play the new way. But at season's end the army team still won the championship because they felt much more comfortable by then. The competition in the CBA is not as good as what the national team faces, so it was easier to make the new ideas work faster with the army team. But I think what it showed is that the new ideas could work with Chinese basketball players.

WANG FEI: *I believe Chinese basketball has to learn a lot from the outside world. In the process, there's not going to be a lot of smooth sailing. There are going to be bumps in the road, but you have to experience them to improve. I still believe that.*

When I got back from the U.S. after my year of basketball study abroad, I totally changed the way we trained and a lot of my offensive and defensive philosophy as well. For example, on defense, in China the philosophy always has been to force people to the middle. But after looking at the NBA, I could see why it was better to force the ball to the baseline, because the passing options are more limited. I made a dramatic change with transition offense and fast breaks, too. There's never been a lot of detail in China. It's all just a running exercise—aimless running, not purposeful running. I tried to teach my Chinese teams a system. For players who had never seen any of this before, especially players good enough to be on the national team, it was kind of shocking. I met a lot of resistance. I was trying to break a lot of old habits. What's important is that players learn why things need to be done a certain way, rather than just being told to do it, and you can only do that through exchange and watching other people play. I tried to make sure everything we did had a purpose. But that's not the way Chinese basketball has been, nor do I think it's that way today. This is something I take some pride in: if Yao never had been exposed to defenses in which the ball is forced to the baseline, I think he'd be a much less effective player in the NBA today.

Changing how the national team plays also takes more time because the players come from different teams with different ideas of how to play. Another problem is that the national team has twelve players, picked from sixteen invited to training camp. It's a long way down to the next level after those sixteen, so they can rest and not play or practice hard because there's nobody good enough to take their place.

The CBA and the national team could learn from the NBA about how to practice. I was very surprised by my first Rockets practice. It was run very tight. We changed from shooting drills to running plays with no time in between. Everybody was 100 percent focused on playing. When you practice in China, the bench players know they won't play much, so they don't work hard. They also know that after the regular practice, the coach will have another practice just for them. So they never practice hard in the first practice. That makes it easy for the first team. That's not the way it is in the NBA.

We don't know how to weight-train in China, either. The first time I broke my foot, I couldn't play, so I just did weight-training. But I had no one to show me what to do. The Rockets have a coach, Anthony Falsone, whose only job is to weight-train us. We had no trainer of any kind with either the Sharks or the national team. And with the Rockets, weight-training is quick. You go from the leg press to the next machine to the next machine, with no stopping or maybe thirty seconds to a minute of rest in between. One day you do your legs, and the next day you work on your back or your arms; you're lifting weights to make something stronger every day. In China, we'd spend all morning weight-training. You would do one set and then take a break for maybe five minutes. Nobody would call you to the next machine. The coach was there, but he couldn't keep track, and there were too many players to watch. Some players were lazy; they'd just sit there and chat. We would be in the weight room for three hours. With no rest, I think we could have finished in forty-five minutes.

We have days off in the NBA, only they're not really days off. If we don't have a game or practice, I still have to go to weight-training. I leave home at 10:00, get back at 12:15. You never know when those days off will be, but under Jeff Van Gundy we have a lot of them. Every four or five days we'd have a day off—or what he'd call a day off. You can tell by looking at Van Gundy's hair and eyes that he doesn't really believe that a day off means doing nothing.

In China, it's a lot different. If they said I had a day off, I wouldn't do anything. You also know when your day off in China is—every Sunday. That's the only day. Play three times a week, practice the other days, Sunday off. So on Saturday night you'd have dinner with a girlfriend or friends, and on Sunday you sleep until noon, then have lunch and go shopping. Or, for me, I'd stay in my room and play video games or spend time with my girlfriend.

Now, I can say all these things about what Chinese basketball needs to do, but that doesn't change how honored I feel about playing for China. I don't care how hard it is trying to play for my country and in the NBA. If there's one thing that bothers me, it's that not everybody thinks about honor when it comes to the national team. Now that the team has become very famous around China, many cities will pay a lot of money to have us play there because a lot of fans will pay a lot of money to see us. Some people are now more worried about making money than doing what's best for the national team. The summer of 2003 is an example; the national team traveled all over the country playing nine exhibition games before the Asian Championships. We played a team of players from the U.S. who had spent a short time in the NBA and another team, the Melbourne Tigers, from Australia. We went 9–0, but we didn't get a lot out of playing those teams. They didn't play like the teams we faced in the Asian Championships, and we practiced things we didn't use in the tournament. The whole tour we played a 1–3–1 zone and then didn't use it in the Asian Championships. I'm glad we didn't because we were terrible at it. Mengke Bateer had to play a wing in the 1–3–1 zone, and that's too much work for him. You can't have someone who weighs 310 pounds trying to play like a defensive small forward. He would get tired running back and forth on defense and then not have any strength to score inside on offense, where we really needed him. I told coach Jiang Xingquan, "Bateer is tired; maybe you can take him out for the final minute of the first quarter, so he can have that minute and the two minutes of the quarter break to rest." That was a good idea, I thought. That's what they do in the NBA with Shaq and other important players. These were also exhibition games, so why not try it?

"No," Jiang said. "That one minute is very important."

Rest is almost like a bad word in Chinese basketball. I don't think there's anything wrong with rest. I think it's important, especially since we practice for long hours that aren't always very productive. Two weeks before the 2000 Olympics, our team doctor said the team was tired and needed rest. We had practiced for six months and played thirty games to get ready. The coach said, "The flight to Australia is twelve hours long. They can rest then."

We also didn't use our bench players very much in the 2003 Asian Championships. Our coach at that time, Jiang Xingquan, believed that unless you foul out or are one foul away, you stay on the floor. That nearly destroyed us in the final game against South Korea because he let Liu Wei pick up four first-half fouls. Liu Wei was our starting point guard and the only one who could break their press. He went to the bench with four fouls late in the first half, started the second half, and fouled out early in the third quarter.

Maybe my favorite part of winning the Asian Championship, other than knowing we would play in the 2004 Olympics, is that Jiao Jian played a part in beating South Korea. He's the player I told you about earlier who had didn't have an up-to-date passport and couldn't go with the junior national team on a trip. He was in the starting five, and they had to cut him on the last day. He's a good friend of mine and Liu Wei's. Someone told me he looks like a Chinese Quentin Tarantino. I didn't know who Quentin Tarantino was when they said it, but if he's handsome with a big nose, that's Jiao Jian.

He almost didn't make the team for the championships, either. On the last day of training camp a decision had to be made to take Jiao Jian or a twenty-one-year-old forward named Mo Ke. Jiao Jian is much older and plays in the CBA for the Beijing Ducks. He plays defense very hard and can rebound, but teams never worry about him scoring. He can score, but not enough to beat you. He's only a jump shooter, and his shot looks very bad. The tip of his first finger on his shooting hand was cut off, so he shoots the ball real fast, as though he can't hold it, but he's not a bad shooter. Sometimes after a game, the reporters will say, "Hey, Jiao Jian played well tonight. How many points did he have, 8?" And then they'd look at the score sheet and say, "What? He had 22?" He's a guy like that. You can't find him on the court, but at the end of the game you see he had a lot of points and a lot of rebounds.

The head coach wanted Mo Ke, but Mr. Li, the CBA manager, wanted Jiao Jian to go. Mr. Li got his way. Now picking between these two guys wasn't very important. It was for the last spot on the team, and that player isn't supposed to play, anyway.

But Jiao Jian did play in the final minutes of the championship game against South Korea and grabbed a very important rebound and scored a layup while being fouled, and then made the extra free throw. In the ceremony after the game, I handed him my tournament MVP trophy and said, "This is for that layup and free throw!"

We played on some very bad floors on the tour to get ready for the Asian Championships, too, and some arenas didn't have air-conditioning, so we were sweating a lot. Sweat on a bad floor is an easy way to get hurt. I strained my calf in one of our two-hour morning workouts before a game, but there was no way the CBA would let me miss the game. I would never have said this, because I always want to be treated the same as my teammates, but I knew people had paid to see me play, not just the team. Although it would have been smarter to rest, I wanted to play if I could because we were in some very small northern cities; for some of those people, this would be their only chance ever to see me play.

The 1–3–1 for Jiang Xingquan was like a very expensive chair you keep in your living room. You don't want to get rid of it, you show it to everybody, but you never actually sit on it. He loves the 1–3–1 zone, and I know why. I was just a boy when I went to watch him coach the national team against South Korea. That was the first time China ever faced a 1–3–1, and we didn't know how to play against it. We still won the game, but only because a great outside shooter, Wu Ching Liu, scored 20 points in the last three or four minutes. This guy, Wu, shot a lot of 3-pointers. Long 3-pointers. Very long 3-pointers. Like 5-feet-behind-the-line 3-pointers. He made six of them in four minutes. The fans went crazy. They were screaming. I was a kid, eating ice cream and screaming, too. It was the first time I saw the Chinese national team at an arena. That's where our coach fell in love with the 1–3–1, because even though South Korea lost, they had led for thirty-six minutes using it.

In my first year with the national team, we had a meeting and the coach talked about that game, about how China played hard and beat them in the last minute. He wanted to point out the players who played in that game for the rest of us, so he asked anyone who was there to stand up. Maybe four guys stood up, and I stood up, too. The coach had a funny look on his face. "You were there?" he asked.

"Yeah," I said. "I was a fan in the stands."

I think maybe Chinese players have to learn basketball English, too, to be better players. In English, you say "elbow" and everybody knows that is near the corner of the top of the paint. But in China it takes many words to describe that spot. Or "the paint." In

China, it is "the three-second area." If I were to go to China and say, "Go to the paint," no one would know what that means.

We play a lot of pick and roll, but that's a little bit different, too. In China, pick and roll is to get the ball to the center going to the basket. The guard almost never shoots, especially not long jump shots. In the U.S., the guard tries first to use the center as a pick to lose his man and drive to the basket to score. The second option is for the point guard to use the center to get open and shoot a jump shot. The third option is to have the center set another pick and try again. Maybe the fourth option is to pass the ball to the center going to the basket, but only if he's wide open. You're almost never wide open near the basket in the NBA.

In the NBA there are also many different names for pick and roll. If the Rockets say "Get" or "Drag" or "Forehead," those are all different pick-and-roll plays. The name tells you where on the floor you should go and what position to take and what the first option is. In China, we run it in different places, but we don't have different names. It would take too long to tell someone in Chinese where they need to go. You'd have a shot-clock violation every time.

So all that was new for me in the NBA. I understand why they play that way, just like I understand why there's more one-on-one basketball in the NBA than anywhere else in the world. It's the talent level of the players. Sometimes that's the best chance you have because teams are so good defensively in the NBA. Before I played against U.S. players, I never thought anyone could dribble that fast or make shots from that far away.

For me, one of the biggest differences between playing in the NBA and in China is that NBA players don't ever show they're afraid. I had so many blocks in the CBA that some players just stopped trying to score against me. During the 1999–2000 season, I had triple-doubles in three games in a row. Most triple-doubles are for points, rebounds, and assists, but mine were for points, rebounds, and blocked shots. (A triple-double is getting 10—double digits—in three different categories.) After that I had only one more triple-double, that coming in the next season for the rest of my CBA career. Almost everybody in the CBA stopped trying to shoot over me. I don't think that will ever happen in the NBA. Everybody wants to dunk on me and they're not afraid. If I block them once, twice, they will still keep trying. I like that. Even though it's more work for me, that's the way it should be.

14

THE DREAM

My dream is to have a home in Hawaii for when I'm not playing. I've never been to Hawaii, but I like the way it sounds. My house would have two floors, and all the furniture would be Scandinavian. I like the color of it. It makes me feel at peace and comfortable. The house would have a swimming pool, too. It would be a place where I can always feel quiet. I can't remember the last time I felt like that, completely quiet, other than in my dreams.

My dream is to go to the South Sea of China on vacation. I went there once as a boy. It's so beautiful. I had no money then but lots of time. Now I have money but no time to go. That's life.

One dream already has come true—that LeBron James, the number-one NBA pick the year after me, went to the right team and became a big star. I was tired of being the focus after my first year. It looks like LeBron enjoys it. I hope that he always enjoys it.

Until I can get to the South Sea or Hawaii, my dream is just to live for six months in the same place and live the same life for a while. Have the same routine. Now no two days are the same. In the NBA, even if you have a home game, you wake up early to go to shootaround. Then you go back home and take a nap. Then you go to the arena in the evening for the game. If there's no game and you're at home, you can sleep a little later and then go to practice. If you're on the road, and we travel *a lot,* you never can be sure how the day will be. Just for a few months I'd like to wake up every day at eight or nine o'clock, go to practice, and come home and do something I want to do. But I can't do that in the NBA. I can't do it in China anymore, either, except for a few weeks a year—and then I do nothing because it's my one chance to rest.

But I wouldn't want life to be the same for too long.

My dream is to be an adventure traveler someday, too. I would visit different countries, see different kinds of people. I wouldn't do it as a job, but just to go and do it. I've already been on a show in America, *National Geographic Ultimate Explorer,* where they pay people to do that, but I was the subject for a story, not the traveler. TV host Lisa Ling came to China to show how the country is changing and to talk to me about that on the show. If I could make money adventure traveling, that would be nice, but more than anything I just want to see the world.

My dream is to go bungee-jumping. I wanted to go the summer after my rookie year. The national team was training in Xie Wan Dao, which is near the sea in northern China. We went there because of the SARS problem in Beijing, where our regular training center is. On our off day in Xie Wan Dao, we all went to the beach where they had a bungee-jumping tower.

The people running it said, "How much do you weigh?"

"About three hundred pounds," I said.

"You can't bungee-jump here," they said. "No one over two hundred and thirty pounds is allowed."

Since I couldn't bungee-jump, I took photos and took a ride in a speedboat. The water was too cold to swim.

My dream is to one day sell cars in Shanghai. That way I could have many different cars and learn about each one. I look at cars as big toys but also interesting tools. I know that some players in the NBA have many, many cars, including collector's cars. I don't have the money to do that now. Would I someday if I did? I don't think so, because I don't want to drive the collector's cars. I'm not interested in having really old cars. I want cars that are very modern, cars that have all the newest technology. That way I can learn about something new in the world, and if I sell them, I can learn for free. Maybe not ever having had a car in China is the reason I think about them so much. When we were at the World Championships in Indianapolis, the team had a day to go shopping. Everybody else went to look at clothes and shoes and things like that. I went to a Mercedes dealership. I didn't have any money, but they still tried to sell me one. At that time I didn't have more than $20 in my pocket. And when I got a cut over my eye playing for the national team the summer after my first NBA season and they had to shave my eyebrow, I looked at the scar and thought, "Hey, that looks like the Mercedes Benz symbol." If I do become a car dealer, I will have to tell my customers the cars are secondhand, because I will drive all of them first.

I don't dream about owning a basketball team. Owning a team is not just business and not just sports. There's too much politics, too much of a dark side, and I really don't like any of that.

My dream is that people in America will learn what China is really like, what people from China are really like. After my rookie year, the city of Shanghai picked me to be its official ambassador.

Helping people learn about China or Shanghai is not my primary job, but it's something I'm glad to do.

My dream is that China will find a new way to identify its athletes at a young age. Picking basketball players by measuring their bones when they are very young and taking only those who will be tall is why China has good forwards and centers but not very many good guards. Talented athletes are being missed and not getting a chance.

My dream is that more people in China will learn about basketball. Right now they don't care how you play, just if you win or lose. If you win, they'll say you played well. If players fight or run hard for the ball and fall on the floor, they laugh instead of cheer. Or if a small player tries to guard a big player, they laugh at him instead of admiring his courage. Not all shots that score are good shots, and not all shots that miss are bad shots, but people don't understand that. I think that's because they don't know the game. More Chinese need to watch all forty-eight minutes, not just the last few seconds.

My dream is that Chinese basketball will develop its own style. If you look at the way Korea plays, with everyone shooting 3-pointers off the dribble, even the big men, and using a full-court press, you can see that their approach is not from the NBA or anyplace else. Korea came up with this style to fit its players. China must do the same.

My dream is that Chinese players won't make excuses. Something I didn't like when I was in the CBA was that a lot of players would say, "The Shanghai Sharks win only because they have Yao Ming. If Yao Ming is out, they are nothing." I think they should have faced that I was with the Shanghai Sharks. You can't say "if" Yao Ming wasn't there. I was there. Charles Barkley might say, "If Michael Jordan had left, I could have won a championship."

No "if." You missed your chance. The army team won five championships in a row before we won. In every game they beat the other team by 20 points, at least. My rookie year they beat the Shanghai Sharks by 40 points. That was our first year to reach level A in the CBA. The second year they beat us by 20 points. The third year they beat us by 15 one time, but we beat them the other time. Then the last year we got the championship by beating them three out of five. I didn't do it all by myself. The entire Shanghai Sharks team worked to get better until the day we could beat the Bayi Rockets, something no one had ever done.

My dream is for athletes in China to be treated as individuals. Sports should always be played for the good of the country; I'm not against that. But a player also should be allowed to benefit from it himself. He should be allowed to make decisions about where he will play and what he thinks will make him a better player.

Chinese players should also be free to wear whatever brand of shoe they want. Right now, shoe companies usually sign contracts with teams, not individual players. I wore Reeboks at the 2003 Asian Championships even though Nike sponsors the Chinese national team. Mengke Bateer and one of our other players have contracts with Adidas, but they still have to wear Nike when they're with the national team. I want to be the first not to do that, not for myself but for the players who come after me. If I don't do that, they can always say to every other player, "Yao Ming didn't wear his own shoes, so why do you think you should?" If I don't do that, shoe companies won't try to sign players, they'll just try to sign teams. But if I succeed, then maybe shoe companies will not only pay star players but even bench players for wearing their shoes. I don't need the money, but the players that come after me might.

I took Coca Cola to court in China for the same reason. They signed a contract to pay the Chinese national team, but they were using my picture on collector's bottles. But I already have a contract with Pepsi. This is all new for athletes in China, and I know that whatever happens to me will open or close doors for the players who follow me. I asked Coca Cola for only 1 yuan, which is about 12 U.S. cents, because I don't want their money. I went to court so a law can be passed that might stop Coca Cola, or any other company, from doing that again.

My dream is to carry the Chinese flag at the Olympics, either in 2004 or in 2008 in Beijing. You know who carried the flag for China at the 2000 Olympics in Sydney? Wang Zhi Zhi. My dream is that Wang Zhi Zhi will return to the national team and help us win a gold medal in the 2008 Olympics in Beijing. This may be my biggest dream of all.

My dream is to win an NBA championship. That dream may be just as big as a gold medal in 2008. I don't know which one is closer. If I play ten or more years in the NBA, that would be a successful career. Lots of players have done that, but it would mean more because I'm a Chinese professional player. Maybe if I win a championship or I am an MVP, NBA teams will feel more comfortable signing or drafting Chinese players. I have seen some young guys in China who I think are good enough. They play tough and are aggressive; they just need coaching and competition.

These may seem like a lot of dreams for someone who hasn't had much time for daydreaming since coming to the NBA, but I dream in two countries and two languages now. Maybe I'm becoming more American in thinking about what I can get out of life, even while the life I already have is pretty good. My dream is that Rudy T., my first NBA coach, stays healthy, lives a long life, and gets another job as head coach, if that's what he wants. A few months after my first season ended, Rudy met with CD and the Rockets owner, Les Alexander, and decided he needed to focus on getting better. That's why they made Rudy a scout and hired Jeff Van Gundy. The doctors said the cancer is gone, but I think Rudy has taken away from the experience that there is more to life than basketball. I believe that, too, which is why I will always think of him as my friend, even if he goes to work for another team.

There is a saying in English, "You can't have your cake and eat it, too." We say something like this in Chinese as well. Since bears catch fish with their paws and Chinese like to eat bear paws, we say, "You can't have your bear paw and fish, too." Maybe not. But I'm going to try.

EPILOGUE

n the summer of 2002, the Houston Rockets acquired Yao Ming, at 7'5" the tallest and at 296 pounds the second-heaviest player ever drafted number one in the NBA. In the summer of 2003 they acquired the ingredients to help him continue to grow.

That began with the hiring of Coach Jeff Van Gundy, who immediately transformed the Rockets' freelancing, guard-oriented offense into a precision attack built around Yao. Hall of Fame center Patrick Ewing, who played under Van Gundy for the New York Knicks, joined the coaching staff as Yao's mentor. The overhauled offensive strategy, combined with a stifling defense—another Van Gundy staple—propelled the Rockets to the seventh seed in the Western Conference playoffs, ending a five-year postseason drought.

As luck would have it, the first round of the playoffs pitted the Rockets in a best-of-seven series against the second-seeded Los Angeles Lakers and the daunting Shaquille O'Neal. "I would never ask to face Shaq if I didn't have to," Yao said. "But there are not a lot of chances to face the most dominant center in the NBA, so I knew that playing him in the playoffs only would help me for the future. Facing Shaq in the playoffs was different from the regular season, too, because during the regular season he'd try to

have fun, like trying to do the point guard's job or taking a different kind of shot. In the playoffs, he just played his way, trying to
find the easiest way to score every time."

Yao learned a painful lesson late in Game 1, when Shaq beat
him to an airball shot by Kobe Bryant and dunked it with one second remaining on the 24-second shot clock and less than 20 seconds left in the game. It turned out to be the deciding basket in a
72-71 Lakers victory. Making matters worse, Yao belatedly hacked
Shaq on the play for his sixth and final foul, forcing him to watch
the Rockets' futile last possession from the bench.

"You can't have any excuses for your mistakes in the playoffs,
and one mistake can kill you," Yao said. The Rockets made adjustments after that first, devastating defeat—with little effect. "What
we did in one game, the Lakers had an answer for it the next game,
so Jeff would put in something new," Yao said. But the Lakers had
answers for that as well. In the end, the Rockets did manage to win
one game before being ousted from the series. Finishing with re-
spectable averages of 15 points and 7.4 rebounds, Yao called the
playoffs "a test of mind and body." Once the sting of the season's
conclusion eased, Yao took comfort in the Rockets' overall improvement.

"There was much more team play my second year," Yao said. "We
played hard on defense and our fast breaks were much better. My
first year our fast breaks were one guy going by himself. He
wouldn't care if there was a teammate with him. Or you'd have two
guys run down the same sideline. If that happened the second year,
the first guy would run the baseline and go to the other side. We
didn't do any of that my first year. We still didn't always play the
right way my second year, but we played the right way more often.
During my second year, when we lost, we knew why we lost. My
first year, we never quite knew how we won or lost."

Yao's consistency improved dramatically in the new system. In his first season, he failed to score in double figures twenty-two times and had fewer than 6 rebounds twenty-one times. The second year, he scored fewer than 10 points only six times and never two games in a row. His rebounding total in 2003–2004 dropped below 6 in just ten games, and it happened in back-to-back games only once. He not only improved his minimal standards but raised the bar on his best, scoring a career-high 41 points to go with 16 rebounds against the Atlanta Hawks on February 22, 2004, and blocking a career-high 7 shots against the Miami Heat on November 11, 2003.

Ewing helped by setting standards. "Sometimes he would say, 'Man, if I was playing and faced this guy, I'd get twenty-five points and fifteen rebounds,'" Yao recounted. "So then I'd know, 'OK, that's the standard.' So my goals now are different. Now it's easier for me to believe I can play good basketball, that on any night I can be The One. My first year, out of six games, maybe I'd have one nice game and the rest would be so-so. That one game I'd be happy, but it was as though I had gotten lucky or won a prize. I didn't know why in that game I was so good or if I could play the same way the next game. Now out of the six, I can play four or five nice games. But the first thing I know is, I have to play really, really hard every night."

During his second season, Yao proved more capable of playing "really, really hard every night" than he had in his rookie year. Proper weight-training made a noticeable difference. Arms once as undefined as fire hoses now had clefts and bulges. As a rookie, once he got tired, he was nearly useless and needed a long rest on the bench to recover. In his second season, he'd fade at times but recover without having to leave the floor.

There also was an attitude change. As a rookie Yao shied away from initiating contact and attempted to finesse his way to the basket. "After we played in Utah the first time my second season," Yao said, "someone asked the Jazz center, Greg Ostertag, about the difference between playing Shaq and playing me. Ostertag said Shaq wants to go through you, while Yao tries to go around you. Now I know you can't always go around. Sometimes— maybe most times—you have to go through the other player."

Yao's elevated confidence was particularly evident over the 2004 All-Star weekend in Los Angeles. His first year, in Atlanta, he looked uncomfortable, as if he didn't think he belonged. The second year he had a swagger and perfunctorily launched two 3s early in the game, an indulgence he wouldn't have dared as a rookie.

"Right before the second All-Star Game, I played both Shaq and the Spurs' Tim Duncan," he said. "I beat Shaq and I played well against the Spurs. That's why I felt more relaxed over All-Star weekend. I felt like I should be there."

Ah, yes, Shaq. Yao faced him only twice as a rookie and, while the opening minutes of the first battle belonged to Yao, Shaq dominated the matchup both times. Even without Shaq for two games, the Lakers split the four-game series. The Lakers and Rockets split their series during Yao's second year as well, and Yao still couldn't defend Shaq by himself. But Shaq also couldn't handle Yao defensively one-on-one, particularly in a 102–87 Houston win in which Yao outscored Shaq 29–24 and outrebounded him 11–9.

"The summer after my rookie year, I went home and thought about having to play Shaq again," Yao said. "When I was with the Shanghai Sharks, my coach told me how to play against Li Nan, a very good outside shooter on the army team. Whatever we did, we couldn't stop him. So we thought about getting the two points back with our offense. I stopped worrying about how to keep Li Nan from scoring and tried to quickly score so my basket canceled his. That's how I tried to play against Shaq my first year. I couldn't stop him, so I'd try to run quick to the other end and score myself—at least until I got tired.

"I didn't think that would work my second year because the Lakers added Gary Payton and Karl Malone. But Malone was hurt when we played the first time, so I concentrated on doing the same thing, and it was very successful. I had 18 points and so did Shaq. The rest of our team was better than the rest of their team, so we won. Late in the game, I was very tired and we were going on a fast break. I was walking under their basket, thinking, 'I'm too tired. I can't catch up.' Then I looked behind me and it was Shaq, walking, too. I thought, 'This is my chance!' and started running. I got a dunk out of it. Maybe that's the answer: no matter what—if you see Shaq behind you, run!"

Yao also adjusted to the NBA's impersonal business side. He was shocked when the Rockets traded Kenny Thomas his rookie year because teams in China don't trade players or even change their rosters in midseason. During his second season, when Houston traded Moochie Norris—a player popular with his teammates and fans, and someone who had gone out of his way to help a shy Chinese rookie feel a part of the team—Yao was hurt, but it didn't linger. Similarly, Yao's concern about the possibility of being traded carried over from the first season, but the difference in 2003–2004 was his confidence that he could make the grade, no matter where he played.

"I got over Moochie being traded faster, even though I was closer to him than to Kenny," Yao said. "My second year I was ready for one day waking up and having a teammate leave and a new teammate come in. I'm less worried about being traded because you never know what is going to happen tomorrow. All you can do is work hard and make your coach believe in you. Besides, being traded is still much better than being fired."

Life off the court became easier for Yao as well. With a driver's license, a custom-fitted BMW 745i, and a familiarity with Houston's highways and Chinese restaurants, Yao expanded his circle beyond home and arena. "After practice as a rookie, I would come right home," he said. "Now I can call my parents and say, 'Don't wait for me for lunch.' And I'll go somewhere to have lunch and relax. I have favorite places now, where I can go and have a green-bean iced drink or something like that."

The final step will be mastering English. He's comfortable enough to go out for dinner without anyone who speaks Chinese, but he still hopes to become so fluent that talking to his teammates is seamless. He was made painfully aware of the language barrier after the Norris trade, when the Rockets faced their former teammate for the first time against the Knicks in New York.

"Moochie played really well," Yao said. "After the game, I just wanted to say hello, good luck, and take care. I went and so did Steve Francis and Cuttino Mobley. Those three talked like I wasn't there. That was hard. It was a bad feeling. It was like I wasn't part of the group. But I think that if one day I can use the language well, that won't happen anymore."

There's also a matter of keeping the two languages straight.

"When I went back and played for the Chinese national team after my rookie year, I was using English words," Yao said. "I'd just played eighty-two games saying 'Switch' and 'Baseline.' My Chinese teammates looked at me pretty strange."

The changes promise to continue. After the 2003–04 season, the Rockets overhauled their roster, trading three of five starting players, including Steve Francis and Cuttino Mobley. Nothing could have prepared Yao for "Stevie Franchise," "Cat," and Kelvin Cato being sent to Orlando in a seven-player trade that brought the league's two-time reigning top scorer Tracy McGrady to Houston. The Chinese national team happened to be in Dallas on a pre-Olympic tour when the deal transpired, but out of respect for his former teammates and in order to gather his thoughts, Yao declined to answer questions from the media until all concerned had had a chance to come to grips with the new order.

"I will miss them," Yao said later. "All three helped me in every way my first two seasons. Stevie, as the team leader, looked out for me like a brother and I will always think of them all as friends. But I also know now this is a business and anyone can be traded. Maybe I will be traded one day, too. For now, all I can say is I'm excited about playing with Tracy McGrady. He can do some amazing things and I am looking forward to seeing him do them every day with me, instead of a couple times a year against me."

The move also meant, of course, the full-bore return of the intense focus that shifted slightly off Yao his second season, with debate immediately arising as to whether or not Yao and McGrady could succeed Shaquille O'Neal and Kobe Bryant as the league's most potent inside-outside combination.

Yao sucked in his breath when he first heard of such talk, still preferring to see himself as part of a 12-man, rather than two-man, team. But, as with every turn of events, he also vowed not to be deterred from moving forward and realizing his full potential—whatever that might be. After his first two seasons in the NBA, it's not hard to imagine Yao pursuing championships as a star on both the Chinese national team and the Houston Rockets. They are lofty goals, Yao says, but they are not impossible.

ACKNOWLEDGMENTS

Telling Yao Ming's story would not have been possible without the cooperation of all those quoted in the book—to each and all, many thanks. A debt of gratitude is also owed many people beyond those who are quoted or appear in the book. The collaborator is forever grateful to the Melbourne Tigers of Australia's NBL, who graciously gave him a place at their training table, a ride on their bus and a seat on their bench during a two-week exhibition tour playing against the Chinese national team in remote parts of China; said collaborator might still be in one of those faroff cities without the unconditional kindness of Coach Lindsay Gaze, his staff and players. Thanks to Brian McIntyre, Tim Frank, Helen Wong and Brenda Spoonemore of the NBA for their assistance. Thanks also to the entire Houston Rockets' media relations staff for providing background material and facilitating interviews, most notably Nelson Luis, Dan McKenna, Tracey Hughes and Matt Rochinski. Special thanks to Colin Pine, for coordinating times and dates for the author and collaborator to meet and translating and clarifying questions or answers when necessary. Miramax's Jonathan Burnham lent his support in a variety of ways, including approval of an unconventional format. Mark Lasswell offered sound advice and a deft touch as the book's primary editor. Kristin Powers of Miramax kept the proverbial ball rolling at critical junctures with her prompt attention to details, large and small. Thanks to the team at Miramax: Kathy Schneider, JillEllyn Riley, Andrew Bevan, Jaime Horn, Bruce Mason, Jennifer Sanger, Isabelle Smeall, Caroline Clayton, Matt Sims, and Hannah Schneider. Many thanks to the collaborator's editors at *ESPN The Magazine*—John Papanek, Gary Hoenig, Jon Pessah and David Cummings—who were extraordinarily accommodating and supportive. Ursula Liang, an American-born Chinese and gifted writer, served as a valuable early sounding board. Thanks to Shari Wenk, the collaborator's agent, for her support and encouragement. Thanks also to Angie Ying and Matt Zhang for their translating services and general knowledge of Chinese custom and culture as well as John Huizinga, Bill Sanders, Bill Duffy, and Lu Hao. On more than one occasion the collaborator kept tabs on the author and all that was said and written about him through Yaomingmania.com; founder and webmaster John Ball's passion and dedication to his hero's exploits were both invaluable and inspiring. Finally, the deepest gratitude to: Corrine Bucher, for not only holding down the fort but critiquing and proofreading and, above all else, always believing; and Chance, whose first year in the world provided limitless inspiration—as well as a second reason to stay up working through the night.